Lab Manual for
Network+ Guide to Networks, Fifth Edition

**Michael Grice and
Todd Verge**

COURSE TECHNOLOGY
CENGAGE Learning

Australia • Brazil • Japan • Korea • Mexico • Singapore • Spain • United Kingdom • United States

COURSE TECHNOLOGY
CENGAGE Learning

Lab Manual for Network+ Guide to Networks, Fifth Edition
Author: Michael Grice and Todd Verge

Vice President, Career and Professional Editorial: Dave Garza

Executive Editor: Stephen Helba

Acquisitions Editor: Nick Lombardi

Managing Editor: Marah Bellegarde

Senior Product Manager: Michelle Ruelos Cannistraci

Developmental Editor: GreenPen

Editorial Assistant: Sarah Pickering

Vide President, Career and Professional Marketing: Jennifer Ann Baker

Marketing Director: Deborah S. Yarnell

Senior Marketing Manager: Erin Coffin

Associate Marketing Manager: Shanna Gibbs

Production Director: Carolyn Miller

Production Manager: Andrew Crouth

Senior Content Project Manager: Andrea Majot

Art Director: Jack Pendleton

Cover illustration: Veer

For product information and technology assistance, contact us at
Cengage Learning Customer & Sales Support, 1-800-354-9706

For permission to use material from this text or product, submit all requests online at **cengage.com/permissions**
Further permissions questions can be emailed to
permissionrequest@cengage.com

Example: Microsoft ® is a registered trademark of the Microsoft Corporation.

Library of Congress Control Number: 2010923751

ISBN-13: 978-1-4354-9673-6
ISBN-10: 1-4354-9673-6

Course Technology
20 Channel Center Street
Boston, MA 02210
USA

Cengage Learning is a leading provider of customized learning solutions with office locations around the globe, including Singapore, the United Kingdom, Australia, Mexico, Brazil, and Japan. Locate your local office at: **international.cengage.com/region**

Cengage Learning products are represented in Canada by Nelson Education, Ltd.

For your lifelong learning solutions, visit **course.cengage.com**
Visit our corporate website at **cengage.com.**

Printed in the United States of America
1 2 3 4 5 6 7 14 13 12 11 10

TABLE OF CONTENTS

PREFACE

Hands-on learning is the best way to master the networking skills necessary for both CompTIA's Network+ exam and a networking career. This book contains dozens of hands-on exercises that apply fundamental networking concepts as they would be applied in the real world. In addition, each chapter offers multiple review questions to reinforce your mastery of networking topics. The organization of this book follows the same organization as Course Technology's *Network+ Guide to Networks, Fifth Edition*, and using the two together will provide an effective learning experience. This book is suitable for use in a beginning or intermediate networking course. As a prerequisite, students should have at least six months of computer experience and should be familiar with some basic networking components, such as NICs and patch cables. Passing CompTIA's A+ certification exam would suffice in lieu of this experience.

FEATURES

To ensure a successful experience for instructors and students alike, this book includes the following features:

- **Network+ Certification Objectives**—Each chapter lists the relevant objectives from the latest CompTIA Network+ Exam.
- **Lab Objectives**—Every lab has a brief description and list of learning objectives.
- **Materials Required**—Every lab includes information on network access privileges, hardware, software, and other materials you will need to complete the lab.
- **Completion Times**—Every lab has an estimated completion time, so that you can plan your activities more accurately.
- **Step-by-Step Instructions**—Logical and precise step-by-step instructions guide you through the hands-on activities in each lab.
- **Review Questions**—Questions help reinforce concepts presented in the lab.

Note for instructors: Answers to review questions are available on the Course Technology Web site at www.cengage.com/coursetechnology. Search on this book's ISBN, which is on the back cover.

HARDWARE REQUIREMENTS

The following is a list of hardware required to complete all the labs in the book. The hardware requirements for many of the individual labs are less than what is listed here.

Note that none of the labs require more than three computers at any one time, so all of the labs could be performed with only three computers. As well, many of the labs can be installed in a virtual environment on a single computer with sufficient resources. Alternatively, you might choose to install multiple network operating systems on each computer, as this will allow you to boot into a particular operating system when needed for a lab and reduce the number of computers needed. Disk space requirements will increase on computers with multiple operating systems.

The minimum requirements for at least two server computers are as follows:

- Pentium or compatible processor running at 2 GHz or higher

- 1 GB of RAM

- At least 40 GB of available storage

- A CD or DVD-ROM drive

- At least one installed NIC (network interface card)

- Hardware compatible with Windows Server 2008, Standard Edition (see *www. microsoft.com/whdc/hcl/default.mspx*)

The minimum requirements for the workstation computers are as follows:

- Pentium or compatible processor running at 500 MHz or higher

- 512 MB of RAM minimum

- At least 2 GB of available storage

- A CD or DVD-ROM drive

- At least one installed NIC (network interface card)

- Hardware compatible with Vista or Windows XP Professional (see *www.microsoft. com/whdc/hcl/default.mspx*)

In addition, at least two computers compatible with a current version of Fedora Linux, which is free for download from *http://fedoraproject.org/* and a variety of other sources are required. The minimum requirements for these computers are the same as the workstation requirements.

Other hardware required for various labs include the following:

- Internet access (cable, DSL, or faster preferred)

- One wireless router that can function as a DHCP server and a compatible wireless NIC

- At least five PCI Ethernet network interface cards with RJ-45 connectors

- Category 5 (or better) UTP cabling (or better) to make cables

- At least six straight-through Category 5 (or better) UTP patch cables

- At least three crossover Category 5 (or better) UTP patch cables
- RJ-45 connectors
- A computer professional's toolkit that includes a Phillips screwdriver, a ground strap, and a ground mat
- A networking professional's kit that includes a cable tester, crimper, wire stripper, and a wire cutting tool
- One network printer
- Four 10/100 (or better) Ethernet hubs
- Two switches with fiber uplink ports and a compatible fiber cable
- Two modems and a dial-up Internet account
- Access to two analog outside phone lines (or two digital lines and two digital-to-analog converters)

SOFTWARE/SETUP REQUIREMENTS

The following is a list of software required to complete all the labs in the book:

- At least two copies of Windows Server 2008, Standard Edition
- At least two copies of Windows Vista or Windows XP Professional
- At least one current copy of Fedora Linux (note that one copy can be used for each computer)

NOTES ON THE LABS

Unless otherwise stated, at the beginning of each lab it is assumed that the student has turned on each computer but has not yet logged on.

On Windows Vista/XP computers, Control Panel should be set to Category View, which is the default; the default Start menu should also be used.

On Windows Server 2008 computers, the default Start menu should be used.

ACKNOWLEDGMENTS

I'd like to thank John Bosco for his patience and attention to detail throughout the editorial process. Thanks also to Nick Lombardi, Michelle Ruelos Cannistraci, Andrea Majot, and the rest of the Course Technology/Cengage staff. Finally, I'd like to thank my friends and colleagues at the Nova Scotia Community College for inspiring me with their love of learning.

AN INTRODUCTION TO NETWORKING

Labs included in this chapter

- Lab 1.1 Understanding Elements of a Network
- Lab 1.2 Building a Simple Peer-to-Peer Network
- Lab 1.3 Building a Simple Client/Server Network
- Lab 1.4 Sharing a Network Printer

Net+ Exam Objectives

Objective	Lab
Explain common logical network topologies and their characteristics	1.1, 1.2, 1.3, 1.4
Install, configure, and differentiate between common network devices	1.2

Lab 1.1 Understanding Elements of a Network

Objectives

When first learning about network components, it is often helpful to observe a live network and talk with experienced networking professionals. The concept of segments, connectivity devices, or structured wiring techniques, for example, can be more easily demonstrated on a real network than in a textbook. The goal of this lab is to explore some real-life examples of basic networking concepts. To complete this lab, you will be required to tour your school's computer laboratory or network and identify various networking components at that site. Alternately, your instructor might arrange to allow your class to tour another network, guided by a willing network professional.

After completing this lab, you will be able to:

- Identify and sketch an organization's network topology
- Identify the nodes on a real-life network
- Identify a network's client software and network operating system
- Identify protocols used by a network

Materials Required

This lab will require the following:

- A network professional or instructor willing to give you a tour of your school's computer laboratory or data center, or a network professional willing to give you a tour of a network at a business or other site
- Pencil and paper
- Clipboard

Estimated completion time: **1–3 hours**

Activity

1. If you cannot tour your school's computer laboratory or data center, contact a business, school, or other organization and ask to interview the person in charge of their network. Explain that your purpose is purely educational and that you desire to learn more about networking. Also, explain that you will need to take notes. Because revealing information about a network might pose a security risk, some network professionals might be unwilling to share this information. If this is the case, you might need to ask your instructor to create a fictitious network and play the role of the network administrator.

2. Make the visit and, with the guidance of the network administrator, observe the organization's network. Remember to ask for details about the network's transmission media, physical topology, hardware, operating systems, services, and protocols.

3. On a separate piece of paper, draw the site's network topology, using boxes to represent the components such as computers and printers. Draw lines to connect the components.

You might also use network-diagramming software such as Microsoft Visio to diagram the network.

4. On your diagram, label servers with the letter "S," workstations with the letter "W," and printers with the letter "P." Label devices used to connect other devices together (such as switches) with a "C." If you are unsure about a network component, label the box with the letter "O" for "other."

5. Ask the networking professional or instructor for specifics about the network operating system (NOS) types and versions and the client types and versions used within this network. Record this information.

6. Record the make and model of any network interface cards (NICs). Note how many different types of NICs this network uses. If the number of different types is high (for example, over six), ask the network administrator if this variability affects network maintenance and troubleshooting.

7. Record the protocols used in the network.

8. Ask the networking professional or instructor if any wireless LANs are used on this network. Record this information.

9. Ask the networking professional or instructor what sorts of measures they take to make the network secure. Ask them about the possible effects of an intrusion or the loss of data. Record this information.

10. If you toured an outside organization's network, thank the person you interviewed. Follow up later with a letter of thanks.

Certification Objectives

Objectives for the Network+ Exam:

- Explain common logical network topologies and their characteristics: peer-to-peer, client/server, VPN, VLAN

Review Questions

1. Which of the following best describes a network's physical topology?

   a. the method by which multiple nodes transmit signals over a shared communications channel

   b. the physical layout of a network

   c. the distance spanned by a network's cable and wireless infrastructure

   d. the software used to ensure reliable connections between nodes on a network

2. Which of the following is the most popular type of modern network architecture for business?

   a. client/server

   b. terminal/mainframe

    c. peer-to-peer

    d. mainframe/dial-up

3. Which of the following elements is *not* required for a client to connect to a server on a client/server LAN?

    a. protocols

    b. media

    c. e-mail account

    d. client software

4. Which of the following are examples of client/server network operating systems? (Choose all that apply.)

    a. Windows XP

    b. Windows Server 2008

    c. Windows Vista

    d. Linux/UNIX

5. Network protocols are used to do which of the following? (Choose all that apply.)

    a. to ensure reliable delivery of data

    b. to determine the nearest printer for a print job

    c. to interpret keyboard commands

    d. to indicate the source and destination addresses for data packets

6. True or False? On a client/server network, clients may have only one protocol installed at any time.

7. A significant difference between the peer-to-peer and client/server network types is that a peer-to-peer network:

    a. is more difficult to set up

    b. does not allow for resource sharing between workstations

    c. does not usually provide centralized management for shared resources

    d. is more secure

8. Why is it necessary for each client on a client/server network to have a unique address?

9. Suppose an intruder has broken into the network you visited. Which of the following are potential results? (Choose all that apply.)

    a. loss of data

    b. altered data (such as grades or billing information)

    c. The network might need to be recabled.

    d. The intruder might use this network's resources to abuse other networks.

Lab 1.2 Building a Simple Peer-to-Peer Network

Objectives

Peer-to-peer networks are commonly found in offices where only a handful of users have access to networked computers, as they do not scale well and do not provide good security. However, peer-to-peer networks are an excellent choice in a few situations because they are simple and inexpensive to configure. A home office with three to five computers and only a couple of users, for example, would make a good candidate for peer-to-peer networking. Even in client/server networks, users might find it convenient to allow other users to access files on their computers. This is often a security risk, however, as a user might share files without sufficient security or even without security.

The goal of this lab is to become familiar with the methods for establishing a simple peer-to-peer network. During this lab, you will be introduced to the hardware and software required to connect two workstations so that they can share each other's resources, such as files and DVD drives.

After completing this lab, you will be able to:

- Build a simple peer-to-peer network

Materials Required

This lab will require the following:

- Two computers running Windows XP Professional or Windows Vista, with Ethernet NICs with RJ-45 connectors; neither computer should be configured as a member of a domain
- A DVD/CD-ROM drive for one of the computers
- Access to both computers with an administrative account (with different passwords)
- Client for Microsoft Networks and File and Printer Sharing for Microsoft Networks installed on both computers
- Either a crossover Category 5 (or better) UTP cable with RJ-45 connectors at either end, or two straight-through Category 5 (or better) UTP cables with RJ-45 connectors and a hub compatible with the NICs on both computers
- A DVD/CD with data files on it

Estimated completion time: **45 minutes**

Activity

1. If you are using a crossover cable, plug one end of the crossover cable into the NIC in one machine and the other end into the NIC in the other machine. If you are using straight-through cables and a hub, plug one end of one of the cable into the NIC in one machine and the other end into the hub. Repeat with the second cable and the second computer. A link light on both NICs illuminates, indicating that each NIC has successfully connected.

2. On each machine, if necessary, press **Ctrl+Alt+Del**. The Log On to Windows dialog box opens.

3. Log on to both machines as an administrator. The Windows desktop appears.

4. Insert the DVD or CD in the DVD drive. If both machines have a DVD-ROM drive, select one at random. In this activity, the machine with the DVD or CD in its DVD drive will be referred to as *WORKSTATION1*, and the other will be referred to as *WORKSTATION2*.

If you are using Windows XP, follow these steps:

1. On *WORKSTATION1*, click **Start,** and then click **Control Panel**.

2. Click the **Network and Internet Connections** icon. The Network and Internet Connections window opens.

3. Click **Set up or change your home or small office network**. The Network Setup Wizard opens.

4. Click **Next**. The next wizard window asks you to connect to the network.

5. Click **Next**. The next wizard window asks you to select a connection method.

6. Click the **Other** option button. Click **Next**.

7. Select the **This computer belongs to a network that does not have an Internet connection** option button and then click **Next**. The next wizard window asks you to name your computer.

8. Type **Net+ Lab** in the Computer description text box. Type **WORKSTATION1** in the Computer name text box. Click **Next**. The next wizard window asks you to name your network.

9. Type **NETPLUS** in the Workgroup name text box. Click **Next**. The next wizard window asks you whether or not to turn on file and printer sharing. Verify that the **Turn on file and printer sharing** option button is selected and then click **Next**. A dialog box opens summarizing the settings you have chosen.

10. Click **Next**. A dialog box opens asking you to wait. The next wizard window indicates that you are almost finished.

11. Click the **Just finish the wizard; I don't need to run the wizard on other computers** option button, and then click **Next**. The Completing the Network Setup Wizard dialog box opens.

12. Click **Finish**. The Network Setup Wizard closes, and the System Settings Change dialog box opens.

13. Click **Yes** to restart the computer.

14. Press **Ctrl+Alt+Del**. The Log On to Windows dialog box opens. Log on to *WORKSTATION1* again as an administrator. The Windows XP desktop appears.

15. Click **Start**, and then click **My Computer**. The My Computer window opens.

16. Right-click the icon for the DVD drive, and select **Sharing and Security** from the shortcut menu. The Properties window opens, with the Sharing tab displayed.

17. Click **If you understand the risk but still want to share the root of the drive, click here**. (Because the DVD/CD is read-only, this action does not present a security risk.)

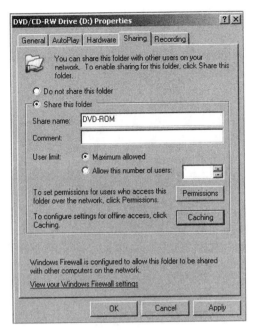

Figure 1-1   Sharing a DVD drive

Courtesy Course Technology/Cengage Learning

18. If necessary, click the **Share this folder on the network** check box. A check mark appears in the box. Replace the existing entry in the Share name text box with **DVD-ROM**. Figure 1-1 shows the Properties window as you share the DVD drive on a computer.

19. If necessary, click the **Allow network users to change my files** check box to remove the check mark.

20. Click **OK**. The Properties window closes.

21. Repeat Steps 1 through 13 on *WORKSTATION2*, using **WORKSTATION2** as the name of the computer in Step 8.

22. On *WORKSTATION2*, click **Start**, and then click **My Network Places**. The My Network Places window opens.

23. Right-click the icon for the DVD-ROM drive on *WORKSTATION1* and click **Explore** in the shortcut menu. If the Connect to workstation1 dialog box opens, go to the next step. Otherwise, go to Step 25.

24. Type **Administrator** in the User name text box, and type the password for *WORKSTATION1* in the Password text box. Click **OK**. A folder containing the files on the CD on *WORKSTATION1* appears.

25. Log off both computers.

In Windows Vista, follow these steps:

1. On *WORKSTATION1*, click **Start**, and then click **Control Panel**.

2. Click **System and Maintenance** and then click **System**.

3. Click **Change settings**. If a User Account Control (UAC) dialog box opens, click **Continue**. The System Properties window opens.

4. Click the **Change** button. Type **WORKSTATION1** in the Computer name text box.

5. In the Member of section, select **Workgroup** and type **NETPLUS** in the Workgroup name text box.

6. Click **OK,** close any open windows, and restart the computer when prompted.

7. Log on with an administrative account. Click **Start**, and then click **Computer**. The Computer window opens.

8. Right-click the icon for the DVD-ROM drive, and select **Share** from the shortcut menu. The Properties window opens, with the Sharing tab displayed.

9. Click the **Advanced Sharing** button. If a UAC box opens, click **Continue**. (Because the DVD/CD is read-only, this action does not present a security risk.)

10. Check the **Share this folder** option button and replace the existing entry in the Share name text box with **DVD-ROM**.

11. Click **OK**. The Advanced Sharing dialog box closes. Click **Close** to close the Properties dialog box.

12. Repeat Steps 1 through 6 on *WORKSTATION2*, using **WORKSTATION2** as the name of the computer in Step 4.

13. On *WORKSTATION2*, click **Start**, and then click **Network**. The Network window opens.

14. Double-click the icon for **WORKSTATION1** to open it. If the Connect to WORKSTATION1 dialog box opens, type **Administrator** in the User name text box, type the password for *WORKSTATION1* in the Password text box, and then click **OK**.

15. Right-click the icon for the CD-ROM drive on *WORKSTATION1* and click **Explore** in the shortcut menu. The files on the CD on *WORKSTATION1* are listed.

16. Log off both computers.

Certification Objectives

Objectives for the Network+ Exam:

- Explain common logical network topologies and their characteristics: peer-to-peer, client/server, VPN, VLAN

- Install, configure, and differentiate between common network devices: hub, repeater, modem, NIC, media converters, basic switch, bridge, wireless access point, basic router, basic firewall, basic DHCP server

Review Questions

1. What physical topology did you use to create your peer-to-peer network?

   a. bus

   b. tree

   c. star

   d. cube

2. Which of the following operating systems will allow you to create a peer-to-peer network from a group of workstations? (Choose all that apply.)

    a. MS-DOS

    b. Windows XP Professional

    c. Windows Server 2008

    d. Windows Vista

3. Which of the following components are *not* necessary to create a peer-to-peer network from a group of workstations? (Choose all that apply.)

    a. client software

    b. NIC

    c. network media

    d. Web browser

    e. network operating system

4. What is the primary difference between peer-to-peer and client/server architectures?

5. True or False? On a peer-to-peer network consisting of four Windows XP workstations, each user can individually control which of her local data files she wants to share with other users.

Lab 1.3 Building a Simple Client/Server Network

Objectives

Client/server networks are found in all but the smallest organizations. Although client/server networks are more difficult to configure than a peer-to-peer network, they are more scalable and can grow larger than peer-to-peer networks can. With more than a handful of computers, a peer-to-peer network quickly becomes unwieldy. In a client/server network, however, you can manage user accounts and network resources such as printers from a single machine. For instance, to change the printer used by all users on a peer-to-peer network, you would need to go to each machine and configure the new printer. Imagine having to do this on 500 machines! In a client/server network, however, you can typically change this setting on the server for all users.

The goal of this lab is to become familiar with the methods for establishing a simple client/server network. During this lab, you will be introduced to the hardware and software required to connect one or more workstations to a server. As part of the setup for this lab, both the server and the workstation need to be configured with an IP address. Computers and other network devices use the IP address to find other computers. You will learn about addressing beginning in Chapter 2.

After completing this lab, you will be able to:

- Build a simple client/server network
- Add a Windows XP or Vista client computer to a Windows Server 2008 domain

Materials Required

This lab will require the following:

- One computer named *WORKSTATION1* running Windows XP Professional or Windows Vista with an Ethernet NIC, configured with an IP address of 192.168.54.2; this computer should not be configured as a member of a domain
- Access to the Windows computer as a regular user
- One computer named *SERVER1* running Windows Server 2008, Standard Edition with an Ethernet NIC, configured with an IP address of 192.168.54.1
- *SERVER1* configured as the domain controller for the netpluslab.net domain
- *WORKSTATION1* configured to use 192.168.54.1 as its DNS server
- Access to the Windows Server 2008 computer and the netpluslab.net domain as the administrator
- On the Windows Server 2008 computer, a DVD/CD-ROM drive with a DVD or CD in it
- A user account named netplus in the Users group in the netpluslab.net domain on the Windows Server 2008 computer
- An Ethernet or Fast Ethernet hub compatible with both NICs
- Two straight-through Category 5 (or better) UTP cables with RJ-45 connectors at either end

Estimated completion time: **60 minutes**

Activity

1. Plug one end of one of the cables into the hub. Plug the other end of the cable into one of the computers. The link light on both the hub and on the NIC in the back of the computer should illuminate.
2. Repeat Step 1 to connect the other computer to the hub.
3. On the Windows Server 2008 computer, press **Ctrl+Alt+Del**. The Log On to Windows dialog box opens.
4. Type **Administrator** in the User name text box, and type the password for this account in the Password text box. Click the **Log on to** list button and then click **NETPLUSLAB**. Click **OK**. The Windows Server 2008 desktop appears.
5. Click **Start**, and then click **Computer**.
6. Right-click the icon for the DVD/CD-ROM drive and then click **Share** in the shortcut menu.
7. Click the **Advanced Sharing** button and then check the **Share this folder** option button. Record the name that appears in the Share name text box. This is the name by which the shared DVD/CD-ROM drive will be identified on the other computer. Click **OK** and then click **Close**.

On a Windows XP computer:

1. Press **Ctrl+Alt+Del** to display the Log On to Windows dialog box. Log on as an administrator. The Windows desktop appears.

2. Click **Start**, and then click **Control Panel**. The Control Panel opens. Click the **Performance and Maintenance** icon.

3. Click the **System** icon. The System Properties window opens.

4. Click the **Computer Name** tab.

5. Click **Network ID**. The Network Identification Wizard opens. Click **Next**.

6. Click the **This computer is part of a business network, and I use it to connect to other computers at work** option button. Click **Next**.

7. Click the **My company uses a network with a domain** option button. Click **Next**.

8. Click **Next**.

9. Enter **netplus** in the User name text box. Enter the password for the netplus account in the Password text box. Enter **NETPLUSLAB.NET** in the Domain text box. Figure 1-2 shows the Network Identification Wizard. Click **Next**.

10. Now you will enter information about the Windows XP computer itself. In the Computer name text box, enter **WORKSTATION1**. In the Computer domain text box, enter **NETPLUSLAB.NET**. Click **Next**. The Domain User Name and Password dialog box opens.

11. In the User name text box, enter **Administrator**. Enter the password for this account in the Password text box. Enter **NETPLUSLAB.NET** in the Domain text box. Click **OK**.

12. The wizard asks you to add a user account to this computer. The wizard should have already selected the **Add the following user** option button, displayed **netplus** in

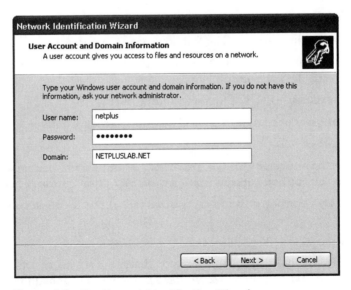

Figure 1-2 The Network Identification Wizard

Courtesy Course Technology/Cengage Learning

the User name text box, and displayed **NETPLUSLAB.NET** in the User domain text box. If not, complete these settings now. Click **Next**.

13. The wizard asks you what sort of access the netplus user should have to this computer. Make sure the **Standard user** option button is selected, and click **Next**.

14. Click **Finish**. The Computer Name Changes dialog box opens, informing you that you must restart the computer for the changes to take effect.

15. Click **OK**. The Computer Name Changes dialog box closes.

16. Click **OK** again. The System Properties dialog box closes.

17. The System Settings Change dialog box opens, asking if you want to restart your computer now. Click **Yes** to reboot the computer.

18. When the computer has rebooted, press **Ctrl+Alt+Del** to display the Log On to Windows dialog box. If the Log on to drop-down menu is not visible, click **Options**. In the User name text box, enter **netplus**. In the Password text box, enter the password for this account. Select **NETPLUSLAB** from the Log on to drop-down menu. Click **OK**.

19. Click **Start**, and then click **My Computer**. The My Computer window opens.

20. Click **My Network Places** in the left pane.

21. Click **Entire Network** in the left pane.

22. Double-click the **Microsoft Windows Network** icon.

23. Double-click the **Netpluslab** icon.

24. Double-click the **SERVER1** icon. A list of all the folders shared on *SERVER1* appears.

25. Right-click the folder name you recorded earlier in this lab. Click **Explore** in the shortcut menu. The files and folders on the disc are displayed.

26. Log off both computers.

On a Windows Vista computer:

1. Log on as an administrator. The Windows desktop appears.

2. Click **Start**, and then click **Control Panel**. The Control Panel opens. Click the **System and Maintenance** icon.

3. Click the **System** icon. The System window opens.

4. Click **Change settings**. If a UAC box opens, click Continue.

5. Click **Network ID**.

6. Select the **This computer is part of a business network; I use it to connect to other computers at work** option button. Click **Next**.

7. Click the **My company uses a network with a domain** option button. Click **Next**.

8. Click **Next**.

9. Enter **netplus** in the User name text box. Enter the password for the netplus account in the Password text box. Enter **NETPLUSLAB.NET** in the Domain text box. Click **Next**.

10. Now you will enter information about the Windows Vista computer itself. In the Computer name text box, enter **WORKSTATION1**. In the Computer domain text box,

enter **NETPLUSLAB.NET**. Click **Next**. The Domain User Name and Password dialog box opens.

11. In the User name text box, enter **Administrator**. Enter the password for this account in the Password text box. Enter **NETPLUSLAB.NET** in the Domain text box. Click **OK**.

12. The wizard asks you to add a user account to this computer. The wizard should have already selected the **Add the following user** option button, displayed **netplus** in the User name text box, and displayed **NETPLUSLAB.NET** in the User domain text box. If not, complete these settings now. Click **Next**.

13. The wizard asks you what sort of access the netplus user should have to this computer. Make sure the **Standard account** option button is selected, and click **Next**.

14. Click **Finish**. A window opens, informing you that you must restart the computer for the changes to take effect.

15. Click **Restart Now** to reboot the computer.

16. When the computer has rebooted, enter **netplus** in the User name text box. In the Password text box, enter the password for this account. Select **NETPLUSLAB** from the Log on to drop-down menu. Click **OK**.

17. Click **Start**, and then click **Network**. If an information bar appears at the top of the window indicating that network discovery and file sharing are turned off, click **Turn on network discovery and file sharing**.

18. Double-click the **SERVER1** icon. A list of all the folders shared on *SERVER1* appears.

19. Right-click the folder name you recorded for the CD on the server. Click **Explore** in the shortcut menu. You see a list of the contents of the CD.

20. Log off both computers.

Certification Objectives

Objectives for the Network+ Exam:

- Explain common logical network topologies and their characteristics: peer-to-peer, client/server, VPN, VLAN

Review Questions

1. Which of the following are or could be shared as resources across a network? (Choose all that apply.)

   a. Microsoft Word and other Office software

   b. printers

   c. documents

   d. network interface cards

2. True or False? Even in a client/server network, it is possible to share documents between individual users' computers as you can in a peer-to-peer network.

3. You are the network administrator for a small company. When users take vacations, they would like to allow other users to update the files stored on their computers.

Additionally, several users have complained that they have accidentally deleted important files on their local computer, and would like some way to recover them. How would you recommend that they store their files?

a. Make multiple copies on their local hard drive.

b. Store the files on the server, which is backed up nightly.

c. Make copies of the file on a floppy disk.

d. Burn the files onto a CD.

4. A very large organization might have thousands of servers. Do the benefits of client/server networks still apply to such an organization?

a. No, because managing so many servers is difficult.

b. No, because the organization can rely on a large peer-to-peer network to share files instead.

c. Yes, because it is easier to manage thousands of servers than it is to manage the hundreds of thousands of workstations that such an organization might have.

d. Yes, because managing thousands of servers is no more difficult than managing a few servers.

5. In this lab, what kind of network service did you configure on your client/server network?

a. management service

b. mail service

c. Internet service

d. file service

6. Which two of the following issues make peer-to-peer networks less scalable than client/server networks?

a. Each time a new user is added, the peer-to-peer network cabling must be reinstalled between nodes.

b. Adding nodes to a peer-to-peer network results in diminished overall network performance.

c. Adding nodes to a peer-to-peer network increases the risk that an intruder can compromise a shared data folder.

d. Adding new resource-sharing locations and ensuring that all authorized users have access to new resources becomes less manageable as the peer-to-peer network grows.

Lab 1.4 Sharing a Network Printer

Objectives

The ability to share network resources among all the users in an organization is an important reason why networks are so widely used. To print a document without a network, a user would need a printer directly attached to her computer, or she would need to copy the document to a form of portable media such as a CD-R or USB drive and find a computer with an attached printer. In an organization with even a few employees, this can be both expensive and time consuming. In an organization with thousands of employees, this can waste an enormous amount of time and cost a great deal of money.

In this lab, you will share a network printer so that users can access it. In the process, you will become familiar with the methods used to share network resources. Depending on the make and model of the printer, the steps required to install printer drivers might vary from the steps provided here.

After completing this lab, you will be able to:

- Share a networked printer on a Windows Server 2008 client/server network

Materials Required

This lab will require the following:

- The network and computers required for Lab 1.3
- A printer that is compatible with Windows Server 2008, Standard Edition
- Drivers for the printer that are compatible with Windows Server 2008; these drivers should be available either among the default drivers installed with Windows Server 2008 or in a known location on a disk or DVD/CD
- Drivers for the printer that are compatible with Windows XP/Vista, and knowledge of their location; these drivers should be available either among the default drivers installed with Windows or in a known location on a CD
- A printer cable that you can use to attach the printer to the Windows Server 2008 computer
- A printer port, such as USB or LPT1, available on the Windows Server 2008 computer
- Paper in the appropriate printer tray

Estimated completion time: **30 minutes**

Activity

1. Attach one end of the printer cable to the printer. Attach the other end of the printer cable to the Windows Server 2008 computer.

2. If necessary, power on the printer.

3. Press **Ctrl+Alt+Del** and log on to the Windows Server 2008 computer as the administrator. The Windows Server 2008 desktop appears.

4. Windows Server 2008 might detect and install the printer automatically. If it does, read through the steps and then skip to Step 19. Otherwise, continue with the following steps.

5. Click **Start**, click **Control Panel**, and then double-click **Printers**. The Printers window opens.

6. Double-click the **Add Printer** icon. The Add Printer window opens.

7. Select **Add a local printer**.

8. Select the appropriate printer port from the drop-down menu and click **Next**.

9. Now you must select a printer driver. If the printer drivers are known to be among the default drivers installed with Windows Server 2008, select the manufacturer for the printer in the Manufacturer list, select the printer model in the Printers list, click **Next**, and then skip ahead to Step 11. If the drivers for the printer are on a CD, insert the CD into the appropriate drive and click **Have Disk**. The Install From Disk dialog box opens.

10. Click **Browse**, select the location of the printer drivers, highlight the name of the printer driver, and click **Open**. Click **OK**, and then click **Next**.

11. Enter a name for the printer, for example, type **NetplusPrinter** in the Printer name text box. Click **Next**.

12. On the Printer Sharing screen, accept the default share name of NetPlusPrinter, enter **Network+ Laboratory** in the Location text box, and click **Next**.

13. Click **Print a test page**. The NetplusPrinter dialog box opens, indicating that the test page is being printed. The test page prints. Click **Close** and then click **Finish** to close the Add Printer window.

14. Right-click the printer's icon and click **Sharing** to open the Properties window to the Sharing tab. Click the **List in the directory** check box to select it and then click **OK**.

In Windows XP:

1. On *WORKSTATION1*, press **Ctrl+Alt+Del** to display the Windows XP logon screen. Enter **netplus** in the User name text box and the password for this account in the Password text box. Make sure that **NETPLUSLAB** is selected from the drop-down menu next to Log on to. Click **OK**. The Windows XP desktop appears.

2. Click **Start**, and then click **Printers and Faxes**. The Printers and Faxes window opens.

3. Below the Printer Tasks heading, click **Add a printer**. The Add Printer Wizard opens.

4. Click **Next**.

5. Make sure that the **A network printer, or a printer attached to another computer** option button is selected. Click **Next**.

6. Now you must select a printer. Make sure that the **Find a printer in the directory** option button is selected, and click **Next**. The Find Printers dialog box opens.

7. Enter **NetplusPrinter** in the Name text box. Verify that **Entire Directory** is selected in the In drop-down menu. Click **Find Now**. The printer you just added to the Windows Server 2008 computer appears in the window at the bottom of the Find Printers dialog box, as shown in Figure 1-3.

8. Click **NetplusPrinter** to highlight it and click **OK**. Click the **No** option button when asked if you want to make this the default printer, and then click **Next**.

9. Click **Finish**. The Add Printer Wizard closes, and the "NetplusPrinter on SERVER1" icon appears in the Printers and Faxes window.

Figure 1-3 Finding a printer

Courtesy Course Technology/Cengage Learning

10. Right-click the **NetplusPrinter on SERVER1** icon and select **Properties** from the shortcut menu.

11. Click **Print Test Page**. The NetplusPrinter on SERVER1 dialog box opens, indicating that you have printed a test page. The test page prints.

12. Click **OK**.

13. Click **OK** again. You have successfully accessed a printer shared on a Windows Server 2008 computer from a client workstation.

14. Log off both computers.

In Windows Vista:

1. On *WORKSTATION1*, press **Ctrl+Alt+Del** to display the Windows Vista logon screen. Make sure that **NETPLUSLAB.NET\netplus** is displayed as the user name and enter the password for this account in the Password text box. Click the **arrow** to log on. The Windows Vista desktop appears.

2. Click **Start, Control Panel, Hardware and Sound,** and then click **Printers**. The Printers window opens.

3. Click **Add a printer**. The Add Printer window opens.

4. Click **Add a network, wireless or Bluetooth printer**.

5. Now you must select a printer. The printer you just added to the Windows Server 2008 computer appears in the list of available printers.

6. Select **NetplusPrinter on SERVER1** and click **Next**.

7. Make sure the Set as the default printer check box is checked and click **Next**.

8. Click **Print a test page**. The NetplusPrinter on SERVER1 dialog box opens, indicating that you have printed a test page. The test page prints.

9. Click **Close** and then click **Finish** in the Add Printer dialog box.

10. Close any open windows. You have successfully accessed a printer shared on a Windows Server 2008 computer from a client workstation.

11. Log off both computers.

Certification Objectives

Objectives for the Network+ Exam:

- Explain common logical network topologies and their characteristics: peer-to-peer, client/server, VPN, VLAN

Review Questions

1. Many printers come with network cards so that they do not need to be attached to a computer. How would the process of sharing such a printer differ from sharing a printer attached to a computer? (Choose all that apply.)

   a. You would need to configure the printer with an address so that other computers can find it.

   b. The process would not differ.

   c. You would have to add the printer to the Windows Server 2008 domain, just as you did the Windows computer in Lab 1.3.

   d. You would not need to connect the printer to another computer via a cable.

2. Users may share printers in a peer-to-peer network. What are the potential disadvantages of this? (Choose all that apply.)

   a. A user could easily misconfigure or turn off his workstation, preventing all other users from accessing the attached printer.

   b. No one will be able to use the printer if the network is down.

   c. The printer will not be backed up.

   d. The printer will not be under centralized control.

3. In this lab, what kind of network service did you configure on your client/server network?

   a. management service

   d. mail service

   c. print service

   d. file service

4. Suppose that you configured software on a Windows Server 2008 computer, which checked printers on the network to make sure that they were operating correctly. What sort of network service would this software provide?

a. file service

b. print service

c. management service

d. mail service

5. How can you tell whether a printer is shared or not?

a. The word "shared" is written on the printer icon.

b. There is no way to tell.

c. There is a small icon at the bottom of the printer icon.

d. Each shared printer appears in the Shared Printers folder.

NETWORKING STANDARDS AND THE OSI MODEL

Labs included in this chapter

- Lab 2.1 IP Address Assignments
- Lab 2.2 Configuring TCP/IP for a Windows Computer
- Lab 2.3 Finding the MAC Address of Another Computer
- Lab 2.4 Looking at Network Connections on a Windows Computer
- Lab 2.5 Viewing Ethernet Frames

Net+ Exam Objectives

Objective	Lab
Explain the function of common networking protocols	2.4
Identify the following address formats	2.1, 2.2, 2.3
Explain the function of each layer of the OSI model	2.5
Given a scenario, select the appropriate command line interface tool and interpret the output to verify functionality	2.1, 2.2, 2.3, 2.4, 2.5

Lab 2.1 IP Address Assignments

Objectives

A Regional Internet Registry (RIR) is an organization that assigns IP addresses to public and private organizations. At the time of this writing, there are five RIRs: the American Registry for Internet Numbers (ARIN), the Asia Pacific Network Information Centre (APNIC), the Latin American and Caribbean Internet Addresses Registry (LACNIC), Réseaux IP Européens (RIPE), and the African Network Information Centre (AfriNIC). Each RIR assigns IP addresses in a different area.

As a network administrator, you might sometimes find that you need to track down the owner of a particular IP address. For instance, you might discover that a host at an IP address outside of your network is generating excessive amounts of traffic to your Web server, sending your mail server unsolicited commercial e-mail, or otherwise abusing your network. To ask whoever owns this host to stop, you must be able to contact the owner. You can use the Web site of an RIR to find this. All of the RIRs maintain a Web site and a WHOIS database, which tracks IP assignments. You can find the Web sites for each organization at *www.arin .net*, *www.apnic.net*, *www.lacnic.net*, *www.ripe.net,* and *www.afrinic.net*. Often IP address assignments are divided further. An Internet service provider (ISP), for instance, will usually delegate some of its IP addresses to its customers.

In this lab, you will use the nslookup command to find the IP address of a site. Then you will look up that IP address on the ARIN site.

Note that the steps in this lab were correct at the time this book was published. If ARIN changes its Web site significantly, the steps might not work exactly as written. However, you should still be able to go to *www.arin.net* and follow the links for WHOIS.

After completing this lab, you will be able to:

- Describe the function of an RIR
- Track down the organization owning an IP address

Materials Required

This lab will require the following:

- A computer running Windows XP Professional or Vista with a connection to the Internet (and instructions on how to access it, if necessary)
- Internet Explorer configured as needed to access Web sites on the Internet
- A Web site address (such as *www.cisco.com*) whose IP address was assigned by ARIN; your instructor should tell you which Web site to use

Estimated completion time: **20–25 minutes**

Activity

1. Log on to the Windows computer. The desktop appears. If necessary, perform whatever steps are needed to access the Internet.

Figure 2-1 Typical output from the `nslookup` command

Courtesy Course Technology/Cengage Learning

2. In Windows XP, click **Start**, point to **All Programs**, point to **Accessories**, and then click **Command Prompt**. (In Windows Vista, click **Start**, type **cmd** in the Start Search text box, and then press **Enter**.) A command prompt window opens.

3. In the command prompt window, type **nslookup** followed by a space and then the name of the Web site assigned to you by your instructor. (For instance, if you were assigned *www.cisco.com*, you would type **nslookup www.cisco.com**.) Press **Enter**. The output of this command should look similar to Figure 2-1.

4. You should see the IP address of the Web site directly under the name of the Web site. In Figure 2-1, for instance, the IP address of *www.cisco.com* is 198.133.219.25. Below, record the IP address you found. Some Web sites might have multiple IP addresses. If this is the case, record the last IP address found.

5. Click **Start**, and then click **Internet Explorer**. Internet Explorer opens.

6. In the Address bar, type **http://www.arin.net/whois/** and then press **Enter**. The ARIN WHOIS Database Search page opens.

7. In the Search ARIN WHOIS for text box, type the IP address you recorded in Step 4. Click **Submit Query**. The query results appear.

8. Record the name of the organization to which the IP address belongs. In some cases, more than one organization might be listed. For instance, an organization and its ISP might be listed.

9. Close any open windows and log off the computer.

Certification Objectives

Objectives for the Network+ Exam:

- Identify the following address formats: IPv6, IPv4, MAC addressing
- Given a scenario, select the appropriate command line interface tool and interpret the output to verify functionality: Traceroute, Ipconfig, Ifconfig, Ping, Arp, Nslookup, Host, Dig, Mtr, Route, Nbtstat, Netstat

Review Questions

1. A host has been overwhelming your Web server. You look up the IP address on *www .arin.net* to determine its owner, but ARIN's Web site tells you that LACNIC owns the IP address. What should you do?

   a. Complain to the owner of the *www.lacnic.net* Web site.

   b. Look up LACNIC in the Regional Internet Registry.

   c. Look up the owner of the IP address on the LACNIC Web site.

   d. Look up the owner of the IP address on the APNIC Web site.

2. What might happen if no organization were responsible for IP addressing on the Internet? (Choose all that apply.)

   a. Organizations might try to use the same ranges of IP addresses.

   b. Addressing on the Internet would be physically impossible.

   c. nothing

   d. The Internet would use another protocol besides IP.

3. You look up an IP address on *www.arin.net* and two organizations are listed. What does this mean?

   a. The two organizations share the IP address assignment.

   b. One organization sold the IP address to the second.

   c. The RIR made a mistake.

   d. One organization delegated the IP address to the second.

4. What is a Regional Internet Registry responsible for?

   a. maintaining Internet connectivity

   b. registering Internets

   c. assigning IP addresses

   d. signing up users with ISP accounts

5. Which of the following are situations where contacting the owner of an IP address would be useful? (Choose all that apply.)

   a. A host outside your network has been attempting to log on to your servers without your permission.

   b. A host inside your network has been attempting to log on to your servers without your permission.

   c. A host outside your network has been attempting to send large amounts of unsolicited commercial e-mail, or spam.

   d. A host outside your network has been accessing your Web site once an hour.

Lab 2.2 Configuring TCP/IP for a Windows Computer

Objectives

Whereas addressing at the Data Link layer usually does not require configuration, addressing at the Network layer usually does. Without properly configured network addresses, two hosts can't communicate with each other over the network using Network layer protocols. The network address is a logical address, and does not correspond to any physical attribute of the computer.

On a TCP/IP network, the Network layer address is the IP address. It consists of four numbers with values between 0 and 255 separated by dots. For instance, 10.172.255.93 is a valid IP address. When written in binary, each number in an IP address is eight bits long, and these numbers are often called octets. The subnet mask is also important. The subnet mask also consists of four octets separated by dots. However, only certain values are allowed. A host with an improperly configured subnet mask might not be able to communicate with some or any hosts. In this lab, you will use the Ipconfig utility to display a computer's IP configuration.

In this lab, you will configure an IP address and subnet mask on a host so that it can communicate with other hosts on a network. You will then use the ping (Packet Internetwork Groper) command to verify that two hosts can communicate with each other at the Network layer in a TCP/IP network. The ping command sends one or more packets using the Internet Control Message Protocol (ICMP) to a remote computer. If the remote computer receives these packets, it sends a reply. If the sender receives the replies, the ping command was successful. After completing this lab, you will be able to:

- Configure an IP address on a Windows computer

Materials Required

This lab will require the following:

- A hub
- A computer running Windows Server 2008, Standard Edition, Windows XP Professional, or Windows Vista configured with an IP address of 192.168.54.1 and with a NIC connected to the hub with a straight-through Category 5 (or better) cable
- A computer named *WORKSTATION1* running Windows XP Professional or Vista with a NIC connected to the hub with a straight-through Category 5 (or better) UTP cable but with no IP address configured
- Access to the Windows XP or Vista computer as an administrator

Estimated completion time: **20 minutes**

Activity

1. On the Windows XP or Vista computer, log on as an administrator. The Windows desktop appears.

2. Click **Start**, point to **All Programs**, point to **Accessories**, point to **Communications**, and then click **Network Connections**. (In Windows Vista, click

Start, right-click **Network**, and select **Properties**. Click **Manage network connections**.) The Network Connections window opens.

3. Right-click the **Local Area Connection** icon, then click **Properties** in the shortcut menu. (In Windows Vista, if a UAC box opens, enter your network credentials if necessary and then click **Continue**.)

4. Double-click **Internet Protocol (TCP/IP)**. (In Windows Vista, double-click **Internet Protocol Version 4 (TCP/IPv4)**.) The Internet Protocol (TCP/IP) Properties dialog box opens.

5. Click the **Use the following IP address** option button.

6. Enter **192.168.54.2** in the IP address text box.

7. Enter **255.255.255.0** in the Subnet mask text box.

8. Enter **192.168.54.1** in the Default gateway text box.

9. Click the **Use the following DNS server addresses** option button.

10. In the Preferred DNS server text box, enter **192.168.54.1**. Figure 2-2 shows the Internet Protocol (TCP/IP) Properties dialog box in Windows XP as an IP address is configured.

11. Click **OK** to close the Internet Protocol (TCP/IP) Properties dialog box.

12. Click **OK** to close the Local Area Connection Properties window.

13. Now you will verify that you have successfully configured an IP address for the Windows computer. Click **Start**, point to **All Programs**, point to **Accessories**, and then click **Command Prompt**. (In Windows Vista, click **Start**, type **cmd** in the Start Search text box, and then press **Enter**.) A command prompt window opens.

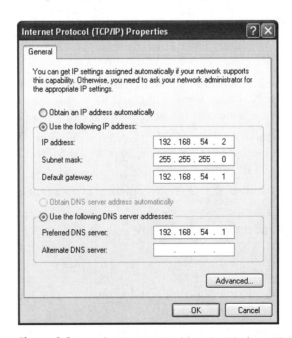

Figure 2-2   Configuring an IP address in Windows XP

Courtesy Course Technology/Cengage Learning

14. Type **ping 192.168.54.1** and press **Enter**. The Windows XP computer sends four ICMP packets to 192.168.54.1, and indicates that it has received four replies from the remote computer.

15. Type **ipconfig** and press **Enter**. The computer prints its IP address, subnet mask, and default gateway. Does this match the information you entered in the Internet Protocol (TCP/IP) Properties dialog box in Steps 6, 7, and 8?

16. Log off.

Certification Objectives

Objectives for the Network+ Exam:

- Identify the following address formats: IPv6, IPv4, MAC addressing
- Given a scenario, select the appropriate command line interface tool and interpret the output to verify functionality: Traceroute, Ipconfig, Ifconfig, Ping, Arp ping, Arp, Nslookup, Host, Dig, Mtr, Route, Nbtstat, Netstat

Review Questions

1. Which of the following information is included in the results of the ping command? (Choose all that apply.)

   a. the operating system used by the remote computer

   b. the IP address or name of the remote computer

   c. the number of packets that were lost

   d. the time it took for the reply to be received

2. Which of the following commands can you use to print information about a computer's Network layer configuration?

   a. netstat

   b. ipconfig

   c. arp

   d. ping

3. How can you verify that two hosts are connected and communicating properly?

   a. From one host, run the ping command to the other host.

   b. From a third host, run the ping command to both hosts.

   c. Run the arp command on both hosts.

   d. Run the ipconfig command on both hosts.

4. What type of protocol does the ping command use?

   a. TCP/IP

   b. UDP

   c. ICMP

   d. ARP

5. A Dynamic Host Control Protocol (DHCP) server can be used to assign IP addresses automatically. Why might this be useful to a network administrator?

6. On many networks, DHCP is used to assign workstations their IP addresses. However, DHCP is rarely used to assign addresses for servers. Why?

   a. DHCP is too expensive.

   b. DHCP is not scalable enough.

   c. Servers are frequently moved around, whereas workstations are not.

   d. Workstations are frequently moved around, whereas servers are not.

Lab 2.3 Finding the MAC Address of Another Computer

Objectives

The MAC address operates at the Media Access Control sublayer of the Data Link layer. It is a unique address assigned by the manufacturer when the NIC is built. In TCP/IP networks, the Address Resolution Protocol (ARP) allows a computer to associate another computer's MAC address at the Data Link layer with its IP address at the Network layer. A computer keeps track of these associations in its ARP cache. If a computer does not see packets from one of the computers whose MAC address is in its ARP cache for a certain period of time, the computer removes that MAC address from its ARP cache. This is called the ARP cache timeout.

A MAC address consists of two parts. The first part consists of six characters assigned to the vendor by the IEEE, known as the block ID. The second part consists of six characters assigned by the vendor, known as the device ID. Each MAC address should be unique. Each character in a MAC address is a hexadecimal number, consisting of numbers from 0 through 9 and letters from *a* through *f*. A MAC address is often represented with colons or dashes between every pair of characters, such as 00:60:97:7F:41:A1 or 00-60-97-7F-41-A1.

You can use the arp command to look at the entries in a computer's ARP cache and to find the MAC addresses of other computers it has communicated with on its local network segment. Incorrect ARP entries can prevent two computers from communicating. For instance, on very rare occasions, two computers will be found on the same network with identical MAC addresses (generally due to manufacturer error). These computers will have difficulty communicating with other computers on that network. More commonly, replacing a computer's NIC might prevent that computer from communicating with other computers on the network until their ARP cache entries time out.

In this lab, you will use the arp command to find the MAC address of another computer. After completing this lab, you will be able to:

- Use the arp command to find and set the MAC address of another computer

Materials Required

This lab will require the following:

- The network required in Lab 1.4, consisting of a computer named *SERVER1* running Windows Server 2008, Standard Edition with an IP address of 192.168.54.1, a computer named *WORKSTATION1* running Windows XP or Vista with an IP address of 192.168.54.2, a hub, and two straight-through Category 5 (or better) UTP cables connecting the NICs on the computers to the hubs

- Access to the Windows Server 2008 computer as an administrator
- Access to the Windows XP or Vista computer as an ordinary user

---

Estimated completion time: **20–30 minutes**

Activity

1. Log on to *WORKSTATION1* as an ordinary user. The Windows desktop appears.

2. Click **Start**, point to **All Programs**, point to **Accessories**, and then click **Command Prompt**. (In Windows Vista, click **Start**, type **cmd** in the Start Search text box, and then press **Enter**.) A command prompt window opens.

3. You will now test network connectivity between *WORKSTATION1* and *SERVER1*. Type **ping 192.168.54.1** in the command prompt window and press **Enter**. The computer indicates that it has received four replies from 192.168.54.1. See Figure 2-3 for an example of the output produced in Windows XP. This indicates that the two computers can communicate with each other over the network. If they could not, the ping command would display an error message such as "Request timed out."

4. Repeat Steps 1 through 3 on *SERVER1*, logging on as an administrator. Use the IP address **192.168.54.2** in Step 3.

5. On *SERVER1*, type **arp -a** in the Command Prompt window and press **Enter**. The computer prints a list of IP addresses and the physical addresses, or MAC addresses, associated with each. Record the MAC address for 192.168.54.2, the Windows XP or Vista computer.

6. Now you will replace the actual MAC address of the Windows XP or Vista computer with a bogus MAC address and see how it affects the ability of the two machines to communicate with each other.

```
Command Prompt                                              _ □ X
Microsoft Windows XP [Version 5.1.2600]
(C) Copyright 1985-2001 Microsoft Corp.

C:\Documents and Settings\netplus.WORKSTATION1>ping 192.168.54.1

Pinging 192.168.54.1 with 32 bytes of data:

Reply from 192.168.54.1: bytes=32 time<1ms TTL=128
Reply from 192.168.54.1: bytes=32 time<1ms TTL=128
Reply from 192.168.54.1: bytes=32 time<1ms TTL=128
Reply from 192.168.54.1: bytes=32 time<1ms TTL=128

Ping statistics for 192.168.54.1:
    Packets: Sent = 4, Received = 4, Lost = 0 (0% loss),
Approximate round trip times in milli-seconds:
    Minimum = 0ms, Maximum = 0ms, Average = 0ms

C:\Documents and Settings\netplus.WORKSTATION1>
```

Figure 2-3 Typical output from the `ping` command

Courtesy Course Technology/Cengage Learning

7. In the command prompt window, type **arp -s 192.168.54.2 00-11-22-33-44-55** and press **Enter**. The Windows Server 2008 computer changes the MAC address it knows for *WORKSTATION1*.

8. Type **arp -a** and press **Enter**. What is the MAC address for *WORKSTATION1* now?

9. On the Windows XP or Vista computer, repeat Step 3. Are you able to ping *SERVER1* successfully?

10. In the command prompt window, type **ipconfig /all**. The computer prints detailed information about its network configuration, including its MAC address. Does this MAC address match the one for *WORKSTATION1* that you found in Step 5?

11. Now you will delete the ARP entry you created for *WORKSTATION1*. On *SERVER1*, type **arp -d** and press **Enter**. All ARP entries are deleted. For your reference, Table 2-1 lists some options for the arp command in Windows.

Table 2-1   Options for the arp command in Windows

Command	Action
arp -a	Displays all the addresses in the ARP cache
arp -s	Adds a static, or permanent, entry to the ARP cache
arp -d	Deletes entries from the ARP cache

12. On *WORKSTATION1*, repeat Step 3. Are you able to communicate with the Windows Server 2008 computer successfully now?

13. Log off both computers.

Certification Objectives

Objectives for the Network+ Exam:

- Identify the following address formats: IPv6, IPv4, MAC addressing
- Given a scenario, select the appropriate command line interface tool and interpret the output to verify functionality: Traceroute, Ipconfig, Ifconfig, Ping, Arp ping, Arp, Nslookup, Host, Dig, Mtr, Route, Nbtstat, Netstat

Review Questions

1. What do the first six characters of a MAC address indicate?

   a. the device ID assigned by the vendor

   b. the block ID assigned by IEEE

   c. the logical address assigned by DHCP

   d. the logical address assigned by DNS

2. Which of the following is a valid MAC address?

   a. 01-ba-cd-dh-83-21

   b. 01-ba-cd-de-83-21-42

    c. 01-ba-cd-de-83-21-42-a0

    d. 01-ba-cd-de-83-21

3. Which of the following commands can you use to find a Windows XP computer's MAC address from a command prompt window on that computer?

    a. ipconfig

    b. ipconfig /all

    c. arp -a

    d. netstat

4. Which of the following commands can you use to find the MAC address of another computer on the same network?

    a. ipconfig

    b. ipconfig /all

    c. arp -a

    d. netstat

5. Under what circumstances is it possible for a computer to have more than one MAC address?

    a. never

    b. if a computer has more than one NIC

    c. if a computer has more than one NIC, but only if it is acting as a router

    d. if a computer is a router

6. You have just replaced the NIC on a server, making no other changes. It can communicate with all the computers on its network but one. What is the most likely explanation for this?

    a. The new NIC is not working properly.

    b. Both computers have the same MAC address.

    c. The remote computer has the old MAC address entry in its ARP cache.

    d. The remote computer has a bad NIC.

7. Which of the following is a function of the Data Link layer?

    a. arranging data in proper sequence at the destination

    b. encrypting data prior to transmission

    c. dividing data into distinct frames

    d. issuing electrical signals onto a wire

8. What part of a data frame checks to make sure that the data arrived exactly as it was sent?

    a. CRC

    b. start delimiter

    c. payload

    d. padding

Lab 2.4 Looking at Network Connections on a Windows Computer

Objectives

The Transport layer ensures that data travels from the source host to the destination host. Transport layer protocols might check for errors. They also might ensure that data arrives in the proper order. In the TCP/IP stack, TCP is the protocol operating at the Transport layer. Because TCP is a connection-oriented protocol, the computers on both ends of a TCP connection must keep track of the status of the connection.

You can use the netstat command on Windows, UNIX, and other operating systems to look at active connections. This command can show detailed information about active network connections, including their status, the number of bytes sent over the network, and other information. UDP, on the other hand, is a connectionless protocol and does not keep track of the connection. As a result, the netstat command provides much less information about UDP connections.

After completing this lab, you will be able to:

- Use the netstat command to view information about the Transport layer

Materials Required

This lab will require the following:

- The network required in Lab 1.4, consisting of a computer named *SERVER1* running Windows Server 2008, Standard Edition with an IP address of 192.168.54.1, a computer named *WORKSTATION1* running Windows XP or Vista with an IP address of 192.168.54.2, a hub, and two straight-through Category 5 (or better) UTP cables connecting the NICs on the computers to the hubs

- Terminal Services running on *SERVER1*, and the computer configured to allow users to log on remotely

- Access to both computers as an administrator

> Estimated completion time: **20 minutes**

Activity

1. On the Windows XP or Vista computer, press **Ctrl+Alt+Del,** if necessary.

2. Log on to *WORKSTATION1* as an administrator. The Windows desktop appears.

3. Click **Start**, point to **All Programs**, point to **Accessories**, and then click **Command Prompt**. (In Windows Vista, click **Start**, type **cmd** in the Start Search text box, and then press **Enter**.)

4. Type **netstat** and press **Enter**. The computer displays information about all open connections on the computer, or returns to the prompt if there are none.

5. Now you will open a new TCP connection by using the Remote Desktop Connection. This program is used to log on to Windows machines remotely. In this lab, you will just use it to create a TCP connection. Click **Start**, point to **All Programs**, point

to **Accessories**, point to **Communications**, and then click **Remote Desktop Connection**. You might not have to point to Communications if Remote Desktop Connection appears on the Accessories menu. (In Windows Vista, click **Start**, click **All Programs**, click **Accessories**, and then click **Remote Desktop Connection**.) The Remote Desktop Connection window opens.

6. Type **192.168.54.1** in the Computer text box. Click **Connect**. The Windows Security dialog box for the Windows Server 2008 computer opens.

7. Log on as an administrator. The Windows Server 2008 desktop appears.

8. Click the Minimize button on the horizontal bar at the top of the window to minimize the Remote Desktop session.

9. In the command prompt window, type **netstat** and press **Enter**. The computer displays information about the connection, indicating the protocol used, the state of the connection, the local address, the destination address, and the ports or service name used by each side of the connection. The state of the connection should be ESTABLISHED. What is the protocol used by the Remote Desktop Connection? Figure 2-4 shows the output of the netstat command.

10. On *SERVER1*, press **Ctrl+Alt+Del** and log on as an administrator. The Windows Server 2008 desktop appears and the Remote Desktop connection from WORKSTATION1 is automatically ended.

11. Open the command prompt.

12. In the command prompt window, type **netstat** and press **Enter**. How are the results of the netstat command different when run on the server?

13. Type **netstat -e** and press **Enter**. The computer displays information about the number of bytes sent and received, and about the number of packets sent and received. Table 2-2 shows options for the netstat command.

14. Type **ping 192.168.54.2** and press **Enter**. The computer indicates that it has received four replies from 192.168.54.2.

15. Type **netstat -e** again and press **Enter**. Has the number of packets sent and received increased?

Figure 2-4 Typical output from the **netstat** command

Courtesy Course Technology/Cengage Learning

Table 2-2   Options for the netstat command

Command	Action
`netstat -a`	Displays all connections and listening ports
`netstat -e`	Displays Ethernet statistics
`netstat -s`	Displays statistics per protocol
`netstat -r`	Displays the routing table
`netstat -n`	Displays numbers instead of names (usually used with the **-a** or **-r** options)

16. Type **netstat -s** and press **Enter**. The computer displays information about individual protocols used.

17. Close the Remote Desktop Connection dialog box and log off both computers.

Certification Objectives

Objectives for the Network+ Exam:

- Explain the function of common networking protocols: TCP, FTP, UDP, TCP/IP suite, DHCP, TFTP, DNS, HTTP(S), ARP, SIP (VoIP), RTP (VoIP), SSH, POP3, NTP, IMAP4, Telnet, SMTP, SNMP2/3, ICMP, IGMP, TLS

- Given a scenario, select the appropriate command line interface tool and interpret the output to verify functionality: Traceroute, Ipconfig, Ifconfig, Ping, Arp, Nslookup, Host, Dig, Mtr, Route, Nbtstat, Netstat

Review Questions

1. What protocol is used by Remote Desktop Connection?

   a. ICMP

   b. TCP

   c. UDP

   d. IP

2. About which protocols does the netstat –s command print information? (Choose all that apply.)

   a. ARP

   b. ICMP

   c. TCP

   d. UDP

3. At what layer of the OSI model does TCP work?

   a. Physical layer

   b. Data Link layer

c. Network layer

    d. Transport layer

  4. At what layer of the OSI model does IP work?

    a. Physical layer

    b. Data Link layer

    c. Network layer

    d. Transport layer

  5. A user is having difficulty connecting to a remote Web site. After the user attempts to connect, the netstat command tells you that the connection state is established. Where in the OSI model is the problem probably located?

    a. at the Data Link layer

    b. at the Network layer

    c. at the Transport layer

    d. somewhere above the Transport layer

  6. Why doesn't the netstat command display any information about ICMP connections?

    a. ICMP does not function at the Transport layer.

    b. ICMP is not a true protocol.

    c. ICMP is a connectionless protocol.

    d. ICMP is considered unimportant.

Lab 2.5 Viewing Ethernet Frames

Objectives

A network protocol analyzer is a software program or hardware device that reads packets or frames directly from a computer's NIC and allows you to view them or to save them for later viewing. This process is called capturing the frames. A network protocol analyzer also decodes the frames captured so that you can look at the individual parts of the frame. Even though a network protocol analyzer captures frames, the packets are typically of the most interest to a network administrator.

    Microsoft Network Monitor is a network protocol analyzer available on Windows Server 2008, as well as on other versions of Windows. You can use a network protocol analyzer to examine the traffic on a network one frame at a time, or one part of a frame at a time. As you gain experience at looking at network traffic, you can also use Network Monitor to look for potential problems. For instance, you can look at Transport layer information in a series of packets to determine if the computer on the other end is sending data too quickly. With a little experience, Network Monitor or other network protocol analyzers can be invaluable troubleshooting tools.

    It is important to keep in mind that a network protocol analyzer such as Network Monitor can be used to violate a user's privacy. As such, it should not be used carelessly or lightly.

    After completing this lab, you will be able to:

- Use Network Monitor to look at captured frames

Materials Required

This lab will require the following:

- The network required in Lab 1.4, consisting of a computer named *SERVER1* running Windows Server 2008, Standard Edition with an IP address of 192.168.54.1, a computer named *WORKSTATION1* running Windows XP or Vista with an IP address of 192.168.54.2, a hub, and two straight-through Category 5 (or better) UTP cables connecting the NICs on the computers to the hubs

- The latest version of Network Monitor downloaded from Microsoft's download center and installed on *SERVER1*

- Access to *SERVER1* as an administrator

- Access to *WORKSTATION1* as any ordinary user

Estimated completion time: **60 minutes**

Activity

1. Log on to *WORKSTATION1* as an ordinary user. The Windows desktop appears.

2. Open the command prompt.

3. Type **ping -t 192.168.54.1** and press **Enter**. This sends ICMP packets continuously to *SERVER1*, and ensures that packets are available when you open Network Monitor.

4. Log on to SERVER1 as an administrator. The Windows Server 2008 desktop appears.

5. Click **Start**, point to **All Programs**, click **Microsoft Network Monitor 3.3**, and then click **Microsoft Network Monitor 3.3** on the submenu. (Your version number might be different.) The Microsoft Network Monitor window opens, as shown in Figure 2-5.

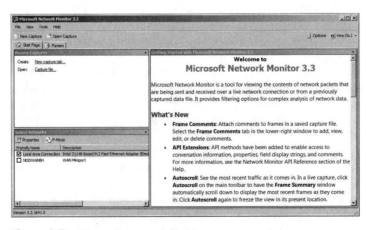

Figure 2-5   Microsoft Network Monitor

Courtesy Course Technology/Cengage Learning

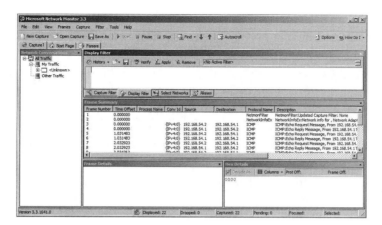

Figure 2-6   A network capture

Courtesy Course Technology/Cengage Learning

6. In the Select Networks pane, ensure that **Local Area Connection** is checked.

7. Click **New Capture** on the toolbar, and then click **Start**. Network Monitor begins to capture packets, as shown in Figure 2-6. The Frame Summary pane shows information about the packets captured by Network Monitor.

8. When the number of frames captured is above 100, click **Stop** on the toolbar.

9. Locate a frame with "ICMP" in the Protocol field and click that row. The list of frames remains in the Frame Summary pane, while a detailed description of each part of the selected frame appears in the Frame Details pane and a representation of the frame in hexadecimal appears in the Hex Details pane. See Figure 2-7 for an example of a captured frame.

10. By clicking the plus signs (+) in the Frame Details pane, you can display detailed information about each part of the packet. In the Frame section, Network Monitor shows detailed information about the frame itself. What is the total frame length for the frame you've chosen?

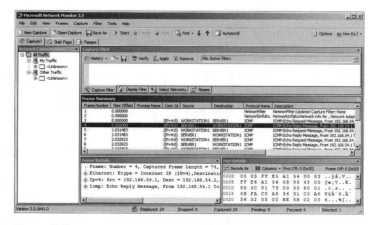

Figure 2-7   An individual frame in a network capture

Courtesy Course Technology/Cengage Learning

11. Click the `plus sign (+)` next to Ethernet. Network Monitor shows detailed information about the Ethernet portion of the frame. What is the source address of the packet? What is the destination address of the packet? What is the Ethernet type?

12. Click the `plus sign (+)` next to Ipv4. Network Monitor shows detailed information about the IP portion of the packet. What is the source address of the packet? What is the destination address of the packet? Is there a checksum in the IP portion of the packet?

13. Click the `plus sign (+)` next to Icmp. Network Monitor shows detailed information about the ICMP portion of the packet. Is there another checksum for this portion of the packet?

14. Close Network Monitor. Click **No** when asked if you want to save the capture. Click **No** if asked to save unsaved entries in the database. On *WORKSTATION1*, press `Ctrl+C` to stop the ping command.

15. Log off both computers.

Certification Objectives

Objectives for the Network+ Exam:

- Explain the function of each layer of the OSI model: Layer 1—Physical, Layer 2—Data Link, Layer 3—Network, Layer 4—Transport, Layer 5—Session, Layer 6—Presentation, Layer 7—Application

- Given a scenario, select the appropriate command line interface tool and interpret the output to verify functionality: Traceroute, Ipconfig, Ifconfig, Ping, Arp, Nslookup, Host, Dig, Mtr, Route, Nbtstat, Netstat

Review Questions

1. At what layer in the OSI model were the source and destination addresses for the packet in Step 11 located?

   Answer: The Data Link layer

2. In the frame you examined in Steps 9 through 14 which portions of the packet calculated a CRC checksum? What layers of the OSI model do they correspond to?

   Answer: Ethernet (Data Link) and ICMP (Transport)

3. A user is unable to reach your company's Web site. From the user's workstation, you can ping the remote Web server. How might you use Network Monitor or another network protocol analyzer to troubleshoot the problem? (Choose all that apply.)

   a. by checking to see if the workstation is sending packets to the Web server

   b. by checking to see if the server is sending packets to the workstation

   c. by checking the workstation's IP configuration

   d. by checking the workstation's ARP configuration

4. Which protocols can be seen using Network Monitor? (Choose all that apply.)

   a. ICMP

   b. ARP

    c. TCP

    d. UDP

5. About which OSI layer does Network Monitor *not* provide information?

    a. Physical layer

    b. Data Link layer

    c. Network layer

    d. Transport layer

TRANSMISSION BASICS AND NETWORKING MEDIA

Labs included in this chapter

- Lab 3.1 Learning Media Characteristics
- Lab 3.2 Creating a UTP Crossover Cable to Connect Two Computers
- Lab 3.3 Comparing Throughput
- Lab 3.4 Understanding How a Category 5 Cable Fails
- Lab 3.5 Connecting Two Switches with Fiber-Optic Cable

Net+ Exam Objectives

Objective	Lab
Categorize standard cable types and their properties	3.1, 3.2, 3.5
Identify common connector types	3.1, 3.2, 3.4, 3.5
Identify common physical network topologies	3.5
Given a scenario, differentiate and implement appropriate wiring standards	3.2
Install components of wiring distribution	3.2
Install, configure, and differentiate between common network devices	3.2, 3.3, 3.5
Explain the function of each layer of the OSI model	3.4
Given a scenario, troubleshoot common connectivity issues and select an appropriate solution	3.2, 3.3, 3.4
Given a scenario, utilize the appropriate hardware tools	3.2, 3.4

Lab 3.1 Learning Media Characteristics

Objectives

In this lab, you will learn about the costs and characteristics of network media and networking and computer equipment. This will give you experience in comparing costs of network components and network media. It will also give you an idea of the equipment needed to set up a network and of the total costs involved in doing so.

Bear in mind that the cost of a certain medium includes not only the cost of the cable, but also the installation cost, the maintenance costs, and the cost of replacing the medium if it becomes obsolete in the future. Additionally, the cost of networking and computer equipment and software will vary widely, depending on the vendor, the equipment chosen, and the licensing terms.

After completing this lab, you will be able to:

- Identify the costs and characteristics of Category 3 and Category 5 cable

Materials Required

This lab will require the following:

- Access to a retail store that sells computer networking equipment or access to the Internet
- Pencil and paper

Estimated completion time: **30–90 minutes**

Activity

1. Visit a retail computer store (such as Best Buy or CompUSA) that sells Ethernet Category 5 cable, computers, software, and networking supplies. Alternately, visit a Web site (such as *www.cdw.com*) of a company that specializes in computers, software, and networking supplies. Record the Web address or the name of the store.

2. Record the cost of Category 5 cable sold by the foot. If the store does not sell cable by the foot, divide the price of the longest Category 5 cable you can find by its length in feet.

3. Record the cost of Category 3, Category 5e, Category 6, or Category 7 cable as you did in the previous step.

4. Record the cost and model information for an Ethernet, 100-Mbps, four-port hub with an RJ-45 connection for a workstation.

5. Record the cost and model information for an Ethernet, 100-Mbps, 16-port hub with an RJ-45 connection.

6. Record the cost and model information for an 802.11g wireless access point.

7. Record the cost and model information for a typical desktop computer. If you have difficulty deciding on a model, choose one that is intermediate in price.

8. Record the cost and model information for a typical laptop computer. If you have difficulty deciding on a model, choose one that is intermediate in price.

9. If not already included, record the cost of an Ethernet 100-Mbps NIC with an RJ-45 connection for a desktop.

10. If not already included, record the cost and model information for a 100-Mbps PCMCIA or USB NIC with an RJ-45 connection for a laptop.

11. If not already included, record the cost and model information for a compatible wireless network card for a laptop.

12. If not already included, record the cost of the full version of the operating system.

13. Assume that you need to connect 50 workstations and 20 laptops to a network. Calculate and record the cost of these computers.

14. Assume that each workstation and each laptop requires 50 feet of cable. Calculate and record the cost of the total amount of Category 5 cable needed for each computer. For comparison, calculate and record the cost of the total amount of the Category 3, Category 5e, Category 6, or Category 7 cable you found in Step 3.

15. Assume tha t each workstation will use a NIC and that each laptop will use both a network card and a wireless network card. Calculate and record the total cost.

16. Assume that one wireless access point will be required. (Additional wireless access points might be required depending on the physical layout of the building and other factors.) How many hubs are required to connect all the workstations and all the laptops to the network at the same time? Calculate and record the total cost for hubs and the wireless access point.

17. Assume that each computer requires a copy of Windows XP Professional, Windows Vista, or Windows 7. (Although they might buy computers with an operating system already installed, many companies reinstall the operating system. The terms of their licensing agreement with Microsoft might require them to purchase it a second time.) Calculate and record the cost of the new operating system for each workstation and laptop.

18. Calculate and record the total cost of the network using Category 5 cable by adding up the totals you calculated in Steps 13 through 17. Do not include in the total the cost of the other cabling you calculated in Step 14.

19. For comparison, calculate and record the total cost of the network using the highest quality cable you could find (Category 6 or 7). Do this by summing the totals you calculated in Steps 13 through 17. Do not include in the total the cost of the Category 5 cabling.

Certification Objectives

Objectives for the Network+ Exam:

- Categorize standard cable types and properties: CAT3, CAT5, CAT5e, CAT6, STP, UTP, multimode fiber, single-mode fiber, coaxial RG-59 and RG-6, serial, and plenum vs. non-plenum, transmission speeds, distance, duplex, noise immunity (security, EMI), and frequency

- Identify common connector types: RJ-11, RJ-45, BNC, SC, ST, LC, RS-232, RG-59, and RG-6

Review Questions

1. What type of connector does a 100Base-T network require?

   a. RJ-11

   b. BNC

   c. AUI

   d. RJ-45

2. Which of the following is commonly used to protect UTP cable from EMI?

   a. conduit

   b. STP

   c. crossover cable

   d. lead shielding

3. What is the maximum throughput of a 100Base-TX network?

   a. 5 Mbps

   b. 10 Mbps

   c. 50 Mbps

   d. 100 Mbps

4. On a 10Base-T network, attenuation is addressed through the use of which of the following?

   a. amplifiers

   b. multiplexers

   c. repeaters

   d. RF generators

5. What is the maximum allowable segment length on a 1000Base-T network?

   a. 85 feet

   b. 85 meters

   c. 185 feet

   d. 100 meters

6. Which of the following will contribute to latency?

   a. the twist ratio of the cable

   b. cable length

   c. EMI

   d. attenuation

Lab 3.2 Creating a UTP Crossover Cable to Connect Two Computers

Objectives

You might find it necessary to make cables from time to time. The phrase "making cables" actually refers to the process of properly attaching connectors to the ends of a length of cable. Many companies make their own cables to save money. Additionally, knowing how to make cables makes it easier to troubleshoot cabling problems.

Normal patch cables, also known as straight-through cables, have wire terminations on either end that are identical. Another kind of cable is a crossover cable. In this type of cable, the transmit and receive pins in one of the cable's plugs must be reversed. A crossover cable allows two workstations to connect directly to each other (without a connectivity device between them).

After completing this lab, you will be able to:

- Make a crossover Category 5 cable

- Directly connect two computers with an RJ-45 crossover cable by plugging one end of the cable into the NIC of one computer and the other end of the cable into the NIC of the second computer

- Use a cable tester to ensure cable integrity

Materials Required

This lab will require the following:

- At least 10 feet of Category 5 (or better) UTP cable without connectors

- Two RJ-45 connectors (or more if necessary)

- Two computers named *WORKSTATION1* and *WORKSTATION2* running Windows XP Professional or Vista, configured to be in a workgroup named NETPLUS, with Ethernet NICs with RJ-45 connectors

- Administrative access to both computers

- A network crimper

- A wire stripper

- A cable tester

- A wire cutting tool

Estimated completion time: **60 minutes**

Activity

1. Use the wire cutter to make a clean cut at both ends of the UTP cable.

2. Use the wire stripper to remove one inch (or less) of the sheath from one end of the UTP cable. Do not strip the insulation from the individual wires inside the UTP cable, and take care not to damage the insulation on the twisted pairs inside.

Table 3-1   Pin numbers and color codes for creating a straight-through cable end

Pin number	Pair number	Use	Color
1	2	Transmit	White with green stripe
2	2	Receive	Green
3	3	Transmit	White with orange stripe
4	1	Receive	Blue
5	1	Transmit	White with blue stripe
6	3	Receive	Orange
7	4	Transmit	White with brown stripe
8	4	Receive	Brown

3. Slightly separate the four wire pairs, but keep the pairs twisted around each other.

4. Hold the RJ-45 connector so that the opening faces you and the plastic flap is on the bottom. Push the wires into the RJ-45 connector so that each wire is in its own slot in the connector, in the order shown in Table 3-1. Use a crimping tool to punch down the cable. You have now completed one end of the cable.

5. Repeat Steps 2 and 3 for the other end of the twisted-pair cable.

6. Hold the RJ-45 connector so that the opening faces you and the plastic flap is on the bottom, just as you did in Step 4. If you flip the RJ-45 connector over, the cable will not work. Push the wires into the RJ-45 connector so that each wire is in its own slot in the order shown in Table 3-2. Use a crimping tool to punch down the cable. This crosses the transmit and receive wires (both positive and negative), which allows the computers to communicate when connected. After completing this step, your crossover cable will be ready to use. Figure 3-1 shows an example of a crossover cable.

Table 3-2   Pin numbers and color codes for creating a crossover cable end

Pin number	Pair number	Use	Color
1	3	Transmit	White with orange stripe
2	3	Receive	Orange
3	2	Transmit	White with green stripe
4	1	Receive	Blue
5	1	Transmit	White with blue stripe
6	2	Receive	Green
7	4	Transmit	White with brown stripe
8	4	Receive	Brown

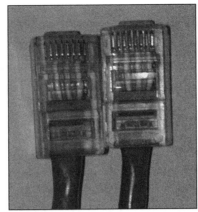

Figure 3-1   Crossover cable

Courtesy Course Technology/Cengage Learning

7. Plug each end of the cable into the cable tester. If the cable tester determines there are any problems with your cable, remove the ends of the cable with a wire cutter and repeat the first six steps of this lab. Otherwise, skip to the next step. Making a cable properly on the first try is difficult.

8. Remove the cable ends from the cable tester.

9. Connect one end of the cable to the NIC of *WORKSTATION1*.

10. Connect the other end of the same cable to the NIC of *WORKSTATION2*. The lights on each NIC turn on.

11. Log on to *WORKSTATION1* using an administrative account. The Windows desktop appears.

12. Click **Start**, point to **All Programs**, point to **Accessories**, point to **Communications**, and then click **Network Connections**. (In Windows Vista, click **Start**, right-click **Network** and select **Properties**. Click **Manage network connections**.)

13. Right-click the **Local Area Connection** icon. Select **Properties** from the shortcut menu that appears. (In Windows Vista, if a UAC box opens, click **Continue**.) The Local Area Connection Properties window opens.

14. Double-click **Internet Protocol (TCP/IP)**. (In Windows Vista, double-click **Internet Protocol Version 4 (TCP/IPv4)**.) The Internet Protocol (TCP/IP) Properties dialog box opens.

15. Click the **Use the following IP address** option button. In the IP address text box, enter **192.168.54.2**. In the Subnet mask text box, enter **255.255.255.0**. Click **OK** and then click **Close**. (In Windows Vista, click **OK** twice.)

16. Repeat Steps 11 through 15 on *WORKSTATION2*, using an IP address of 192.168.54.3.

17. On *WORKSTATION2*, click **Start**, point to **All Programs**, point to **Accessories**, and then click **Command Prompt**. (In Windows Vista, click **Start**, type **cmd** in the Start Search text box, and then press **Enter**.) A command prompt window opens.

18. Type **ping 192.168.54.2** and press **Enter**. The computer indicates that it has received four replies, demonstrating that the two computers can communicate with each other over the new cable.

19. On *WORKSTATION1*, open a command prompt window.

20. Type **ping 192.168.54.3** and press **Enter**. The computer indicates that it has received four replies from the remote computer.

21. Log off both computers.

Certification Objectives

Objectives for the Network+ Exam:

- Categorize standard cable types and properties: CAT3, CAT5, CAT5e, CAT6, STP, UTP, multimode fiber, single-mode fiber, coaxial RG-59 and RG-6, serial, and plenum vs. non-plenum, transmission speeds, distance, duplex, noise immunity (security, EMI), and frequency

- Identify common connector types: RJ-11, RJ-45, BNC, SC, ST, LC, RS-232, RG-59, RG-6

- Given a scenario, differentiate and implement appropriate wiring standards: 568A, 568B, straight vs. crossover, rollover, loopback

- Install, configure, and differentiate between common network devices: hub, repeater, modem, NIC, media converters, basic switch, bridge, wireless access point, basic router, basic firewall, basic DHCP server

- Given a scenario, troubleshoot common connectivity issues and select an appropriate solution. *Physical issues*: cross talk, nearing cross talk, attenuation, collisions, shorts, open impedance mismatch (echo), interference. *Logical issues*: port speed, port duplex mismatch, incorrect VLAN, incorrect IP address, wrong gateway, wrong DNS, wrong subnet mask. *Issues that should be identified but escalated*: switching loop, routing loop, route problems, proxy arp, broadcast storms. *Wireless issues*: interference (bleed, environmental factors), incorrect encryption, incorrect channel, incorrect frequency, ESSID mismatch, standard mismatch (802.11 a/b/g/n), distance, bounce, incorrect antenna placement

- Given a scenario, utilize the appropriate hardware tools: cable testers, protocol analyzer, certifiers, TDR, OTDR, multimeter, toner probe, butt set, punch down tool, cable stripper, snips, voltage event recorder, temperature monitor

Review Questions

1. What is one use for a crossover cable?

   a. to connect a hub and a workstation

   b. to connect a workstation to a wall jack

   c. to connect two workstations directly

   d. to connect a workstation to a modem

2. Which of the following tools would be useful in creating a patch cable for a 100Base-T network?

   a. screwdriver

   b. crimper

   c. soldering iron

   d. pliers

3. In twisted-pair wire, how does the twist ratio affect transmission? (Choose all that apply.)

   a. The more twists per inch, the less cross talk transmission will suffer.

   b. The more twists per inch, the slower the transmission.

   c. The more twists per inch, the more attenuation transmission will suffer.

   d. The more twists per inch, the faster the transmission.

4. What is the maximum speed at which Category 3 UTP can transmit data?

   a. 1 Mbps

   b. 10 Mbps

   c. 100 Mbps

   d. 1 Gbps

5. What type of cable would connect a workstation to the wall jack in the work area of a 100Base-T network?

   a. straight-through cable

   b. crossover cable

   c. coaxial cable

   d. punch-down cable

6. What type of cable is required for 100Base-FX?

   a. coaxial cable

   b. UTP

   c. STP

   d. fiber-optic cable

7. Which of the following would be the best medium for an environment that is subject to heavy EMI?

   a. fiber-optic cable

   b. RF

   c. infrared

   d. UTP

Lab 3.3 Comparing Throughput

Objectives

As a network administrator, you will often have to choose between different types of media, even within the same network. Throughput is often an important consideration in choosing between different network media. For instance, servers typically require faster media than most workstations, and some workstations will require faster media than others. Additionally, the types of applications in use on the network will also play a role in the types of media used. Some applications, such as streaming video, require more bandwidth than others.

When comparing media types, it is often helpful to look at the actual transmission rates under realistic conditions. First, the actual transmission rates will often be different from the theoretical transmission rates. Many factors will prevent a computer from transmitting or receiving data at the theoretical rate. These include the quality of the cabling, noise, and the ability of the computer on either end to send or receive data. Additionally, the bandwidth used by other computers on the network can limit the available bandwidth. Also, you will often need to verify that many applications work as expected with the intended media. With applications such as streaming video or IP telephony (VoIP), factors such as latency and transmission rate make a big difference in whether users can successfully use the application. Testing new applications under realistic conditions can help you make the best decision possible about the type of network media you will use in your network.

After completing this lab, you will be able to:

- Measure the throughput on an Ethernet network
- Compare throughput on networks using different media
- Recognize that actual throughput might not reach the maximum throughput specified for a network

Materials Required

This lab will require the following:

- A computer named *SERVER1* running Windows Server 2008, Standard Edition and configured as a domain controller for the netpluslab.net domain with an IP address of 192.168.54.1 and a subnet mask of 255.255.255.0
- A computer named *WORKSTATION1* running Windows XP Professional or Vista in the netpluslab.net domain and configured with an IP address of 192.168.54.2 and a subnet mask of 255.255.255.0
- Access as the Administrator to *SERVER1*
- Two hubs capable of 100 Mbps (such as a 100-Mbps hub or a 10/100 hub), or two switches with RJ-45 ports configured so that each port is in the same VLAN
- Ethernet NICs with RJ-45 connectors in each computer, so that each computer can transmit data at the rate of the hubs or switches
- Two straight-through Category 5 (or better) UTP cables that can be used to connect the computers to a hub
- One crossover Category 5 (or better) UTP cable that can be used to connect the two hubs directly

- On *SERVER1*, a shared folder named NETPLUS that can be accessed by the netplus user in the netpluslab.net domain; this folder should contain a large file (>50MB) such as driver.cab copied from the Windows XP C:\WINDOWS\Driver Cache\i386 folder.

Estimated completion time: **25–30 minutes**

Activity

1. Connect the computers to the first hub.

2. On *SERVER1*, log on as the Administrator. The Windows Server 2008 desktop appears.

3. Click **Start**, point to **All Programs**, point to **Administrative Tools**, and then click **Reliability and Performance Monitor**.

4. Select the **Performance Monitor** icon in the left pane.

5. Right-click the graph in the right pane. Select **Add Counters** from the shortcut menu. The Add Counters dialog box opens, as shown in Figure 3-2.

6. Click **Network Interface** in the list of available counters and then click the computer's NIC in the Instances of selected object list box.

7. Expand the **Network Interface** category and click **Bytes Total/sec** in the list below Network Interface. Click **Add**. The Bytes Total/sec counter is added to the list of counters that will be monitored.

8. Click **OK**. The Add Counters dialog box closes.

9. If the Performance window shows any counters besides Bytes Total/sec at the bottom of the right pane of the Performance window, click these counters to highlight them. Press the **Delete key** to delete them. You now see the NIC's current bandwidth.

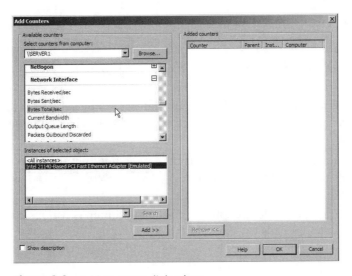

Figure 3-2   Add Counters dialog box

Courtesy Course Technology/Cengage Learning

10. Log on to *WORKSTATION1* with an administrative account. The Windows desktop appears.

11. Click **Start**, and then click **My Computer (Computer** in Windows Vista**)**. The My Computer window (Computer window in Windows Vista) opens.

12. Click **Tools** on the menu bar, and then click **Map Network Drive**. (In Windows Vista, simply click **Map network drive** on the toolbar.) The Map Network Drive window opens.

13. If necessary, choose drive letter **Z:** from the drop-down menu next to the Drive list box. Type **\\192.168.54.1\netplus** in the Folder text box and then click **Finish**.

14. A message box is displayed, indicating that you are attempting to connect to \\192.168.54.1\netplus. The Connect to 192.168.54.1 window opens. (The window might not appear if the password is the same on both computers. If so, go to Step 16.)

15. In the User name text box, enter **netplus@netpluslab.net**. In the Password text box, enter the password for the netplus account. Click **OK**. A window showing the contents of the shared netplus folder on the server is displayed.

16. Click **Start**, point to **All Programs**, point to **Accessories**, and then click **Command Prompt**. (In Windows Vista, click **Start**, type **cmd** in the Start Search text box, and then press **Enter**.) A command prompt window opens.

17. Type **mkdir C:\temp** and press **Enter**. The computer creates a new directory.

18. Type **notepad test.bat** and press **Enter**. A dialog box opens asking if you want to create the file.

19. Click **Yes**. The Notepad window opens.

20. In Notepad, enter the following three lines, substituting the correct filename for *driver.cab*:

    ```
    :Copy

    copy Z:\driver.cab C:\temp

    goto COPY
    ```

21. Exit Notepad. A dialog box opens, asking if you want to save your changes. Click **Yes**. (In Windows Vista, click **Save**.)

22. At the command prompt, type **test** and press **Enter**. The batch file continuously copies the file to *WORKSTATION1* from the shared folder on the Windows Server 2008 computer.

23. Look at the graph on *SERVER1*. If the line is flat and at the very bottom or the very top of the graph, right-click the graph and select **Properties** from the shortcut menu. Otherwise, go to Step 26.

24. On *SERVER1*, click the **Graph** tab. In the Maximum text box, enter **500** and click **OK**. The computer redraws the graph with the new scale. If the line on the graph is still flat, repeat the previous step and this step using 5000 and then 50,000 until the line is in the middle of the graph.

25. After a minute, look at the Average box at the bottom of the graph and record the number of bytes received per second. Multiply this number by 8 to find the number of

bits received per second. Record the number of bits received per second and compare it with the bandwidth of the hub.

26. At the command prompt on *WORKSTATION1*, press **Ctrl+C** to stop the batch file. Type **Y** and press **Enter** when asked to terminate the batch job.

27. Leave *WORKSTATION1* connected to the first hub but connect *SERVER1* to the second hub. Connect the two hubs directly with a crossover cable. The lights on each NIC turn on.

28. At the command prompt on *WORKSTATION1*, type **test** and press **Enter**.

29. Watch the graph on *SERVER1*. After a minute, record the number of bytes received per second. Multiply this number by 8 to find the number of bits received per second and compare it with the bandwidth of the hubs.

30. At the command prompt on *WORKSTATION1*, press **Ctrl+C** to stop the batch file. Type **Y** and press **Enter** when asked to terminate the batch job. On *SERVER1*, close the Reliability and Performance Monitor window.

31. Compare the number of bits received per second through the single hub you recorded in Step 25 with the number of bits received per second through two hubs you recorded in Step 29.

32. Log off both computers.

Certification Objectives

Objectives for the Network+ Exam:

- Install, configure, and differentiate between common network devices: hub, repeater, modem, NIC, media converters, basic switch, bridge, wireless access point, basic router, basic firewall, basic DHCP server

- Given a scenario, troubleshoot common connectivity issues and select an appropriate solution. *Physical issues*: cross talk, nearing cross talk, attenuation, collisions, shorts, open impedance mismatch (echo), interference. *Logical issues*: port speed, port duplex mismatch, incorrect VLAN, incorrect IP address, wrong gateway, wrong DNS, wrong subnet mask. *Issues that should be identified but escalated*: switching loop, routing loop, route problems, proxy arp, broadcast storms. *Wireless issues*: interference (bleed, environmental factors), incorrect encryption, incorrect channel, incorrect frequency, ESSID mismatch, standard mismatch (802.11 a/b/g/n), distance, bounce, incorrect antenna placement

Review Questions

1. What might cause a 100Base-TX network to experience an average throughput of less than 100 Mbps? (Choose all that apply.)

   a. heavy traffic on the network

   b. excessive noise

   c. too many protocols bound on the server

   d. a mix of different network operating systems on the servers

2. What is the maximum number of repeaters a data packet may traverse on a 100Base-T network?

   a. 2

   b. 3

   c. 4

   d. 5

3. What does the "T" in 10Base-T and 100Base-T stand for?

   a. transmission

   b. Transport layer

   c. twisted-pair

   d. transparent

4. Which of the following is not capable of full duplexing?

   a. 10Base-T

   b. 100Base-TX

   c. 100Base-T4

   d. 100Base-FX

5. What type of media do wireless networks use? (Choose all that apply.)

   a. UTP

   b. alpha wave

   c. infrared

   d. radio frequency

6. What type of cable is required for a 100Base-T network?

   a. CAT 3 or higher

   b. CAT 5 or higher

   c. CAT 6 or higher

   d. CAT 7 or higher

7. Where would you find a plenum cable?

   a. above the ceiling tiles in an office

   b. in an outdoor cable trench that leads to a building

   c. between a hub and a punch-down panel

   d. between a workstation and a wall jack

Lab 3.4 Understanding How a Category 5 Cable Fails

Objectives

Verifying the integrity of network cabling is often an important first step in solving network problems. In the OSI model, the network media is at the Physical layer. If the network media is not functioning properly, the layers above the Physical layer will not function properly either. It is important to keep in mind that damage to cabling might not be immediately obvious, and might result in odd or intermittent problems. For instance, a damaged cable might cause excess noise. Although data might be transmitted through the cable, protocols at higher levels of the OSI model will need to retransmit data. The problem might also become worse over time, eventually preventing data from being transmitted through the cable at all.

Network cabling should be protected as much as possible. It can be damaged slowly over time by factors such as excessive heat or pressure, or it can be damaged quickly by a user's foot or a backhoe. The better protected network cabling is, the longer it will last.

In this lab, you will simulate a failed cable by building an incorrectly made cable. Although cables can be damaged in many different ways, it is also important to verify that network cabling is properly installed in the first place. If you do not verify proper installation of network cabling, you might find it difficult to distinguish between a problem with the original installation and cabling damaged after the installation. This can prevent you from finding the ultimate source of the problem and fixing it properly.

After completing this lab, you will be able to:

- Identify the problem associated with an incorrectly wired Category 5 (or better) UTP cable

Materials Required

This lab will require the following:

- At least 10 feet of Category 5 (or better) UTP cable
- Four RJ-45 connectors
- A computer named *WORKSTATION1* running Windows XP Professional or Vista in the NETPLUS workgroup with an Ethernet NIC with RJ-45 connectors, configured with an IP address of 192.168.54.2 and a subnet mask of 255.255.255.0
- A computer named *WORKSTATION2* running Windows XP Professional or Vista in the NETPLUS workgroup with an Ethernet NIC with RJ-45 connectors, configured with an IP address of 192.168.54.3 and a subnet mask of 255.255.255.0
- File and Printer Sharing for Microsoft Networks installed on both computers
- Administrative access to both computers
- A network crimper
- A wire stripper
- A wire cutting tool
- Completion of Lab 3.2

Estimated completion time: **60 minutes**

Activity

1. Perform Steps 1 through 4 of Lab 3.2 for one end of the twisted-pair cable.
2. Repeat Steps 1 through 3 of Lab 3.2 for the other end of the twisted-pair cable.

Table 3-3   Pin numbers and color codes for creating an incorrect cable end

Pin number	Pair number	Color
1	4	Brown
2	4	White with brown stripes
3	1	White with blue stripes
4	3	White with orange stripes
5	3	Orange
6	1	Blue
7	2	White with green stripes
8	2	Green

3. On the second end of the twisted-pair cable, push the wires into the RJ-45 connector so that each wire is in its own slot and so that the colors match the pin numbers listed in Table 3-3. Using a crimping tool, punch down the end of the cable. This results in an incorrectly made cable.

4. Connect one end of the cable to each computer. If the network adapter lights on each computer do not illuminate, proceed with the next step. If they do, you accidentally made a correctly wired cable, and you need to begin this lab again.

5. Log on to *WORKSTATION1* with an administrative account. The Windows desktop appears.

6. Click **Start**, point to **All Programs**, point to **Accessories**, and then click **Command Prompt**. (In Windows Vista, click **Start**, type **cmd** in the Start Search text box, and then press **Enter**.) A command prompt window opens.

7. Type **ping 192.168.54.3** and press **Enter**. The computer indicates that the request timed out four times.

8. Repeat Steps 5 through 7 on *WORKSTATION2*, attempting to ping the IP address 192.168.54.2 instead.

9. Using the wire cutting tool, cut the incorrectly wired end of the cable about one inch from the RJ-45 connector. The RJ-45 connector should drop off.

10. Rewire and recrimp the connector to make a crossover cable as described in Lab 3.2; this connector should be wired according to Table 3-2. Connect one end of the cable to the NIC in each of the computers.

11. In the command prompt window on *WORKSTATION1*, type **ping 192.168.54.3** and press **Enter**. The computer indicates that it has received four replies from *WORKSTATION2*.

12. In the command prompt window on *WORKSTATION2*, type **ping 192.168.54.2** and press **Enter**. The computer indicates that it has received four replies from *WORKSTATION1*.

13. Log off both computers.

Certification Objectives

Objectives for the Network+ Exam:

- Identify common connector types: RJ-11, RJ-45, BNC, SC, ST, LC, RS-232, RG-59, RG-6

- Given a scenario, troubleshoot common connectivity issues and select an appropriate solution. *Physical issues*: cross talk, nearing cross talk, attenuation, collisions, shorts, open impedance mismatch (echo), interference. *Logical issues*: port speed, port duplex mismatch, incorrect VLAN, incorrect IP address, wrong gateway, wrong DNS, wrong subnet mask. *Issues that should be identified but escalated*: switching loop, routing loop, route problems, proxy arp, broadcast storms. *Wireless issues*: interference (bleed, environmental factors), incorrect encryption, incorrect channel, incorrect frequency, ESSID mismatch, standard mismatch (802.11 a/b/g/n), distance, bounce, incorrect antenna placement

- Given a scenario, utilize the appropriate hardware tools: cable testers, protocol analyzer, certifiers, TDR, OTDR, multimeter, toner probe, butt set, punch down tool, cable stripper, snips, voltage event recorder, temperature monitor.

Review Questions

1. What pin number is used for transmitting a positive signal on an RJ-45 straight-through patch cable?

   a. 1

   b. 2

   c. 5

   d. 6

2. Which of the following could be a symptom of a damaged patch cable between a workstation and the wall jack on a UTP network? (Choose all that apply.)

   a. The workstation cannot send or receive data to or from the network.

   b. The workstation and other workstations in the same office cannot send or receive data to or from the network.

   c. The workstation can send data to the network, but cannot receive data from the network.

   d. All workstations on the same segment can send data to the network, but cannot receive data from the network.

3. How does bend radius affect transmission?

   a. Transmission will not be successful until the bend radius has been reached.

   b. Transmission cannot occur at the bend radius.

   c. Transmission will be unreliable after the bend radius is exceeded.

   d. Transmission will be less secure after the bend radius is exceeded.

4. How many wire pairs are in a typical Category 5 cable?

   a. 2

   b. 3

   c. 4

   d. 6

5. What problem could be caused by laying cable in the ceiling tiles six inches above a bank of fluorescent lights?

   a. increased latency

   b. EMI

   c. fire hazard

   d. decreased bend radius

6. What organization is responsible for establishing structured wiring standards?

   a. TIA/EIA

   b. ANSI

   c. ITU

   d. FCC

Lab 3.5 Connecting Two Switches with Fiber-Optic Cable

Objectives

In this lab, you will connect two switches with fiber-optic cable. Although UTP cable is less fragile, less expensive, and easier to handle than fiber, fiber can allow the transfer of more information over greater distances than UTP cable. Additionally, electrical interference does not affect fiber.

A port used to connect two switches is often called an uplink port. An uplink port often uses faster media than the other ports on the switch, but not always. Traffic between the two switches will be transmitted through the uplink ports. If the other ports on the switch transmit a lot of traffic between the two switches, the uplink port might become saturated. This will reduce throughput for any traffic that must go through the two switches. If the uplink ports use a faster media than the other ports on the switch, it becomes more difficult (or impossible) to saturate the link between the two ports.

After completing this lab, you will be able to:

- Connect two switches using multimode fiber

Materials Required

This lab will require the following:

- A computer named *WORKSTATION1* running Windows XP Professional or Vista with a NIC and with an IP address of 192.168.54.2 and a subnet mask of 255.255.255.0
- A computer named *WORKSTATION2* running Windows XP Professional or Vista with a NIC and with an IP address of 192.168.54.3 and a subnet mask of 255.255.255.0

- Administrative access to both computers
- A shared folder on *WORKSTATION2* named NETPLUS
- Two switches, named *SWITCH1* and *SWITCH2*, with fiber uplink ports (with any necessary configuration to act as uplink ports), the appropriate connectors, and all ports configured in the same VLAN
- Installation of any adapters, such as Gigabit Interface Converters (GBICs), necessary for operation of the uplink ports
- A length of fiber-optic cable with the appropriate connectors to attach to the two switches
- Two Category 5 (or better) UTP cables with RJ-45 connectors

Other fiber connectors may be used as appropriate.

Estimated completion time: **20 minutes**

Activity

1. Plug the RJ-45 connector at one end of a UTP cable into the NIC of *WORKSTATION1*. Plug the RJ-45 connector at the other end of the cable into one of the RJ-45 ports on *SWITCH1*. Link lights on the switch and on the NIC light up.

2. Repeat the previous step, connecting *WORKSTATION2* to *SWITCH2*.

3. If necessary, remove the plugs from one of the fiber uplink ports on *SWITCH1*. Fiber ports often come with a plug to protect the port from dust and other damage.

As fiber ports may emit invisible laser radiation when they do not contain a cable, do not stare into an open port. Avoid looking into one if possible while the switch is powered on.

4. Grasp the connector at one end of the fiber-optic cable. Making sure that the SC connector is properly oriented, push it into the uplink port on *SWITCH1* until the connector snaps into place. Link lights on both switches light up.

5. Log on to WORKSTATION1 using an administrative account. The Windows desktop appears.

6. Click **Start**, point to **All Programs**, point to **Accessories**, and then click **Command Prompt**. (In Windows Vista, click **Start**, type **cmd** in the Start Search text box, and then press **Enter**.) A command prompt window opens.

7. Type **ping 192.168.54.3** and press **Enter**. The computer indicates that it has received four replies.

8. Repeat Steps 5 through 7 on *WORKSTATION2*, and then ping the IP address 192.168.54.2.

9. Log off both computers.

Certification Objectives

Objectives for the Network+ Exam:

- Categorize standard cable types and properties: CAT3, CAT5, CAT5e, CAT6, STP, UTP, multimode fiber, single-mode fiber, coaxial RG-59 and RG-6, serial, and plenum vs. non-plenum, transmission speeds, distance, duplex, noise immunity (security, EMI), and frequency
- Identify common connector types: RJ-11, RJ-45, BNC, SC, ST, LC, RS-232, RG-59, RG-6
- Install, configure, and differentiate between common network devices: hub, repeater, modem, NIC, media converters, basic switch, bridge, wireless access point, basic router, basic firewall, basic DHCP server

Review Questions

1. Which of the following is *not* an advantage of fiber cables over UTP cables?

   a. Fiber is not susceptible to electric interference, whereas UTP cable is.

   b. Fiber is less fragile than UTP cable.

   c. Fiber is less expensive than UTP cable.

   d. Fiber can transmit data over longer distances than UTP cable.

2. In which of the following situations would it be possible to use a UTP cable standard such as 1000Base-CX over a fiber-optic cable standard such as 1000Base-LX or 1000Base-T?

   a. when connecting two data centers over distances of 2 km or less

   b. when connecting short distances of 25 meters or less between network devices and servers inside a single data center

   c. when connecting short distances of 200 meters or less between network devices and workstations inside a building

   d. when connecting buildings inside a campus over distances of 500 meters or less

3. Which of the following problems could cause optic loss in fiber-optic cable?

   a. cross talk between strands of fiber in multimode fiber cables

   b. cross talk between cables in single-mode fiber cables

   c. electromagnetic interference caused by power lines near the cables

   d. oil accidentally placed in a connection during splicing

4. 100Base-FX requires multimode fiber cable with two or more strands. How are these strands used to transmit and receive data? (Choose all that apply.)

   a. One strand is used for both transmission and reception in both full and half duplex.

   b. Both strands are used for transmission and reception in full duplex.

   c. One strand is used for transmission and the other is used for reception in half duplex.

   d. Both strands are used for transmission and reception in full duplex, whereas there is no half duplex for 100Base-FX.

5. You work for a small ISP. Which fiber technology would be best for connecting to your telecommunications carrier over a distance of 2.8 miles?

   a. 1000Base-LX

   b. 1000Base-SX

   c. 10 GBase-SR

   d. 1000Base-T

INTRODUCTION to TCP/IP PROTOCOLS

Labs included in this chapter

- Lab 4.1 Configuring IP Addresses and Subnet Masks
- Lab 4.2 Automatically Assigning IP Addresses with DHCP
- Lab 4.3 Configuring Domain Name System (DNS) Properties
- Lab 4.4 Using FTP
- Lab 4.5 Understanding Port Numbers
- Lab 4.6 Disabling Unnecessary Protocols

Net+ Exam Objectives

Objective	Lab
Explain the function of common networking protocols	4.2, 4.4, 4.6
Identify commonly used TCP and UDP default ports	4.5
Identify the following address formats	4.1
Given a scenario, troubleshoot common connectivity issues and select an appropriate solution	4.1, 4.3, 4.6
Given a scenario, select the appropriate command line interface tool and interpret the output to verify functionality	4.1
Explain issues that affect device security	4.6

Lab 4.1 Configuring IP Addresses and Subnet Masks

Objectives

To address a TCP/IP host properly, you need both an IP address and a subnet mask. The subnet mask is used to further divide a network. This allows a network administrator to control access or traffic between two subnetworks (or subnets). A router or layer-3 switch is required to route network traffic between the two subnets. For instance, you might want to prevent users from directly accessing a Web server. If you put the users and the Web server on different subnets, you can then use a router to control user access to the Web server.

An IP address consists of four numbers separated by dots. Each individual number in the address is called an octet. For instance, in the IP address 10.172.11.145, the first octet is 10, the second octet is 172, and so on. IP addresses have traditionally been divided into classes based on the first octet. The first octet of Class A addresses is between 1 and 126, the first octet of Class B addresses is between 128 and 191, and the first octet of Class C addresses is between 192 and 223. Class D addresses, whose first octet ranges from 224 to 239, are reserved for multicast. Class E addresses, whose first octet ranges from 239 to 254, are reserved for experimental purposes. Finally, addresses whose first octet is 255 are reserved for broadcasts.

Subnet masks can be used to conserve IP addresses. The size of a subnet mask determines the number of hosts that can be placed on a network. Using subnet masks, you can allocate IP address blocks that fit the number of hosts you have. The default subnet mask of a Class B network is 255.255.0.0, and it can have up to 65,534 hosts. A Class A network has a default subnet mask of 255.0.0.0, and it can have up to 16,777,214 hosts. Without subnetting, you would be unable to divide these very large networks into smaller networks. With subnetting, you can carve a larger network into many different subnets. For instance, suppose you were assigned a Class B network. If you subdivided this network into smaller networks with subnet masks of 255.255.255.0 (the default subnet mask for Class C networks), you would be able to divide the Class B network into 256 smaller networks.

After completing this lab, you will be able to:

- Configure IP addresses and subnet masks in Windows XP or Vista
- Discuss the purpose of subnet masks

Materials Required

This lab will require the following:

- Two computers running Microsoft Windows XP or Vista, both configured as members of the NETPLUS workgroup
- Access to each computer as an administrator
- Both computers connected to a hub with Category 5 (or better) UTP cables

Estimated completion time: **20 minutes**

Activity

1. Log on to both computers as an administrator.

2. On one computer, click **Start**, point to **All Programs**, point to **Accessories**, point to **Communications**, and then click **Network Connections**. (In Windows Vista,

click **Start**, right-click **Network**, and click **Properties**. Click **Manage network connections**.) The Network Connections window opens.

3. In the Network Connections window, right-click **Local Area Connection** and select **Properties** from the shortcut menu. (In Windows Vista, if a UAC box opens, click **Continue**.) The Local Area Connection Properties window opens.

4. Double-click **Internet Protocol (TCP/IP)**. (In Windows Vista, double-click **Internet Protocol Version 4 (TCP/IPv4)**.) The Internet Protocol (TCP/IP) Properties dialog box opens.

5. Click the **Use the following IP address** option button.

6. Enter **172.20.1.1** in the IP address text box.

7. Enter **255.255.255.0** in the Subnet mask text box. See Figure 4-1. If necessary, clear the Default gateway and DNS server fields.

8. Click **OK** and then click **Close**. The Local Area Connection Properties window closes.

9. Now you will configure the second computer in a different network. Repeat Steps 2 through 8 on the second computer, using 172.20.2.1 as the IP address and 255.255.255.0 as the subnet mask. Table 4-1 shows the IP addresses and subnet masks on each computer.

10. You now have configured the two computers on two different subnets. To demonstrate this, on the second computer click **Start**, point to **All Programs**, point to **Accessories**, and then click **Command Prompt**. (In Windows Vista, click **Start**, type **cmd** in the Start Search text box, and then press **Enter**.) A command prompt window opens.

11. In the command prompt window, type **ping 172.20.1.1** and press **Enter**. You see a message indicating that the remote computer is unreachable. The message appears on the screen four times.

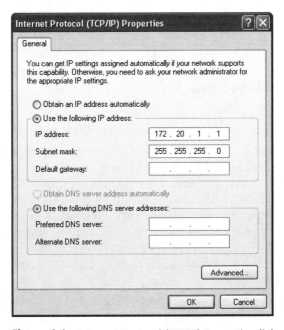

Figure 4-1 Internet Protocol (TCP/IP) Properties dialog box

Courtesy Course Technology/Cengage Learning

Table 4-1   IP address and subnet mask assignments in different networks

Computer	IP address	Subnet mask
First computer	172.20.1.1	255.255.255.0
Second computer	172.20.2.1	255.255.255.0

12. Repeat Steps 10 and 11 on the first computer, attempting to ping 172.20.2.1.

13. Now you will change the subnet mask so that both computers are on the same network. Repeat Steps 3 through 8 on the first computer, keeping the IP address the same but changing the subnet mask to 255.255.0.0.

14. Repeat Steps 3 through 8 on the second computer, keeping the IP address the same but changing the subnet mask to 255.255.0.0. Table 4-2 summarizes the new IP address assignments for the network.

15. Repeat Step 11 on the second computer, attempting to ping 172.20.1.1. The computer receives four replies, indicating that there is network connectivity between the two computers.

16. Repeat Step 11 on the first computer, attempting to ping 172.20.2.1.

17. Log off both computers.

Table 4-2   New IP address assignments in the same network

Computer	IP address	Subnet mask
First computer	172.20.1.1	255.255.0.0
Second computer	172.20.2.1	255.255.0.0

Certification Objectives

Objectives for the Network+ Exam:

- Identify the following address formats: IPv6, IPv4, MAC addressing

- Given a scenario, troubleshoot common connectivity issues and select an appropriate solution. *Physical issues*: cross talk, nearing cross talk, attenuation, collisions, shorts, open impedance mismatch (echo), interference. *Logical issues*: port speed, port duplex mismatch, incorrect VLAN, incorrect IP address, wrong gateway, wrong DNS, wrong subnet mask. *Issues that should be identified but escalated*: switching loop, routing loop, route problems, proxy arp, broadcast storms. *Wireless issues*: interference (bleed, environmental factors), incorrect encryption, incorrect channel, incorrect frequency, ESSID mismatch, standard mismatch (802.11 a/b/g/n), distance, bounce, incorrect antenna placement

- Given a scenario, select the appropriate command line interface tool and interpret the output to verify functionality: Traceroute, Ipconfig, Ifconfig, Ping, Arp ping, Arp, Nslookup, Host, Dig, Mtr, Route, Nbtstat, Netstat

Review Questions

1. What is the class of network that you configured in this activity?

   a. Class A

   b. Class B

   c. Class C

   d. Class D

2. What is the purpose of a subnet mask?

   a. to indicate which protocols a particular network uses

   b. to further subdivide a network

   c. to mask, or prevent access to, portions of a network

   d. to limit the protocols used in a particular network

3. A network has a subnet mask of 255.255.255.0. How many usable IP addresses are available for network hosts?

   a. 65,535

   b. 65,534

   c. 256

   d. 254

4. Assuming that it has the default subnet mask, why can't you assign the IP address 192.168.54.255 to a host?

   a. This address is reserved for multicast.

   b. This address is reserved for experimental uses.

   c. This address describes the network.

   d. This address is the broadcast address.

5. Which of the following commands can you use in Windows to display information about the subnet mask configured for a particular NIC?

   a. ipconfig

   b. ping

   c. cmd

   d. netstat

Lab 4.2 Automatically Assigning IP Addresses with DHCP

Objectives

In this lab, you will assign IP addresses to client workstations automatically with a Dynamic Host Configuration Protocol (DHCP) server. DHCP allows you to assign IP addresses from a central location, without having to configure each workstation individually. In all but the smallest networks, this will save you time. You can also configure additional information, such as the default gateway and any DNS or WINS servers to be used.

DHCP works by assigning a pool of IP addresses to a network. When a workstation requests an IP address, the DHCP server assigns one of the available addresses from the pool. Most network administrators do not use DHCP to address their servers, routers, or other network devices like printers. You might find it useful to set aside a range of IP addresses on each network for devices with static IP addresses. Servers and most network devices typically have static IP addresses, and are not often moved. However, you can use DHCP to assign static addresses based on a device's MAC address.

If a Windows computer configured to use DHCP is unable to obtain IP address information from a DHCP server, it will use Automatic Private IP Addressing (APIPA) to assign itself an IP address. However, the DHCP client will periodically attempt to reach the DHCP server until it can obtain an IP address. APIPA addresses are in the range from 169.254.0.0 to 169.254.255.255 and have a subnet mask of 255.255.0.0. The APIPA address pool is a Class B address set aside by the Internet Assigned Numbers Authority (IANA) so that network administrators will not use it for any other purpose. Although APIPA can simplify address assignment on simple networks, it does not work well in networks with more than one subnet or that need to connect to the Internet.

To configure the Windows DHCP server, you create a DHCP scope. Each scope consists of a range of IP addresses to be assigned, addresses to be excluded from the scope, and other information to be assigned to clients. Multiple DHCP scopes are typically used when a DHCP server needs to assign addresses for multiple subnets.

After completing this lab, you will be able to:

- Configure the DHCP server on Windows Server 2008
- Understand DHCP and dynamic addressing

Materials Required

This lab will require the following:

- A computer named *SERVER1* running Windows Server 2008, Standard Edition, configured as a DNS server and a domain controller for the netpluslab.net domain, with an IP address of 192.168.54.1 and a subnet mask of 255.255.255.0
- Access to the computer as the Administrator
- DHCP installed on *SERVER1* but not configured
- A computer running Windows XP Professional or Vista in the netpluslab.net domain, without a specified IP address
- Administrative access to the Windows XP or Vista computer
- Both computers connected to a hub with straight-through Category 5 (or better) UTP cables

Estimated completion time: **30 minutes**

Activity

1. Log on to *SERVER1* as the Administrator. The Windows Server 2008 desktop appears.

2. Click **Start**, point to **Administrative Tools**, and then click **DHCP**. The DHCP window opens.

3. Click **server1.netpluslab.net** in the left pane of the window. Right-click **IPv4** and click **New Scope**. The New Scope Wizard opens.

4. Click **Next**.

5. Enter **Net Plus Lab** in the Name text box. Enter **Test** in the Description text box. Click **Next**.

6. Now you will configure the DHCP server to assign clients IP addresses from 192.168.54.10 to 192.168.54.200. This range allows for servers and network devices with static IP addresses from 192.168.54.1 to 192.168.54.9 and 192.168.54.201 to 192.168.54.254. In the Start IP address text box, enter **192.168.54.10**. In the End IP address text box, enter **192.168.54.200**. In the Subnet mask text box, enter **255.255.255.0**, if necessary. Figure 4-2 shows the New Scope Wizard. Click **Next**.

7. Now you will exclude the IP address 192.168.54.100 from the DHCP scope. In the Start IP address text box, enter **192.168.54.100**. This allows you to reserve this static IP address for the existing server in the middle of the range of IP addresses to be used for the DHCP scope. Click **Add**. The computer excludes the address from the DHCP scope. Click **Next**.

8. Now you can assign the amount of time that a client can use an IP address assigned to it from the DHCP server before it needs to renew the address. Enter **10** in the Days text box. Click **Next**.

9. Now you have the opportunity to configure further options. Click the **Yes, I want to configure these options now** option button, if necessary. Click **Next**.

10. Now you can specify the default gateway used by clients. Click **Next**, as this network has no default gateway.

11. Now you can specify information about domain name resolution for clients. In the Parent domain text box, enter **netpluslab.net**. In the IP address text box, enter **192.168.54.1** and click **Add**. Clients will now use this server as their DNS server. Click **Next**.

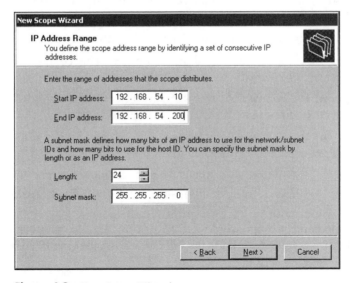

Figure 4-2   New Scope Wizard

Courtesy Course Technology/Cengage Learning

12. In this window, you can specify WINS servers. Click **Next**.

13. Now you must activate the DHCP scope. Make sure that the **Yes, I want to activate this** scope now option button is selected and click **Next**. Click **Finish**.

14. If the server1.netpluslab.net icon is a white circle with a red arrow in the center, right-click **IPv4** in the left pane, and select **Authorize** from the shortcut menu. Wait a few seconds and press **F5**. If the server1.netpluslab.net icon in the left pane is not a white circle with a green arrow in the center, press **F5** every few seconds until it is. A green arrow indicates that the scope is active, whereas a red arrow indicates that it is not. The DHCP server is now authorized to assign IP addresses in the netpluslab.net domain.

15. Log on to the Windows XP or Vista computer as an administrator. The Windows desktop appears.

16. Click **Start**, point to **All Programs**, point to **Accessories**, point to **Communications**, and then click **Network Connections**. (In Windows Vista, click **Start**, right-click **Network**, and click **Properties**. Click **Manage network connections**.) The Network Connections window opens.

17. Right-click the **Local Area Connection** icon and select **Properties** from the short-cut menu. (In Windows Vista, if a UAC box opens, click **Continue**.) The Local Area Connection window opens.

18. Double-click **Internet Protocol (TCP/IP)**. (In Windows Vista, double-click **Internet Protocol Version 4 (TCP/IPv4)**.) The Internet Protocol (TCP/IP) Properties dialog box opens.

19. Click the **Obtain an IP address automatically** and **Obtain DNS server address automatically** option buttons. Click **OK**, and then click **OK** again to close the Local Area Connection Properties window.

20. Click **Start**, point to **All Programs**, point to **Accessories**, and then click **Command Prompt**. (In Windows Vista, click **Start**, type **cmd** in the Start Search text box, and then press **Enter**.) A command prompt window opens.

21. Type **ipconfig** and press **Enter**. What is the current IP address of this computer?

22. Type **ipconfig/release** and press **Enter**. The computer releases any current address assigned by DHCP.

23. Type **ipconfig/renew** and press **Enter**. The computer obtains an IP address from the DHCP server and prints it. What is the new IP address?

24. Type **ipconfig/all** and press **Enter**. Record the name or address of the DNS server, the DHCP server, and the time the DHCP lease expires.

25. Now you will examine what happens when a computer running Windows fails to get an IP address through DHCP. Disconnect the cable connecting *SERVER1* to the hub. (Do not disconnect *WORKSTATION1* from the hub.)

26. In the command prompt window, type **ipconfig/release** and press **Enter**. The computer prints information for the NIC indicating that the IP address and subnet mask are both 0.0.0.0.

27. Type **ipconfig/renew** and press **Enter**. After a couple of minutes, the computer indicates that it was unable to contact the DHCP server.

28. Type **ipconfig/all** and press **Enter**. The computer prints the new IP address and subnet mask for the computer. What are the IP address and subnet mask now? What DNS servers and domain name are now configured for the server?

29. Connect *SERVER1* to the hub again. Wait a couple of minutes and type **ipconfig** in the command prompt window. Repeat this step until the computer is able to obtain an IP address from the DHCP server.

30. Log off both computers.

Certification Objectives

Objectives for the Network+ Exam:

- Explain the function of common networking protocols: TCP, FTP, UDP, TCP/IP suite, DHCP, TFTP, DNS, HTTP(S), ARP, SIP (VoIP), RTP (VoIP), SSH, POP3, NTP, IMAP4, Telnet, SMTP, SNMP2/3, ICMP, IGMP, TLS

Review Questions

1. What was the IP address the Windows computer obtained in Step 23?

2. When does the DHCP lease you obtained in this lab expire?

3. Which of the following are valid methods of assigning IP addresses to workstations, servers, and network devices? (Choose all that apply.)

   a. manual configuration

   b. DHCP

   c. BOOTP

   d. POST

4. You would like to assign a WINS server to each workstation. Can you accomplish this via DHCP?

5. Your colleague placed a second DHCP server on the network by mistake. What might happen as a result? (Choose all that apply.)

   a. The second DHCP server might lease duplicate addresses to some hosts.

   b. The second DHCP server might give out incorrect settings to its clients.

   c. DHCP might stop working on the first DHCP server.

   d. You might need to configure IP addresses on some hosts manually.

6. Which of the following information could not be given out by a DHCP server?

   a. WINS server address

   b. DNS server address

   c. default gateway

   d. additional network protocols to be used

7. All of the following configuration information can be supplied by a DHCP server. Which of the following cannot be supplied by APIPA? (Choose all that apply.)

a. IP address

b. subnet mask

c. DNS servers

d. default gateway

Lab 4.3 Configuring Domain Name System (DNS) Properties

Objectives

The Domain Name System (DNS) is a method of associating an IP address with a host name. It is an alternative to the hosts file, and is much easier to manage and maintain over many servers. For that reason, DNS is used throughout the Internet. When you open a Web browser and attempt to connect to *www.comptia.com*, for example, the Web browser first queries a DNS server to find the IP address of the Web site. If the DNS server your computer is configured to use does not know the IP address associated with *www.comptia.com*, it queries the authoritative name server for the comptia.com domain (or zone). The authoritative name server is the DNS server with the definitive DNS information for that domain. When the authoritative DNS server responds with the IP address to your DNS server, your DNS server sends that information to your computer. The Web browser on your computer then uses that IP address to connect to the Web site.

In addition to finding the IP address belonging to a particular host name (a process known as a forward DNS lookup), DNS is also used to find the host name belonging to a particular IP address. This process is known as a reverse DNS lookup. A computer can use a reverse DNS lookup to determine the name of a computer attempting to access its network resources. However, reverse DNS lookups are not a reliable way of determining this information.

One tool you can use to find DNS information directly is the Nslookup command. This command allows you to find the IP address associated with a particular host name and other information.

Keep in mind that beginning with Windows 2000 Server, DNS has become tightly integrated with Active Directory. Before Windows 2000 Server, making a mistake when configuring DNS might prevent you from accessing a server by name. Now, making a mistake configuring DNS can prevent Active Directory from w orking properly. Keeping DNS working properly is very important in networks that use Windows Server 2008.

After completing this lab, you will be able to:

- Add a DNS server to DNS
- Add a DNS zone
- Add a DNS host
- Configure a computer to refer to the DNS server
- Access a computer using its DNS name

Materials Required

This lab will require the following:

- A computer running Windows Server 2008, Standard Edition named *SERVER1* configured with an IP address of 192.168.54.1 and a subnet mask of 255.255.255.0
- The Windows Server 2008 computer configured as a domain controller for the netpluslab.net domain with the DNS server role installed
- A reverse lookup zone configured for the 192.168.54.x subnet
- A computer running Windows XP Professional or Vista named *WORKSTATION1* configured with an IP address of 192.168.54.3 and a subnet mask of 255.255.255.0, but without a DNS server configured
- A second computer running Windows XP Professional or Vista named *WORKSTATION2* configured with an IP address of 192.168.54.5 and a subnet mask of 255.255.255.0, but without a DNS server configured
- Administrative access to both computers
- Each computer connected to a hub with straight-through CAT 5 (or better) UTP cables

---

Estimated completion time: **30 minutes**

Activity

1. Log on to *SERVER1* as the Administrator. The Windows Server 2008 desktop appears.
2. Click **Start**, point to **Administrative Tools**, and then click **DNS**. The DNS Manager window opens.
3. Click the **plus sign (+)** next to the server name to expand the tree underneath it. Right-click the name of the server. Click **New Zone**. The New Zone Wizard opens.
4. Click **Next**. The next window in the wizard asks you to select the type of zone you want to configure.
5. Make sure that the **Primary zone** option button is selected and click **Next**. The next window in the wizard asks you to choose how DNS data will be replicated through your network.
6. Click **Next** to select the default option. The next window in the wizard asks you to choose whether you want to create a forward or reverse lookup zone.
7. Make sure that the **Forward lookup zone** option is selected and click **Next**. The wizard now asks you to choose a name for the zone.
8. In the Zone name text box, type **otherorg.net**, and then click **Next**. The next window in the wizard asks you to select the type of DNS updates to be used.
9. Click **Next** to select the default option. The next window in the wizard summarizes the options that you have chosen and indicates that you have finished.
10. Click **Finish**. The New Zone Wizard closes.

11. In the left pane of the DNS Manager window, click the **plus sign (+)** next to the Forward Lookup Zones folder. The tree expands, showing a list of domains for which this DNS server is authoritative, including the new otherorg.net domain.

12. In the left pane, click the **otherorg.net** folder to select it. Right-click the **otherorg. net** folder, and click **New Host (A or AAAA)** from the shortcut menu. The New Host dialog box opens.

13. In the Name text box, type **workstation1**. In the IP address text box, type **192.168.54.3.** Place a check in the **Create associated pointer (PTR) record** check box. Figure 4-3 shows the DNS Manager window and the New Host dialog box.

14. Click the **Add Host** button. The DNS dialog box opens, indicating that the host record workstation1.otherorg.net was successfully created.

15. Click **OK**. The DNS dialog box closes.

16. Click **Done**. The New Host dialog box closes.

17. Click the **netpluslab.net** folder to select it. Then right-click the **netpluslab.net** folder, and click **New Host (A or AAAA)** from the shortcut menu. The New Host dialog box opens.

18. In the New Host dialog box, repeat Steps 13 through 15, creating the domain name **workstation2.netpluslab.net** with an IP address of **192.168.54.5**.

19. Click **Done**.

20. Log on to *WORKSTATION1* as an administrator. The Windows desktop appears.

21. Click **Start**, point to **All Programs**, point to **Accessories**, point to **Communications**, and then click **Network Connections**. (In Windows Vista, click **Start**, right-click **Network**, and click **Properties**. Click **Manage network connections**.) The Network Connections window opens.

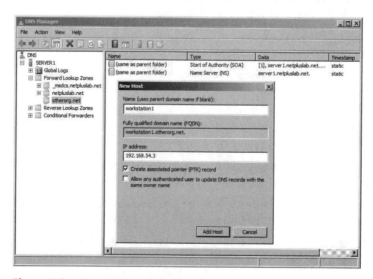

Figure 4-3 The DNS Manager window and New Host dialog box

Courtesy Course Technology/Cengage Learning

22. Right-click **Local Area Connection** and click **Properties** from the shortcut menu. (In Windows Vista, if a UAC box opens, click **Continue**.) The Local Area Connection Properties window opens.

23. Double-click **Internet Protocol (TCP/IP)**. (In Windows Vista, double-click **Internet Protocol Version 4 (TCP/IPv4)**.) The Internet Protocol (TCP/IP) Properties window opens.

24. Click the **Use the following DNS server addresses** option button, if necessary. In the Preferred DNS server text box, type **192.168.54.1**.

25. Click **OK** twice to exit the Local Area Connection Properties window.

26. Click **Start**, point to **All Programs**, point to **Accessories**, and click **Command Prompt**. (In Windows Vista, click **Start**, type **cmd** in the Start Search text box, and then press **Enter**.) A command prompt window opens.

27. In the command prompt window, type **nslookup workstation2.netpluslab. net** and press **Enter**. The computer displays the name *workstation2.netpluslab.net* and its IP address, as well as the IP address of the DNS server answering the request.

28. Type **ping workstation2.netpluslab.net** and press **Enter**. The computer indicates that it has received four replies from the remote computer, and displays its IP address.

29. Repeat Steps 27 and 28, pinging **workstation1.otherorg.net**.

30. Log off all three computers.

Certification Objectives

Objectives for the Network+ Exam:

- Given a scenario, troubleshoot common connectivity issues and select an appropriate solution. *Physical issues*: cross talk, nearing cross talk, attenuation, collisions, shorts, open impedance mismatch (echo), interference. *Logical issues*: port speed, port duplex mismatch, incorrect VLAN, incorrect IP address, wrong gateway, wrong DNS, wrong subnet mask. *Issues that should be identified but escalated*: switching loop, routing loop, route problems, proxy arp, broadcast storms. *Wireless issues*: interference (bleed, environmental factors), incorrect encryption, incorrect channel, incorrect frequency, ESSID mismatch, standard mismatch (802.11 a/b/g/n), distance, bounce, incorrect antenna placement

Review Questions

1. What is the purpose of a name server?

    a. to maintain the DNS database for an entire zone

    b. to supply clients with IP address resolution for requested hosts

    c. to track and record all TCP/IP host name information for a network

    d. to track and record all NetBIOS naming information for a network

2. What is the term for the group of devices that a name server manages?

    a. hierarchy

    b. tree

    c. zone

    d. directory

3. Which of the following are examples of top-level domains? (Choose all that apply.)

   a. .net

   b. .com

   c. .uk

   d. .aut

4. When a DNS server retrieves the host name associated with an IP address, what type of lookup is it accomplishing?

   a. forward

   b. adjacent

   c. backward

   d. reverse

5. What is one advantage of using DNS instead of hosts files?

   a. DNS does not require manual updating of files on multiple networked nodes.

   b. DNS is more compatible with Linux systems.

   c. DNS will map both NetBIOS and TCP/IP host names to IP addresses, whereas hosts files will map only TCP/IP host names to IP addresses.

   d. Using DNS is more secure than using hosts files.

Lab 4.4 Using FTP

Objectives

In this lab, you will connect to a File Transfer Protocol (FTP) server on a remote host. FTP is used throughout the Internet to make files available for downloading. If a network administrator would like to make files available to the general public, she can create an anonymous FTP server. Users can log on to an anonymous FTP server by using a special account named "anonymous" without knowing the password.

FTP servers are available on nearly all platforms. If you run an anonymous FTP server, you should be careful when allowing anonymous users to upload files (that is, transfer files to the server) because malicious users could fill up your server's disk drive with their files. Another potential problem with FTP is that it sends passwords in unencrypted text, so they could be captured by a malicious user.

A variety of FTP clients are available for almost all modern operating systems. Command-line FTP clients are built into most modern operating systems, including Linux and Windows, but various GUI clients are also available. A GUI client will automate the FTP process for you, and might include additional features such as the ability to resume interrupted downloads.

After completing this lab, you will be able to:

- Log on to an FTP site
- Download files from an FTP site
- Copy files to an FTP site
- Define security policies for an FTP site

Materials Required

This lab will require the following:

- A computer running Windows Server 2008, Standard Edition named *SERVER1*, configured as a domain controller for the netpluslab.net domain with an IP address of 192.168.54.1 and a subnet mask of 255.255.255.0

- Internet Information Services (IIS) version 7 installed and running on *SERVER1* with the File Transfer Protocol (FTP) service installed, with a root of C:\Inetpub\ftproot for the FTP service and with the default configuration and sample files in place

- The folder C:\Inetpub\ftproot configured so that users in the Domain Users group have Read, Write, and Execute permissions

- Access to *SERVER1* as the Administrator

- A user account named netplus in the Domain Users group in the netpluslab.net domain

- A computer running Windows XP Professional or Vista named *WORKSTATION1*, configured with an IP address of 192.168.54.3 and a subnet mask of 255.255.255.0

- Both computers connected to a hub with CAT 5 (or better) UTP cables

Estimated completion time: **35 minutes**

Activity

1. Log on to *SERVER1* as the Administrator. The Windows Server 2008 desktop appears.

2. Click **Start**, point to **All Programs**, click **Accessories**, and then click **Command Prompt**. A command prompt window opens.

3. In the command prompt window, type **echo "***your name***" > C:\Inetpub\ftproot\ netplus.txt** and press **Enter**. (Substitute your name for "*your name*.") This creates a file named netplus.txt containing your name in the C:\Inetpub\ftproot directory.

4. At the command prompt, type **copy C:\Inetpub\wwwroot\welcome.png C:\ Inetpub\ftproot** and press **Enter**. The computer copies the file from one directory to the other. This image file now will be available on the FTP site configured on this computer.

5. Log on to *WORKSTATION1* as the netplus user. The Windows desktop appears.

6. Click **Start**, point to **All Programs**, point to **Accessories**, and then click **Command Prompt**. (In Windows Vista, click **Start**, type **cmd** in the Start Search text box, and then press **Enter**.) A command prompt window opens.

7. In the command prompt window, type **ftp 192.168.54.1** and press **Enter**. The computer indicates that you have connected to 192.168.54.1, and that the remote computer is running the Microsoft FTP service. The prompt changes to User (192.168.54.1:(none)):.

8. At the User (192.168.54.1:(none)): prompt, type **anonymous** and press **Enter**. The computer indicates that anonymous access is allowed and asks you to type an e-mail address or other form of identity as a password. The Password prompt also appears. At the Password prompt, type an e-mail address or a brief phrase, and then press **Enter**. Note that the letters you type do not echo to the screen. The computer indicates that you

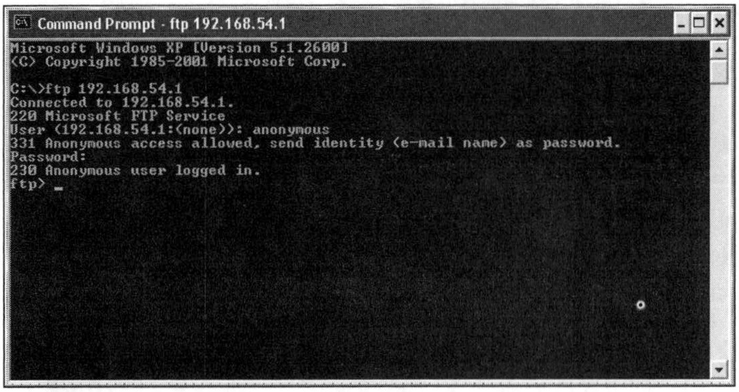

Figure 4-4 Logging on to an FTP server

Courtesy Course Technology/Cengage Learning

have logged on successfully, and the prompt changes to ftp>. Figure 4-4 shows a user logging on to an FTP server.

9. Type **dir** and press **Enter**. A list of the files found on the remote computer, including welcome.png and netplus.txt, is displayed.

10. Type **ls** and press **Enter**. A list of the files found on the remote computer is displayed.

11. At the prompt, type **get netplus.txt** and press **Enter**. The computer indicates that it is opening an ASCII mode data connection. ASCII mode allows FTP to transfer plain text files more quickly, and ensures that a plain text file is readable by the computer that downloads it. An ASCII mode transfer will corrupt files that are not in plain text, such as image or program files. (It will also corrupt many word processor files, such as Microsoft Word documents, because these are not stored as plain text files by the word processor.)

12. To transfer the image file, type **binary** at the prompt, and then press **Enter**. The computer will now transfer files using binary mode. In a binary mode transfer, an exact copy of the file is transferred from the server.

13. Type **get welcome.png** at the prompt, and then press **Enter**. The computer indicates that the file is being transferred in binary mode. The ftp> prompt returns when the transfer is complete.

14. Type **!copy netplus.txt upload.txt** and press **Enter**. The computer displays the message "1 file(s) copied". The exclamation mark (!) tells the FTP program that you want to run a command on *WORKSTATION1* that copies the file netplus.txt to upload.txt in the directory you are working in on *WORKSTATION1*.

15. To try to upload a file to the remote server, type **put upload.txt** and press **Enter**. The computer indicates that access is denied.

16. Type **quit** and press **Enter** to exit the FTP site.

17. Now you will remove anonymous FTP access to the server, and allow users to upload files. On *SERVER1*, click **Start**, point to **Administrative Tools**, and then click **Internet Information Services (IIS) Manager** (not IIS 6.0 Manager). The Internet Information Services (IIS) Manager window opens.

18. Click the **SERVER1 (local computer)** icon in the left pane. Icons for services run by IIS appear in the right pane, including an icon for FTP Sites.

19. Double-click the **FTP Sites** icon in the right pane. An icon for Default FTP Site appears.

20. Right-click **Default FTP Site** and click **Properties**. The Default FTP Site Properties window opens.

21. Click the **Security Accounts** tab. Uncheck the **Allow anonymous connections** check box. The IIS Manager dialog box opens, indicating that the authentication option you have selected will result in unencrypted passwords being transmitted over the network.

22. Click **Yes** to close the IIS Manager dialog box.

23. Click the **Home Directory** tab. Select the **Write** check box. At this point, you are ready to upload files. Click **OK**.

24. Right-click **SERVER1 (local computer)** in the left pane, point to **All Tasks**, and click **Restart IIS**. The Stop/Start/Restart dialog box opens.

25. Make sure that **Restart Internet Services on SERVER1** is selected in the "What do you want IIS to do?" drop-down menu and click **OK**. The Shutting Down dialog box opens briefly, indicating that the computer is shutting down IIS. An hourglass appears while Internet services are restarted, and then the Internet Information Services dialog box reopens.

26. In the command prompt window on *WORKSTATION1*, type **ftp 192.168.54.1** and then press **Enter**. The logon prompt appears. Type **anonymous** and then press **Enter**. Type a password and then press **Enter**. The ftp> prompt indicates that user anonymous cannot log on and that the logon failed.

27. Type **quit** and press **Enter**.

28. Type **ftp 192.168.54.1** and then press **Enter**. The logon prompt appears. Type **netplus** and press **Enter**. At the Password prompt, type the password for the netplus account and press **Enter**. You are now logged on to the remote server.

29. Type **put upload.txt** and press **Enter**. The computer indicates that the file is being uploaded to the remote computer in ASCII mode data connection.

30. Type **quit** and then press **Enter**.

31. On *SERVER1*, click **Start** and then click **My Computer** (**Computer** in Windows Vista). The My Computer (or Computer) window opens.

32. Double-click the **Local Disk (C:)** icon. Double-click the **Inetpub** folder. Double-click the **ftproot** folder. The C:\Inetpub\ftproot folder opens, showing the upload.txt text file and the other files on the FTP server.

33. Log off both computers.

Certification Objectives

Objectives for the Network+ Exam:

- Explain the function of common networking protocols: TCP, FTP, UDP, TCP/IP suite, DHCP, TFTP, DNS, HTTP(S), ARP, SIP (VoIP), RTP (VoIP), SSH, POP3, NTP, IMAP4, Telnet, SMTP, SNMP2/3, ICMP, IGMP, TLS

Review Questions

1. Which of the following commands would you type at the ftp> prompt to copy a file named "textfile.doc" from your C:\ directory to an FTP server?

   a. copy "textfile.doc"

   b. put C:\textfile.doc

   c. get C:\textfile.doc

   d. move C:\textfile.doc

2. On what Transport layer protocol does FTP rely?

   a. TCP

   b. UDP

   c. ICMP

   d. NTP

3. What is the term for an FTP site that allows any user to access its directories?

   a. anonymous

   b. restricted

   c. private

   d. unlimited

4. What command allows you to list the contents of a directory on an FTP server?

   a. list

   b. lf

   c. ls

   d. la

5. What would you type at the ftp> prompt to view a list of available FTP commands? (Choose all that apply.)

   a. list

   b. ?

   c. help

   d. commands

6. What two file types can you specify when transferring files via FTP?

   a. ASCII and binary

   b. alphabetical and numeric

   c. program and data

   d. dynamic and static

Lab 4.5 Understanding Port Numbers

Objectives

In TCP/IP, servers use port numbers to identify processes associated with different services. For instance, a server might run several different services over TCP, including HTTP and FTP. Based only on the IP address, there is no way to distinguish between the two services. However, requests from client computers can connect to different port numbers. The default port number for the HTTP service, for example, is 80, whereas the default port number for the FTP control service is 21.

Most client software is designed to look for the default port number when connecting to a service. For example, by default, Web browsers attempt to find Web servers at port 80. However, you can usually configure a service to run on another port and configure the client software to look for that service on the new port.

You can tell a Web browser to look for a Web server at a nondefault port by adding a colon and the port number after the Web site name or IP address in the URL. For instance, to go to the Microsoft Web site using the default port (80), you would use the URL *www. microsoft.com*. To look for a Web server at the same site on port 7777, you would use the URL *www.microsoft.com:7777* instead. Port numbers in UDP work the same way as port numbers in TCP.

After completing this lab, you will be able to:

- Identify default port numbers for several services
- Modify a service's default port numbers
- Connect to a service using a nondefault port number

Materials Required

This lab will require the following:

- A computer running Windows Server 2008, Standard Edition named *SERVER1*, configured as a domain controller for the netpluslab.net domain with an IP address of 192.168.54.1 and a subnet mask of 255.255.255.0
- Internet Information Services (IIS) installed and running on *SERVER1* with the default configuration; to ensure that the default configuration is enabled, you can remove and reinstall the software
- A text file in *SERVER1*'s Web root (C:\Inetpub\wwwroot) named default.htm and containing the text "This is a test page"
- Access as the Administrator to *SERVER1*
- A computer running Windows XP Professional or Vista named *WORKSTATION1*, configured with an IP address of 192.168.54.3 and a subnet mask of 255.255.255.0
- Access with an ordinary user account to the client computer
- Both computers connected to a hub with straight-through CAT 5 (or better) UTP cables

Estimated completion time: **20 minutes**

Activity

1. Log on to *WORKSTATION1* with an ordinary user account. The Windows desktop appears.

2. Click **Start**, and then click **Internet Explorer**. Internet Explorer opens.

3. In the Address bar, type **http://192.168.54.1** and press **Enter**. A Web page opens containing the text "This is a test page."

4. If you are not already logged on to *SERVER1* as the Administrator, do so now.

5. On *SERVER1*, click **Start**, point to **Administrative Tools**, and then click **Internet Information Services (IIS) 6.0 Manager**. The Internet Information Services (IIS) Manager 6.0 window opens.

6. In the left pane of the window, click **SERVER1 (NETPLUSLAB/Administrator)**. Icons for services controlled by the IIS Manager appear in the right pane.

7. In the right pane, double-click the **Web Sites** icon. The Default Web Site icon appears in the right pane.

8. Right-click the **Default Web Site** icon in the right pane of the window, and then click **Properties**. The Default Web Site Properties dialog box opens.

9. In the TCP port text box, change the number from 80 to **8880**. This tells IIS to run the Web server on port 8880 instead of on port 80. Figure 4-5 shows the Default Web Site Properties dialog box. Click **OK**.

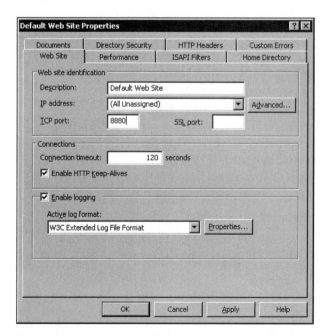

Figure 4-5   The Default Web Site Properties dialog box

Courtesy Course Technology/Cengage Learning

10. In the left pane of the Internet Information Services (IIS) Manager window, right-click **SERVER1**. In the shortcut menu, point to **All Tasks**, and then click **Restart IIS**. The Stop/Start/Restart dialog box opens.

11. Make sure that **Restart Internet Services on SERVER1** is selected in the "What do you want IIS to do?" drop-down menu. Click **OK**. The Shutting Down dialog box opens, indicating that the computer is attempting to shut down IIS, and then closes. An hourglass appears briefly, and then the computer restarts IIS.

12. On the menu bar, click **File** and then click **Exit** to close the IIS Manager.

13. On *WORKSTATION1*, close Internet Explorer. This ensures that Internet Explorer does not use its disk cache of the Web page when you try to load the Web page again.

14. Click **Start**, point to **All Programs**, and then click **Internet Explorer**. Internet Explorer opens.

15. In the Address bar, type **http://192.168.54.1** and then press **Enter**. An error message appears indicating that the page cannot be displayed.

16. In the Address bar, type **http://192.168.54.1:8880** and then press **Enter**. A Web page displays the text "This is a test page."

17. Log off both computers.

Certification Objectives

Objectives for the Network+ Exam:

- Identify commonly used TCP and UDP default ports. *TCP ports*: FTP—20, 21; SSH—22; TELNET—23; SMTP—25; DNS–53; HTTP—80; POP3—110; NTP—123; IMAP4—143; HTTPS—443. *UDP ports*: TFTP—69; DNS—53; BOOTPS/DHCP—67; SNMP—161

Review Questions

1. What symbol is used to separate the computer name from the port number in a URL (assuming that IP version 4 is in use)?

   a. ;

   b. :

   c. #

   d. .

2. What is the default port number for the Telnet service?

   a. 20

   b. 21

   c. 22

   d. 23

3. What is the default port number for the HTTP service?

    a. 40

    b. 44

    c. 60

    d. 80

4. What range of port numbers comprises the well-known port numbers?

    a. 0 to 64

    b. 0 to 128

    c. 0 to 1023

    d. 0 to 8880

5. What is a socket?

    a. a virtual connector that associates a URL with its IP address

    b. a method of identifying the IP addresses belonging to clients as they connect to servers

    c. a logical address assigned to a specific process running on a computer

    d. a discrete unit of data

6. Which of the following addresses could represent the SMTP service using its default port on a mail server?

    a. 188.65.79.80:25

    b. 188.65.79.80...24

    c. 188.65.79.80$24

    d. 188.65.79.80;25

Lab 4.6 Disabling Unnecessary Protocols

Objectives

The goal of this lab is to help you learn how to disable protocols that are not being used. You will often be able to configure multiple network clients to use only one or two network protocols. Disabling or removing a protocol will reduce network traffic and the load on your servers. On a computer with multiple NICs, you might find it useful to disable a protocol on one network interface card and leave it enabled on another. The clients on the network attached to one NIC might need that protocol, whereas the clients on the network attached to the other NIC do not.

   After completing this lab, you will be able to:

- Disable unnecessary protocols

Materials Required

This lab will require the following:

- One computer named *WORKSTATION1* running Windows XP Professional or Vista with an Ethernet NIC, configured with an IP address of 192.168.54.2; this computer should not be configured as a member of a domain

- *WORKSTATION1* should have the Reliable Multicast Protocol already installed

- Access to the Windows computer as an administrator
- One computer named *SERVER1* running Windows Server 2008, Standard Edition with an Ethernet NIC, configured with an IP address of 192.168.54.1
- *SERVER1* should have the Reliable Multicast Protocol already installed
- An Ethernet or Fast Ethernet hub compatible with both NICs
- Two straight-through Category 5 (or better) UTP cables with RJ-45 connectors at either end

Estimated completion time: **15–20 minutes**

Activity

1. Log on to *WORKSTATION1* as an administrator. The Windows desktop appears.

2. Click **Start**, point to **All Programs**, point to **Accessories**, point to **Communications**, and click **Network Connections**. (In Windows Vista, click **Start**, right-click **Network**, and click **Properties**. Click **Manage network connections**.) The Network Connections window opens.

3. Right-click the **Local Area Connection** icon and select **Properties** from the shortcut menu. (In Windows Vista, if a UAC box opens, click **Continue**.) The Local Area Connection Properties window opens.

4. Click **Reliable Multicast Protocol** to highlight it.

5. Click **Uninstall**. A dialog box opens, indicating that uninstalling a network component removes it from all network connections. Figure 4-6 shows the process of uninstalling a network protocol

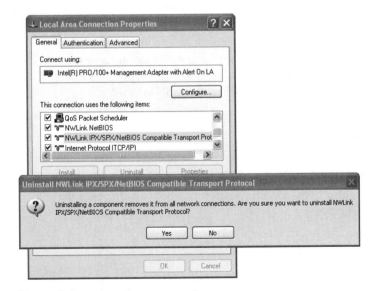

Figure 4-6 Uninstalling a protocol

Courtesy Course Technology/Cengage Learning

6. Click **Yes** to remove the protocol. The computer removes Reliable Multicast Protocol. The Local Network dialog box opens, indicating that you must shut down the computer before the changes will take effect.

7. Click **Yes**. The computer reboots.

8. Log on to *SERVER1* as the Administrator. The Windows Server 2008 desktop appears.

9. Click **Start**, click **Control Panel**, double-click **Network and Sharing Center**, click **Manage network connections**, and then double-click **Local Area Connection**. The Local Area Connection Status window opens.

10. Click the **Properties** button. The Local Area Connection Properties window opens

11. Repeat Steps 4 through 7. You have successfully removed the Reliable Multicast Protocol from the Windows Server 2008 computer.

12. Log off both computers.

Certification Objectives

Objectives for the Network+ Exam:

- Explain the function of common networking protocols: TCP, FTP, UDP, TCP/IP suite, DHCP, TFTP, DNS, HTTP(S), ARP, SIP (VoIP), RTP (VoIP), SSH, POP3, NTP, IMAP4, Telnet, SMTP, SNMP2/3, ICMP, IGMP, TLS

- Given a scenario, troubleshoot common connectivity issues and select an appropriate solution. *Physical issues*: cross talk, nearing cross talk, attenuation, collisions, shorts, open impedance mismatch (echo), interference. *Logical issues*: port speed, port duplex mismatch, incorrect VLAN, incorrect IP address, wrong gateway, wrong DNS, wrong subnet mask. *Issues that should be identified but escalated*: switching loop, routing loop, route problems, proxy arp, broadcast storms. *Wireless issues*: interference (bleed, environmental factors), incorrect encryption, incorrect channel, incorrect frequency, ESSID mismatch, standard mismatch (802.11 a/b/g/n), distance, bounce, incorrect antenna placement

- Explain issues that affect device security: Physical security; restricting local and remote access; secure methods vs. unsecure methods; SSH, HTTPS, SNMPv3, SFTP, SCP; TELNET, HTTP, FTP, RSH, RCP, SNMPv1/2

Review Questions

1. True or False? It is prudent to install and bind all four major protocol suites on your server, regardless of whether they are going to be used.

2. Why would a network administrator choose to disable one of two network interface cards on a server?

   a. because it is infrequently used

   b. because it is faulty

   c. because it is not as fast as the other

   d. because it is incapable of handling certain protocols

3. A computer uses both the IPX/SPX and TCP/IP protocols. Which of the following would be true if IPX/SPX were disabled?

   a. Clients would not be able to access the server's resources via IPX/SPX.

   b. Clients would not be able to access the server at all.

   c. Only those clients running TCP/IP would be able to access the server's resources.

   d. Clients would be able to access the server's resources via both TCP/IP and IPX/SPX, but TCP/IP-based services would be slower.

4. Why would a network administrator choose to unbind a protocol on a server?

   a. because it is only occasionally used, and as long as it remains bound it is using server resources

   b. because it is no longer used, and as long as it remains bound it is using server resources

   c. because it is interfering with traffic using other protocols

   d. because it has proven to be unstable with certain applications

5. Besides TCP/IP, what must be bound to a client's NIC before the client can log on to a Windows Server 2008 server?

   a. Client for Microsoft Networks

   b. Gateway Services for NetWare

   c. IPX/SPX

   d. NWLink

6. Why is NetBEUI not routable?

   a. because it does not contain a subprotocol at the Application layer of the OSI model

   b. because it does not contain Network layer addressing information

   c. because it is incompatible with modern routing techniques

   d. because its data frames are too large and slow to be practically routed

CHAPTER FIVE

TOPOLOGIES AND ETHERNET STANDARDS

Labs included in this chapter

- Lab 5.1 The Parallel Backbone
- Lab 5.2 Building a Daisy Chain
- Lab 5.3 Configuring Ethernet Frame Types
- Lab 5.4 Examining Ethernet Frames

Net+ Exam Objectives

Objective	Lab
Identify common physical network topologies	5.1, 5.2
Categorize LAN technology types and properties	5.3, 5.4
Given a scenario, troubleshoot common connectivity issues and select an appropriate solution	5.4

Lab 5.1 The Parallel Backbone

Objectives

In this lab, you will build a network that includes a variation of the parallel backbone. In a parallel backbone, each network segment has two or more connections to the central router or switch. If one connection fails, each segment can still connect to the rest of the network through the other connection.

The disadvantage to using a parallel backbone is cost. Depending on the type of devices used in the network and on the logical topology, it might require additional cabling, additional network devices, or additional configuration of network devices. As a network administrator, you must often choose between price and reliability. In most networks, only the most important devices have redundant network connections. For instance, a failure of the server that handles a company's billing might cost the company a substantial amount of money. The cost of a parallel backbone can be offset by the money that could be lost during such an outage. For a workstation, however, a parallel backbone might not be cost effective.

After completing this lab, you will be able to:

- Create a parallel backbone network

Materials Required

This lab will require the following:

- Two computers running Windows Server 2008, Standard Edition, one named *SERVER1* and the other named *SERVER2*, each with two NICs with RJ-45 connectors but without IP addresses configured
- Routing and Remote Access Services (RRAS) should be installed but not enabled on both computers
- Access as the Administrator to both computers
- Two 10/100 Ethernet hubs (or better)
- Four straight-through Cat 5 (or better) UTP cables

> Estimated completion time: **60 minutes**

Activity

1. Power on the two computers and the two hubs.

2. Plug one of the cables into a NIC in *SERVER1*. Plug the other end of the cable into one of the hubs. The link light on both the hub and on the NIC illuminate.

3. Plug another cable into the second NIC in *SERVER1*. Plug the other end of this cable into the other hub (that is, the hub you did not use in Step 2). Both NICs on *SERVER1* are now connected to different hubs. The link lights on the hub and on the NIC illuminate.

4. Plug a third cable into a NIC on *SERVER2*. Plug the other end of this cable into one of the hubs.

5. Plug the fourth cable into the second NIC on *SERVER2*. Plug the other end of this cable into the other hub. Both NICs on *SERVER2* are now plugged into different hubs, and

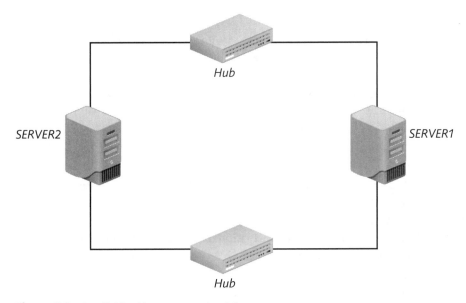

Figure 5-1 Parallel backbone network cabling

Courtesy Course Technology/Cengage Learning

each server is now connected to each hub. Figure 5-1 shows the network cabling for this lab.

6. Log on to *SERVER1* as the Administrator. The Windows Server 2008 desktop appears.

7. Click **Start,** click **Control Panel,** double-click **Network and Sharing Center,** click **Manage network connections,** and then double-click **Local Area Connection.** The Local Area Connection Status window opens.

8. Click **Properties**. The Local Area Connection Properties window opens.

9. Double-click **Internet Protocol Version 4 (TCP/IPv4).** The Internet Protocol (TCP/IP) Properties window opens.

10. Select the **Use the following IP address** option button. Enter **192.168.54.1** in the IP address text box and **255.255.255.0** in the Subnet mask text box. Select the **Use the following DNS Server addresses** option button, and enter **192.168.54.1** in the Preferred DNS server text box.

11. Click the **Advanced** button. The Advanced TCP/IP Settings dialog box opens.

12. Click **Add** beneath the IP addresses list box. The TCP/IP Address dialog box opens.

13. Now you will configure a secondary IP address. Enter **10.1.1.1** in the IP address text box and **255.255.255.0** in the Subnet mask text box.

14. Click **Add**. The dialog box closes, and the new IP address appears below "IP addresses" in the Advanced TCP/IP Settings dialog box.

15. Click **OK** three times to close the Local Area Connection Properties window. Click **Close** to close the Local Area Connection Status window.

16. Double-click **Local Area Connection 2**. The Local Area Connection 2 Status window opens.

17. Click **Properties**. The Local Area Connection 2 Properties window opens.

18. Double-click **Internet Protocol Version 4 (TCP/IPv4)**. The Internet Protocol (TCP/IP) Properties window opens.

19. Select the **Use the following IP address** option button. Enter **192.168.56.1** in the IP address text box and **255.255.255.0** in the Subnet mask text box. Select the **Use the following DNS Server addresses** option button, and enter **192.168.54.1** in the Preferred DNS server text box.

20. Click **OK** twice to close the Local Area Connection 2 Properties window. Click **Close** to close the Local Area Connection 2 Status window.

21. Click **Start**, point to **Administrative Tools**, and click **Routing and Remote Access**. The Routing and Remote Access window opens.

22. Right-click **SERVER1 (local)** in the left pane of the Routing and Remote Access window. Select **Configure and Enable Routing and Remote Access** from the shortcut menu. The Routing and Remote Access Server Setup Wizard opens.

23. Click **Next**.

24. Select the **Custom configuration** option. Click **Next**.

25. Click the **LAN routing** check box to select it. Click **Next**.

26. Click **Finish**. A dialog box opens, indicating that the service has been installed and asking if you would like to start the service. Click **Start service**. The service starts.

27. If necessary, click the **plus sign (+)** next to SERVER1 (local) to expand the tree. In the left pane of the Routing and Remote Access window, click the **plus sign (+)** to expand the tree below IPv4 if the tree is not already expanded. Right-click **General**, then select **New Routing Protocol** from the shortcut menu. The New Routing Protocol dialog box opens.

28. Double-click **RIP Version 2 for Internet Protocol**. The dialog box closes, and RIP appears below IPv4 in the tree in the left pane of the Routing and Remote Access window.

29. Right-click **RIP** in the tree in the left pane. Select **New Interface** from the shortcut menu. The New Interface for RIP Version 2 for Internet Protocol dialog box opens.

30. Double-click **Local Area Connection**. The RIP Properties – Local Area Connection Properties window opens.

31. Click **OK**.

32. Repeat Steps 29 through 31 for Local Area Connection 2.

33. Right-click **SERVER1 (local)** in the left pane. A shortcut menu opens. Point to **All Tasks**, then click **Restart**. The Routing and Remote Access service restarts.

34. On *SERVER2*, repeat Steps 6 through 10 and 15 through 33. (Note that when repeating Step 15, it will be necessary to click **OK** only twice.) However, use **192.168.54.2** in the IP address text box and Preferred DNS server text box in Step 10, and use **192.168.56.2** in the IP address text box and **192.168.54.2** in the Preferred DNS server text box in Step 19.

35. On *SERVER2*, click **Start**, point to **All Programs**, click **Accessories**, and then click **Command Prompt**. A command prompt window opens.

36. Type **ping 10.1.1.1** and press **Enter**. You see a message indicating that the computer has received four replies from the remote computer. (If the ping command is unsuccessful, switch the cables attached to *SERVER2*'s NICs, and verify that the link light on each NIC and hub is illuminated as expected.)

37. Remove one of the cables attached to *SERVER2*. (However, leave all of the cables attached to *SERVER1*.)

38. Type **ping 10.1.1.1** and press **Enter**. You see a message indicating that the computer has received four replies from the remote computer despite the removal of the cable.

39. Log off both computers.

Certification Objectives

Objectives for the Network+ Exam:

- Identify common physical network topologies: star, mesh, bus, ring, point to point, point to multipoint, hybrid

Review Questions

1. What is an advantage of using a parallel backbone over a collapsed backbone?

   a. A collapsed backbone requires too many connecting devices.

   b. A parallel backbone uses redundant connections and is more reliable.

   c. A collapsed backbone uses redundant connections, which costs more money.

   d. A parallel backbone uses fewer redundant connections, which costs less money.

2. What is the purpose of using the routing protocol in this lab?

   a. Each server can choose a different path when the current path fails.

   b. The network administrator does not have to configure static routes.

   c. It has no purpose.

   d. Each server saves the appropriate IP addresses in its ARP cache.

3. Which of the following is true about the use of parallel backbones in real-life networks?

   a. Parallel backbones are used when redundant connections are not possible.

   b. Parallel backbones are used whenever possible because they are so inexpensive.

   c. Parallel backbones only work in Ethernet networks.

   d. Parallel backbones are used for important servers and networks because they are more expensive to build.

4. In this lab, you configured the hubs and the two servers in a ring. How does the topology in this lab differ from a ring topology such as Token Ring? (Choose all that apply.)

   a. Each host transmits when necessary.

   b. A single workstation or server in a simple ring topology could take down the entire ring.

   c. Each host passes a token to the next host.

   d. The topology in this lab is an example of an active topology.

5. Which of the following network technologies has built-in redundancies?

    a. Token Ring

    b. Gigabit Ethernet

    c. FDDI

    d. 10Base-2 Ethernet

Lab 5.2 Building a Daisy Chain

Objectives

In this lab, you will create a daisy chain, which is simply a linked series of devices. You would most likely have several workstations or servers connected to each hub in the daisy chain. Because the hubs are modular and only require Cat 5 (or better) cables, the sort of network built in this lab is cheap and quick.

In any daisy chain, however, you run the risk of expanding the network beyond its physical limitations. That is, your daisy chain might exceed the maximum length for the network technology used. For instance, on a 100Base-TX network, connecting more than three network segments with more than two hubs violates the standards. While on a Gigabit Ethernet network, you can use only one hub. Depending on the network devices involved, overextending a daisy chain can result in serious problems. On a network such as the one in this lab, for instance, overextension can result in high error rates, data transmission problems, or reduced throughput. These problems might also be intermittent and, hence, more difficult to identify and troubleshoot.

Ordinarily, you must use a crossover cable to connect two hubs or switches together. However, many switches and hubs have an uplink port. An uplink port allows you to use a straight-through cable instead. One end of the straight-through cable is attached to an uplink port, and the other end is attached to an ordinary switch or hub port. In other cases, the hub or switch might have a button that determines whether the uplink port functions as an uplink port or as an ordinary port.

After completing this lab, you will be able to:

- Identify common enterprise backbone topologies
- Build a simple version of a common enterprise backbone

Materials Required

This lab will require the following:

- Four Ethernet hubs set at a common speed
- Five straight-through Cat 5 (or better) UTP cables
- Three crossover Cat 5 (or better) UTP cables, if required, to connect the hubs
- A computer running Microsoft Windows XP Professional or Vista named *WORKSTATION1*, with an RJ-45 NIC running at the same speed as the hubs and with an IP address of 192.168.54.2 and a subnet mask of 255.255.255.0

- A computer running Microsoft Windows XP Professional or Vista named *WORKSTATION2*, with an RJ-45 NIC running at the same speed as the hubs and with an IP address of 192.168.54.3 and a subnet mask of 255.255.255.0
- Access as an administrator to both computers

Estimated completion time: **45 minutes**

Activity

1. Power on each hub and each computer.

2. Plug one of the Cat 5 cables into a port in one of the hubs. Plug the other end of this cable into the uplink port of one of the other hubs. On both hubs a link light illuminates. If the hubs do not have uplink ports or if the lights do not illuminate, use a crossover cable to connect the hubs instead. The uplink port is designed to allow two hubs to be connected with a straight-through cable, but not all hubs have uplink ports.

3. Connect one of the remaining two hubs to one of the two hubs you connected in Step 2. Connect the remaining hub to the hub you just connected. Now you have a chain of four hubs. Each connection on each hub should have an illuminated link light.

4. Plug the RJ-45 connector from one of the CAT 5 cables into a data port on one of the hubs on the end. Plug the other end into the NIC in the back of one of the computers. A link light illuminates on both the hub and the NIC.

5. Repeat Step 4 by connecting the other computer into the hub at the other end of the chain. Figure 5-2 shows the network cabling for this lab.

6. Log on to *WORKSTATION1* as an administrator. The Windows desktop appears.

7. Click **Start**, point to **All Programs**, point to **Accessories**, and click **Command Prompt**. (In Windows Vista, click **Start**, type **cmd** in the Start Search text box, and then press **Enter**.) A command prompt window opens.

8. Type **ping 192.168.54.3** and press **Enter**. You see a message indicating that the computer has received four replies. (If you see an error message instead, go to the next step.)

9. Repeat the previous step, examining the lights on each hub for errors. (Typically, a light on a hub will blink red or will not blink at all if the hub is experiencing errors.) Do you see any error lights on any of the hubs?

10. Log off the computer.

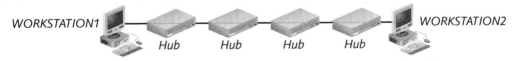

WORKSTATION1   Hub   Hub   Hub   Hub   WORKSTATION2

Figure 5-2   Daisy chain network cabling

Courtesy Course Technology/Cengage Learning

Certification Objectives

Objectives for the Network+ Exam:

- Identify common physical network topologies: star, mesh, bus, ring, point to point, point to multipoint, hybrid

Review Questions

1. Does the network you built in this lab meet the requirements for the hubs that you used? Why or why not?

2. What type of port connects one hub to another in a daisy-chain fashion?

    a. output port

    b. patch panel port

    c. uplink port

    d. external port

3. When connecting hubs in a daisy-chain fashion on a 100Base-T network, what is the maximum number of hubs you may connect?

    a. 2

    b. 3

    c. 4

    d. 5

4. When connectivity devices are connected in a daisy-chain fashion, what type of backbone do they create?

    a. parallel

    b. serial

    c. collapsed

    d. distributed

5. What type of network access method is used on a ring network?

    a. CSMA/CA

    b. CSMA/CD

    c. demand priority

    d. token passing

6. Which of the following is the most popular hybrid topology used on modern Ethernet networks?

    a. star-wired bus

    b. star-wired ring

    c. ring-wired star

    d. bus-wired star

7. What is risky about daisy-chaining hubs on a 100Base-T network? (Choose all that apply.)

   a. Too many hubs will cause errors in addressing data for its proper destination.

   b. Too many hubs will cause the network to exceed its maximum length.

   c. Too many hubs will increase the attenuation of a data signal.

   d. Too many hubs will increase the possibility for errors in data encryption and decryption.

Lab 5.3 Configuring Ethernet Frame Types

Objectives

In most networks, the Ethernet frame type is determined automatically by the NIC and no configuration is necessary. In some cases, however, you might find it necessary to configure the NIC manually to use a particular frame type. Depending on the protocols in question, use of multiple protocols might require multiple frame types. For instance, although recent versions of NetWare use IP by default, the default frame type used when IPX/SPX is configured is Ethernet 802.2. However, Ethernet II is the most commonly used frame type on all modern networks. NetWare servers also support a variety of frame types, and the default has changed over the years. Additionally, NetWare servers may be configured to use multiple frame types to support the use of multiple IPX networks on the same NIC. You might also need to use different frame types to support legacy operating systems or applications.

There are a total of four Ethernet frame types. Besides Ethernet II and Ethernet 802.2, Ethernet networks may also use Ethernet 802.3 and Ethernet SNAP. In general, you should minimize the number of frame types in use on your network. The use of multiple frame types requires each NIC to examine each incoming frame to determine its type. This delays processing of the frame slightly.

Whereas newer versions of NetWare primarily use IP, older versions used IPX/SPX. The IPX/SPX protocol stack is similar to the TCP/IP stack in some ways. For instance, IPX is a connectionless, best-effort protocol similar to IP, whereas SPX is a connection-oriented protocol similar to TCP.

After completing this lab, you will be able to:

- Examine and change Ethernet frame settings for computers running Windows XP Professional

Materials Required

This lab will require the following:

- A computer running Windows XP Professional named *WORKSTATION1*, with a NIC configured with an IP address of 192.168.54.1 and a subnet mask of 255.255.255.0, and with the NWLink IPX/SPX/NetBIOS Compatible Transport Protocol installed

- A computer running Windows XP Professional named *WORKSTATION2*, with a NIC configured with an IP address of 192.168.54.2 and a subnet mask of 255.255.255.0, and with the NWLink IPX/SPX/NetBIOS Compatible Transport Protocol installed

- The network protocol analyzer Wireshark (available from *www.wireshark.org*) installed on *WORKSTATION1*
- Access to both computers as an administrator
- Both computers connected to a hub with straight-through Cat 5 (or better) UTP cables

Estimated completion time: **45 minutes**

Activity

1. Log on to *WORKSTATION1* as an administrator. The Windows desktop appears.

2. Click **Start**, click **Control Panel**, double-click **Network Connections**, click **Manage network connections**, and right-click **Local Area Connection**.

3. Click **Properties**. The Local Area Connection Properties dialog box opens.

4. Double-click **NWLink IPX/SPX/NetBIOS Compatible Transport Protocol**. The NWLink IPX/SPX/NetBIOS Compatible Transport Protocol Properties dialog box opens.

5. Select the **Manual frame type detection** option.

6. Click **Add**. The Manual Frame Detection dialog box opens.

7. From the Frame type drop-down menu, select **Ethernet SNAP**. Click **OK**.

8. Click **OK**, and then click **Close** to close the Local Area Connection Properties dialog box. Click **Close** to close the Local Area Connection Status dialog box.

9. Log on to *WORKSTATION2* as an administrator. The Windows desktop appears.

10. Click **Start**, point to **All Programs**, point to **Accessories**, point to **Communications**, and click **Network Connections**.

11. Right-click the **Local Area Connection** icon. Select **Properties** from the shortcut menu. The Local Area Connection Properties dialog box opens.

12. Double-click **NWLink IPX/SPX/NetBIOS Compatible Transport Protocol**. The NWLink IPX/SPX/NetBIOS Compatible Transport Protocol Properties dialog box opens.

13. In the Frame type drop-down menu, select **Ethernet SNAP**. Click **OK**, and then click **Close** to close the Local Area Connection Properties dialog box.

14. On *WORKSTATION1*, click **Start**, point to **All Programs**, and click **Wireshark.** The Wireshark Protocol Analyzer opens.

15. Click **Interface List**, select your network interface, and then click **Start**.

16. Wireshark begins to capture frames.

17. Now you will generate some frames while Wireshark captures them in the background. Click **Start**, point to **All Programs**, point to **Accessories**, and click **Command Prompt**. A command prompt window opens.

18. Type **ping 192.168.54.2** and press **Enter**. You see a message indicating that the computer has received four replies.

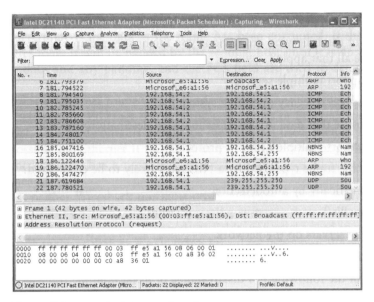

Figure 5-3 Wireshark Protocol Analyzer

Courtesy Course Technology/Cengage Learning

19. Now look at the Wireshark window, which lists the frames captured by protocol. When some IPX frames have been captured, click **Stop**. This might take several minutes. A list of captured frames is displayed in the top pane, while details about the protocol highlighted in the top pane are shown in the bottom two panes. The Wireshark window is shown in Figure 5-3.

20. Scroll through the frames until you see a frame marked IPX or NBIPX in the Protocol column. Click the frame to highlight it. Detailed information about the frame appears in the bottom two panes of the window.

21. In the middle pane, click the **plus sign** next to IEEE 802.3 Ethernet and next to Logical-Link Control. What type of Ethernet frame does this appear to be?

22. Scroll through the frames until you find a frame listed as ICMP in the Protocol column. Click the frame to highlight it. Detailed information about the frame appears in the bottom two panes.

23. In the middle pane, click the **plus sign** next to Ethernet II. What sort of frame is this? How does it differ from the frame you saw in Step 21?

24. Log off both computers.

Certification Objectives

Objectives for the Network+ Exam:

- Categorize LAN technology types and properties. *Types*: Ethernet, 10BaseT, 100BaseTX, 100BaseFX, 1000BaseT, 1000BaseX, 10GBaseSR, 10GBaseLR, 10GBaseER, 10GBaseSW, 10GBaseLW, 10GBaseEW, 10GBaseT. *Properties*: CSMA/CD, Broadcast, Collision, Bonding, Speed, Distance

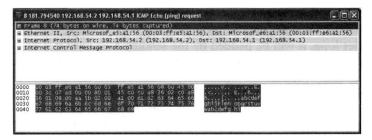

Figure 5-4   Captured frame

Courtesy Course Technology/Cengage Learning

5. Click **Start**, point to **All Programs**, point to **Accessories**, and click **Command Prompt**. A command prompt window opens.

6. Type **ping -t 192.168.54.2** and press **Enter**. The computer begins pinging 192.168.54.2 and will continue to do so until you stop it.

7. Now look at the Wireshark window. When the total number of frames captured is greater than 10, click **Stop**. A list of captured frames appears in the top pane, and details about the highlighted frame appear in the bottom two panes. Figure 5-4 shows an example of a captured frame.

8. Click a frame listed as **ICMP** in the Protocol column to highlight it. Detailed information about the frame appears in the bottom two panes.

9. In the middle pane, click the **plus sign** next to Ethernet II to expand the tree below it. Record the source and destination addresses.

10. Record the destination and source addresses in the Internet Protocol part of the frame. (This is part of the data field of the frame.) Was this frame sent from the Windows Server 2008 computer, or was it sent from the Windows XP or Vista computer?

11. In the command prompt window, press **Ctrl+C** to stop the **ping** command, then type **ipconfig/all** and press **Enter**. What is the MAC address for this host? Does it match one of the addresses you recorded in Step 9?

12. Type **arp -a** and press **Enter**. Look for the IP address of the other computer. Does its associated MAC address match one of the addresses you recorded in Step 9?

13. Look at the type field below "Ethernet II." What is this frame's type? Does it match the protocol listed in Wireshark's protocol column? Why or why not?

14. Log off both computers.

Certification Objectives

Objectives for the Network+ Exam:

- Categorize LAN technology types and properties. *Types*: Ethernet, 10BaseT, 100BaseTX, 100BaseFX, 1000BaseT, 1000BaseX, 10GBaseSR, 10GBaseLR, 10GBaseER, 10GBaseSW, 10GBaseLW, 10GBaseEW, 10GBaseT. *Properties*: CSMA/CD, Broadcast, Collision, Bonding, Speed, Distance

- Given a scenario, troubleshoot common connectivity issues and select an appropriate solution. *Physical issues*: crosstalk, nearing crosstalk, near end crosstalk, attenuation, collisions, shorts, open impedance mismatch (echo), interference. *Logical issues*: port speed, port duplex mismatch, incorrect VLAN, incorrect IP address, wrong gateway, wrong DNS, wrong subnet mask. *Issues that should be identified but escalated*: switching loop, routing loop, route problems, proxy arp, broadcast storms. *Wireless issues*: interference (bleed, environmental factors), incorrect encryption, incorrect channel, incorrect frequency, ESSID mismatch, standard mismatch (802.11 a/b/g/n), distance, bounce, incorrect antenna placement

Review Questions

1. What is the purpose of the checksum?

   a. to ensure that data arrives in the proper sequence

   b. to ensure that data is properly encrypted and decrypted

   c. to ensure that data arrives at its intended destination

   d. to ensure that data arrives whole and intact

2. How many times is a checksum calculated when a frame of data is sent from a source computer to a destination computer that resides on the same segment?

   a. 1

   b. 2

   c. 3

   d. 4

3. What type of address identifies the source of data in a frame?

   a. MAC

   b. logical

   c. network

   d. host

4. What is the purpose of padding in an Ethernet frame?

   a. to ensure that the data in the frame is exactly 1500 bytes long

   b. to ensure that the data in the frame is no more than 46 bytes long

   c. to signal that the frame has ended

   d. to ensure that the data in the frame is at least 46 bytes long

5. What is the minimum size of an Ethernet frame?

   a. 56 bytes

   b. 64 bytes

   c. 128 bytes

   d. 256 bytes

6. Which parts of an Ethernet frame are Wireshark and other protocol analyzers unlikely to capture? (Choose all that apply.)

a. the header

b. the Frame Check Sequence

c. the padding

d. the preamble

CHAPTER SIX

NETWORKING HARDWARE

Labs included in this chapter

- Lab 6.1 Configuring Transmission and Duplex Settings
- Lab 6.2 Creating a Multi-Homed Computer by Installing Two NICs
- Lab 6.3 Activating Routing and Remote Access in Windows Server 2008
- Lab 6.4 Activating a Routing Protocol in Windows Server 2008
- Lab 6.5 Configuring a Bridging Firewall

Net+ Exam Objectives

Objective	Lab
Identify common IPv4 and IPv6 routing protocols	6.4
Explain the purpose and properties of routing	6.2, 6.3, 6.4
Explain the methods of network access security	6.3, 6.5
Install, configure, and differentiate between common network devices	6.1, 6.5
Explain the function of hardware and software security devices	6.5
Explain common features of a firewall	6.5

10. Click **Start**, point to **All Programs**, click **Accessories**, and then click **Command Prompt**. A command prompt window opens.

11. Type **ping 192.168.54.2** and press **Enter**. The computer indicates that it has received four replies from the remote computer. Do you see any red error lights on the hub? (You might not because this network will not have a lot of traffic.)

12. Repeat Steps 3 through 9. When you repeat Step 8, use the value that you recorded in Step 7 instead of 100 Mbps Full Duplex.

13. Log off the computer.

Certification Objectives

Objectives for the Network+ Exam:

- Install, configure, and differentiate between common network devices: hub, repeater, modem, NIC, media converters, basic switch, bridge, wireless access point, basic router, basic firewall, basic DHCP server

Review Questions

1. What effect might an incorrect duplex setting have on a NIC? (Choose all that apply.)

   a. errors

   b. collisions

   c. retransmitted frames

   d. incorrect theoretical transmission speed

2. In the same dialog box in which you configured transmission speed and duplex settings, it is also possible to change the physical address of a NIC. What might happen if you were to do so?

   a. No devices could connect to that NIC because of its new physical address.

   b. TCP/IP communication would be normal immediately after the change.

   c. IPX/SPX communication would be normal after the ARP cache entries on other hosts timed out.

   d. TCP/IP communication would be normal after the ARP cache entries on other hosts timed out.

3. True or False? Changing the duplex setting on a NIC is the same as changing its physical address.

4. You have just attached a server to a new network. However, the server's throughput is lower than expected. Why might this be? (Choose all that apply.)

   a. The server is running the wrong routing protocol.

   b. The server's duplex setting is incorrect, and many frames are retransmitted.

   c. The server's transmission speed setting is incorrect.

   d. The server NIC's physical address is incorrectly configured.

5. What effect do duplex settings have on a server's routing protocols?

   a. None, the routing protocols operate at the Transport layer.

   b. None, the routing protocols operate at the Network layer.

   c. Mismatched duplex settings cause collisions and retransmissions.

   d. Mismatched duplex settings cause TCP/IP to fail altogether.

Lab 6.2 Creating a Multi-Homed Computer by Installing Two NICs

Objectives

Network adapters (also called network interface cards, or NICs) are connectivity devices that enable a workstation, server, printer, or other node to receive and transmit data over the network media. In most modern network devices, NICs contain the data transceiver, which is the device that transmits and receives data signals.

NICs operate at both the Physical layer and Data Link layer of the OSI model because they apply data signals to the wire and assemble or disassemble data frames. They do not, however, analyze the data from higher layers. A router, on the other hand, operates at the Network layer of the OSI model and can interpret higher-layer logical addressing information.

In this lab, you will perform the first step in creating a multi-homed computer consisting of a single computer with two NICs. A multi-homed computer has more than one NIC. Multi-homed computers called routers are used to interconnect dissimilar networks; the presence of two NICs in a computer allows it to connect to two different networks. Other types of networks may be connected by using different types of interfaces.

After completing this lab, you will be able to:

- Physically install NICs

- Make a multi-homed computer using two NICs

- Configure TCP/IP properties on NICs

Materials Required

This lab will require the following:

- A computer named *SERVER1* running Windows Server 2008, Standard Edition without any NICs installed

- At least two PCI bus slots available on the Windows Server 2008 computer

- Access to the Windows Server 2008 computer as the Administrator

- Two Ethernet PCI NICs with RJ-45 connectors listed on the Windows Server Catalog Hardware Compatibility List (HCL); at the time of this writing, you can find the Windows Server Catalog at *www.windowsservercatalog.com*

- Two Ethernet hubs compatible with the NICs

- Two straight-through Cat 5 (or better) UTP cables

- A toolkit with a Phillips-head screwdriver, a ground mat, and a ground strap

4. On a typical 100Base-T network, where would you find transceivers?

   a. in the NICs

   b. in the operating systems

   c. in the UPSs

   d. in the cabling

5. Which of the following is a difference between a router and a hub?

   a. A router is less sophisticated than a hub.

   b. A router operates at the Transport layer of the OSI model, whereas a hub operates at the Data Link layer of the OSI model.

   c. A router operates at the Network layer of the OSI model, whereas a hub operates at the Physical layer of the OSI model.

   d. A router regenerates signals, whereas a hub interprets addressing information to ensure that data is directed to the proper destination.

6. In which of the following networking scenarios would a router be the optimal connectivity device?

   a. a home network with five users who want to share documents that are stored on one of the five workstations

   b. a WAN that connects a college physics department with a classroom in a high school on the other side of town

   c. a LAN that connects 10 users, a server, and a printer at a small business

   d. a peer-to-peer LAN that connects eight users to provide a shared database

7. What is the most likely purpose of the hubs in this lab?

   a. to connect the computer to different networks

   b. to determine by checking the link lights whether the NIC has been installed correctly

   c. to determine by checking the link lights whether you have configured the IP addresses on the NICs correctly

   d. to allow the NICs to operate at the Network layer

Lab 6.3 Activating Routing and Remote Access in Windows Server 2008

Objectives

In this lab, you will configure a multi-homed server to be a simple router and add a static route to its routing table. When a router receives a packet from a computer or another router, it looks in its routing table to see where it must send the packet. A routing table consists of a list of all the networks the router knows about and the next hop for each of these networks. Each route consists of a destination network and the next hop where the router should send packets to reach the destination. The next hop might be the IP address of the next router on the path to the destination or the network interface card closest to it. A router has separate routing tables for each routable protocol (such as TCP/IP or IPX/SPX) it runs.

For instance, suppose a router receives a packet with a destination address of 10.100.17.29. It looks in its routing table for a route that matches this address. It finds the route and sees that packets for 10.100.17.29 should be sent out to the router at 10.100.17.1. Then it sends the packet to 10.100.17.1.

When the router at 10.100.17.1 receives the packet, it looks at its routing table for a matching route. The matching route tells the router to send the packet out its Ethernet NIC. It sends the packet out its Ethernet NIC, where it is received by the destination computer. In this manner, routers can send packets over long paths consisting of many hops.

To fill its routing table, a router must learn the routes it needs to use. One way in which routers learn routes is by looking at the addresses on their own interfaces. Network administrators can also add routes directly into a routing table. Routes configured by a network administrator are known as static routes.

Note that most network administrators will use dedicated routing hardware whenever possible, rather than a software router such as the one you will configure in this lab. Dedicated routing hardware will typically be faster, more stable, and have more features than a software router.

After completing this lab, you will be able to:

- Activate and configure Routing and Remote Access Services on a Windows Server 2008 server

- Show the routing table of a Windows Server 2008 server configured as a network router

- Add a static route to a Windows Server 2008 server configured as a network router

Materials Required

This lab will require the following:

- The network built at the end of Lab 6.2

- A computer named *SERVER1* running Windows Server 2008, Standard Edition with two NICs with Routing and Remote Access Service installed

- One NIC on the *SERVER1* computer configured with an IP address of 192.168.54.1 and a subnet mask of 255.255.255.0

- The other NIC on the *SERVER1* computer configured with an IP address of 172.16.1.1 and a subnet mask of 255.255.255.0

- Two computers running Windows XP Professional or Vista with NICs compatible with the hubs

- One of the Windows XP or Vista computers named *WORKSTATION1* and configured with an IP address of 192.168.54.2 and a default gateway of 192.168.54.1

- The other Windows XP or Vista computer named *WORKSTATION2* and configured with an IP address of 172.16.1.2 and a default gateway of 172.16.1.1

- Access to both Windows XP or Vista computers as the local administrator

- Two straight-through Cat 5 (or better) UTP cables

Estimated completion time: **75 minutes**

Activity

1. Plug in each NIC in *SERVER1* to one of the hubs. Log on to SERVER1 as the Administrator. The Windows Server 2008 desktop appears.

2. On the Windows Server 2008 computer, click **Start**, point to **Administrative Tools**, and then click **Routing and Remote Access**.

3. In the left pane of the dialog box, click the name of the server to select it. Click **Action**, and, if necessary, click **Configure and Enable Routing and Remote Access**. The Routing and Remote Access Server Setup Wizard opens.

4. Click **Next**. The Configuration dialog box opens, listing several options for configuring this computer as a router.

5. Select the **Custom configuration** option, and then click **Next**. The Custom Configuration dialog box opens.

6. Click the **LAN routing** check box to place a check in it. Click **Next**.

7. Click **Finish**. The Routing and Remote Access Server Setup Wizard saves your settings and starts the Routing and Remote Access Service.

8. A dialog box opens, indicating that the Routing and Remote Access Service has been installed. Click **Start service** to start the service. A dialog box indicating that the service is initializing opens briefly. Close the Routing and Remote Access dialog box.

9. Plug the RJ-45 connector of one of the Cat 5 cables into one of the hubs. Plug the other end of the cable into the NIC in the back of one of the Windows XP Professional computers.

10. Repeat the previous step, connecting the other computer to the other hub. The Windows XP computers should each be plugged into different hubs, while *SERVER1* should be plugged into both hubs. This allows traffic from *WORKSTATION1* to travel through *SERVER1* to *WORKSTATION2*. Figure 6-2 shows the network cabling.

11. Log on to *WORKSTATION1* as an administrator. The Windows desktop appears.

12. Click **Start**, point to **All Programs**, point to **Accessories**, and then click **Command Prompt**. (In Windows Vista, click **Start**, type **cmd** in the Start Search text box, and then press **Enter**.) A command prompt window opens.

13. Type **ping 172.16.1.2** and press **Enter**. If the output does not indicate that the computer has received four replies from 172.16.1.2, repeat Steps 9 and 10 before continuing, switching the hubs to which each computer is attached.

14. Repeat Steps 11 and 12 with *WORKSTATION2*. The Windows Server 2008 computer is now acting as a router. This means that it accepts packets from *WORKSTATION1*

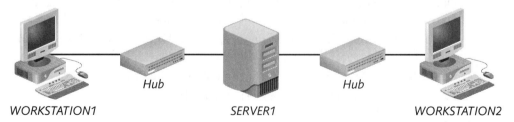

WORKSTATION1   SERVER1   WORKSTATION2

Figure 6-2   Network cabling for Lab 6.3

Courtesy Course Technology/Cengage Learning

and uses its routing table to determine where to send the packets so that they reach their destination, *WORKSTATION2*.

15. At the command prompt, type **ping 192.168.54.2** and press **Enter**. The output indicates that this computer has received four replies from the other computer. You have successfully used the Windows Server 2008 computer as a router.

16. Next, you will configure a secondary IP address on *WORKSTATION2*. Click **Start**, point to **All Programs**, point to **Accessories**, point to **Communications**, and then click **Network Connections**. (In Windows Vista, click **Start**, right-click **Network**, and click **Properties**. Click **Manage network connections**.) The Network Connections dialog box opens.

17. Right-click the **Local Area Connection** icon and then click **Properties** on the shortcut menu. (In Windows Vista, if a UAC dialog box opens, click **Continue**.)

18. Double-click **Internet Protocol (TCP/IP)**. (In Windows Vista, double-click **Internet Protocol Version 4 (TCP/IPv4)**.) The Internet Protocol (TCP/IP) Properties dialog box opens. Click **Advanced**. The Advanced TCP/IP Settings dialog box opens.

19. Click **Add** beneath the IP addresses heading at the top of the dialog box. The TCP/IP Address dialog box opens.

20. Type **10.1.1.1** in the IP address text box. Type **255.0.0.0** in the Subnet mask text box.

21. Click **Add**. You have just configured this computer with a second IP address, which it can also use to communicate with other computers. You return to the Advanced TCP/IP Settings dialog box.

22. Click **OK** to close the Advanced TCP/IP Settings dialog box, click **OK** to close the Internet Protocol (TCP/IP) Properties dialog box, and then click **OK** to close the Local Area Connection Properties dialog box.

23. In the command prompt window for *WORKSTATION1*, type **ping 10.1.1.1** and press **Enter**. You see a reply (displayed four times on the screen) indicating that the destination host is unreachable.

24. Next, you will check to see if a route exists on the Windows Server 2008 computer so that you can reach the secondary IP address on *WORKSTATION2* from *WORKSTATION1*. On the Windows Server 2008 computer, click **Start**, point to **All Programs**, click **Accessories**, and then click **Command Prompt**.

25. Type **route print** and press **Enter**. The computer displays a list of its interfaces and its routing table. Notice that there is no route to any IP address or network beginning with 10. See Figure 6-3 for an example of a routing table on a Windows Server 2008 computer like *SERVER1* in this lab.

26. Recall that when you typed ping 10.1.1.1 in Step 23, the computer responded with "Destination host unreachable" four times. Now you will configure a static route on *SERVER1* so that *WORKSTATION1* can reach 10.1.1.1. Type **route add 10.0.0.0 mask 255.0.0.0 172.16.1.2** and press **Enter**. This tells the router to add a route to any machine with a network number of 10.0.0.0 and a subnet mask of 255.0.0.0 through the computer with the IP address of 172.16.1.2.

27. Type **ping 10.1.1.1** and press **Enter**. The computer responds with "Reply from 10.1.1.1" four times.

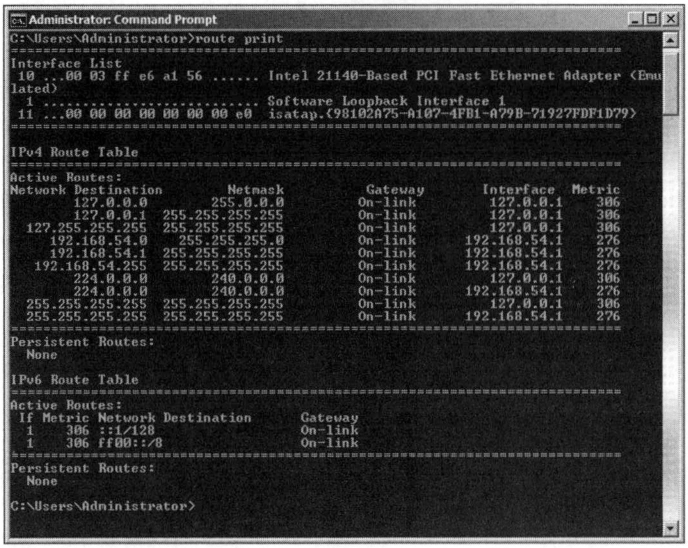

Figure 6-3 Routing table

Courtesy Course Technology/Cengage Learning

28. Type **route print** and press **Enter**. The computer displays its routing table. In the Network Destination column, you should see the route you added in Step 26, 10.0.0.0.

29. Return to the command prompt window you opened earlier on *WORKSTATION1*. Type **ping 10.1.1.1** and press **Enter**. The computer responds with "Reply from 10.1.1.1" four times. You have now successfully used the static route you configured on the Windows Server 2008 computer.

30. Finally, you will look at the route used by packets to reach 10.1.1.1. Type **tracert 10.1.1.1** and press **Enter**. The computer displays the route that packets take to reach the address 10.1.1.1.

31. Log off all three computers.

Certification Objectives

- Explain the purpose and properties of routing: IGP vs. EGP, static vs. dynamic, next hop, understanding routing tables and how they pertain to path selection, explain convergence (steady state)

Review Questions

1. What is the purpose of a routing table on a TCP/IP-based network?

   a. to associate the NetBIOS names of nodes with their IP addresses

   b. to associate the IP addresses of nodes with their host names

   c. to associate the IP addresses of nodes with their locations on the network

   d. to associate the host names of nodes with their MAC addresses

2. Which of the following most fully describes what a successful response from the ping command indicates?

   a. that a node is powered on

   b. that a node is physically connected to the network

   c. that a node is running the Windows Server 2008 operating system

   d. that a node is connected to the network and is running TCP/IP successfully

3. What does the Tracert command show?

   a. the path taken by packets to the destination address

   b. the MAC address of the destination address

   c. whether the remote host supports TCP/IP

   d. the operating system run by the host at the destination address

4. What command would you use to add a node's IP address, subnet mask, and network location interface to a routing table?

   a. route add

   b. add host

   c. add node

   d. route open

5. In the default ping command on a computer running Windows, how many replies will you receive if the test is successful?

   a. 1

   b. 2

   c. 3

   d. 4

6. What menu option sequence would you choose to set up Routing and Remote Access Services on a Windows Server 2008 computer?

   a. Start, Control Panel, Network Connections, Routing and Remote Access

   b. Start, Administrative Tools, Routing and Remote Access

   c. Start, All Programs, Accessories, Routing and Remote Access

   d. Start, Control Panel, Routing and Remote Access

Lab 6.4 Activating a Routing Protocol in Windows Server 2008

Objectives

Configuring more than a handful of static routes on a network is time consuming and error-prone. Many networks consist of hundreds or even thousands of routes. For instance, at the time of this writing, the Internet routing table consists of around 300,000 routes. If you used static routes to maintain the routing tables on your routers, you would need to configure each static route on each router. Imagine configuring 500 or more routes on 50 routers! Additionally, each time you added a new network, you would need to configure a new route on each router.

To simplify network administration, most networks of any size use a routing protocol to help routers learn routes. A router running a routing protocol tells connected routers, or neighbors, about the networks it knows about. In turn, it learns all the routes its neighbors know about. In this way, it can discover all the routes in the network. Routing protocols also allow routers to find the best routes to a destination. Finally, routing protocols allow routers to recover from outages. If a router fails, other routers will learn this from information sent by the routing protocol. If another route to the destination is available, they will use it.

In this lab, you will configure Routing Information Protocol (RIP) version 2 on a computer running Windows Server 2008. RIP is a relatively simple routing protocol, which is supported on many network devices and servers. However, keep in mind that routing protocols can be quite complex and that mistakes with routing protocols can cause large outages.

After completing this lab, you will be able to:

- Explain the function of various routing protocols
- Install a routing protocol on a Windows Server 2008 computer

Materials Required

This lab will require the following:

- A computer named *SERVER1* running Windows Server 2008, Standard Edition with two NICs
- One NIC on the *SERVER1* computer configured with an IP address of 192.168.54.1 and a subnet mask of 255.255.255.0
- The other NIC on the *SERVER1* computer configured with an IP address of 172.16.1.1 and a subnet mask of 255.255.255.0
- A computer named *SERVER2* running Windows Server 2008, with a NIC, an IP address of 192.168.54.2, a subnet mask of 255.255.255.0, and no default gateway
- Routing and Remote Access disabled on both computers
- Two Ethernet hubs
- Three straight-through Cat 5 (or better) UTP cables
- Access as the Administrator to both computers

Estimated completion time: **45 minutes**

Activity

1. Connect each of the NICs in *SERVER1* to a separate hub with Cat 5 cables.

2. Connect the NIC in *SERVER2* to one of the hubs with the remaining Cat 5 cable.

3. Log on to *SERVER2* as the Administrator. The Windows Server 2008 desktop appears.

4. Click **Start**, point to **All Programs**, click **Accessories**, and click **Command Prompt**. A command prompt window opens.

5. Now you will verify that you have network connectivity with *SERVER1*. Type **ping 192.168.54.1** and press **Enter**. The computer indicates that it has received four replies. If instead you see a timeout error (or other error), *SERVER2* is plugged into the wrong hub. Take the cable plugged into *SERVER2*'s NIC, remove the end attached to the hub, and plug it into the other hub. Repeat this step.

6. Now you will attempt to reach the IP address of *SERVER1*'s other NIC. Type **ping 172.16.1.1** and press **Enter**. You see four messages indicating that the destination host is unreachable.

7. Type **route print** and press **Enter** to show the computer's routing table. Record the networks listed in the Network Destination column and the corresponding subnet masks in the Netmask column.

8. Log on to *SERVER1* as the Administrator. The Windows Server 2008 desktop appears.

9. Click **Start**, point to **All Programs**, click **Accessories**, and click **Command Prompt**. A command prompt window opens.

10. Type **route print** and press **Enter**. The computer displays its routing table. Record the routes you see as you did in Step 7.

11. Click **Start**, point to **All Programs**, point to **Administrative Tools**, and click **Routing and Remote Access**. The Routing and Remote Access dialog box opens.

12. In the left pane, select **SERVER1**. Click **Action** on the menu bar, and then click **Configure and Enable Routing and Remote Access**. The Routing and Remote Access Server Setup Wizard appears.

13. Click **Next**. The Configuration dialog box opens, listing several options for configuring this computer as a router.

14. Select the **Custom configuration** option, and then click **Next**. The Custom Configuration dialog box opens.

15. Click the **LAN routing** check box to place a check in it. Click **Next**.

16. Click **Finish**. The Routing and Remote Access Server Setup Wizard saves your settings and starts the Routing and Remote Access Service.

17. A dialog box opens, indicating that the Routing and Remote Access Service has been installed. Click **Start service** to start the service. Dialog boxes indicating that the service is initializing open briefly.

18. In the left pane of the Routing and Remote Access dialog box, click the **plus sign (+)** next to the SERVER1 (local) icon, if necessary. A tree containing several nodes appears below the SERVER1 icon. Click the **plus sign (+)** next to the IPv4 node. More options appear underneath the IPv4 node, including an icon named General.

19. Right-click the **General** icon and then click **New Routing Protocol** on the shortcut menu. The New Routing Protocol dialog box opens, as shown in Figure 6-4.

20. Click **RIP Version 2 for Internet Protocol**, and then click **OK**. A RIP icon appears in the left pane on the same tree as the General icon while the Windows Server 2008 computer installs the Routing Information Protocol.

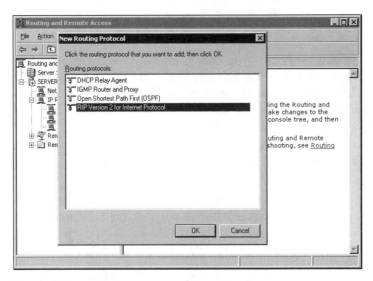

Figure 6-4   Adding a new routing protocol

Courtesy Course Technology/Cengage Learning

21. Right-click the new **RIP** icon in the tree in the left pane, and then click **New Interface**. The New Interface for RIP Version 2 for Internet Protocol dialog box opens.

22. Click **Local Area Connection,** if necessary, and then click **OK** to add the interface. The RIP Properties – Local Area Connection Properties dialog box opens.

23. Click **OK** to close the dialog box and finish adding the interface. If necessary, select RIP in the left pane. An icon for Local Area Connection appears in the right pane of the Routing and Remote Access dialog box.

24. Repeat Steps 21 through 23 for Local Area Connection 2.

25. Right-click the **SERVER1 (local)** icon. On the shortcut menu, point to **All Tasks**, then click **Restart**. A dialog box opens briefly indicating that the Routing and Remote Access Service is restarting.

26. Enable Routing and Remote Access on *SERVER2* by repeating Steps 11 through 23 and Step 25. After RIP for IP is installed on both computers, they will dynamically share their routing tables within a minute.

27. Wait one minute. In the left pane of the Routing and Remote Access dialog box on *SERVER2*, right-click the **RIP** icon, and then click **Show Neighbors**. The SERVER2 – RIP Neighbors dialog box opens, showing the IP address of *SERVER1*. If you do not see the IP address of *SERVER1* in this dialog box, wait another minute and repeat this step.

28. In the command prompt window on *SERVER2*, type **ping 172.16.1.1** and press **Enter**.

29. Type **route print** and press **Enter**. What additional routes do you see now that you didn't see in Step 11?

30. Repeat the previous step on *SERVER1*.

Certification Objectives

Objectives for the Network+ Exam:

- Identify common IPv4 and IPv6 routing protocols: *Link state*: OSPF, IS-IS; *Distance vector*: RIP, RIPv2, BGP; *Hybrid*: EIGRP
- Explain the purpose and properties of routing: IGP vs. EGP, static vs. dynamic, next hop, understanding routing tables and how they pertain to path selection, explain convergence (steady state)

Review Questions

1. What does RIP stand for?

    a. Regulated Interaction Protocol

    b. Routing Information Protocol

    c. Response Interpretation Protocol

    d. Registered Installation Protocol

2. True or False? To determine the best path to transfer data, routers communicate using routing protocols such as TCP/IP.

3. What additional routes did you find in Step 29?

4. Which routing protocol is commonly used for Internet backbones?

    a. OSPF

    b. RIP for IP

    c. EIGRP

    d. BGP

5. Under what circumstances might the best path not equal the shortest distance between two nodes? (Choose all that apply.)

    a. when a communications link has been recently added to the network

    b. when a communications link is suffering congestion

    c. when a router experiences routing protocol errors

    d. when the media on the shortest path is slower than the media on the best path

6. Which protocol was developed by Cisco Systems and has a fast convergence time but is supported only on Cisco routers?

    a. OSPF

    b. RIP for IP

    c. EIGRP

    d. BGP

7. What does OSPF stand for?

    a. open shortest path first

    b. overhead system path forwarding

    c. overlook system packet forwarding

    d. open session peer first

Lab 6.5 Configuring a Bridging Firewall

Objectives

A firewall is a gateway used to connect two or more networks and to control the traffic allowed to cross a network. A firewall is often used to protect a network from potentially malicious traffic on the Internet. For example, the firewall is typically configured to allow users on the protected network, or inside the firewall, to use network resources on the Internet. Many firewalls can control traffic with varying degrees of ease anywhere from the Data Link layer up to the Application layer.

In many ways, the distinction between a firewall and a router is fuzzy. Many routers can also filter traffic. Like a router, a firewall can be a dedicated piece of hardware or software configured on a server. The function of a firewall also overlaps somewhat with that of a router. A firewall can use a handful of static routes, or it can run a routing protocol like a router.

However, a firewall does not need to be a router at all. In this lab, you will configure a computer running Windows Server 2008 as both a bridge and a firewall. A bridge is a gateway device that operates at Layer 2 of the OSI model, and does not require Layer 3 configuration. However, a bridging firewall can use information at Layer 3 and higher in the packets it receives to decide whether to forward them.

In this lab, you will configure the firewall to selectively prevent one computer from being able to ping the other. When one computer pings a second computer, it sends an ICMP echo request packet. The second computer sends an ICMP echo reply packet to acknowledge the ping. When the first computer receives the ICMP echo reply packet from the second computer, it knows that the ping has been successful. A firewall can prevent computers outside the firewall from pinging computers inside the firewall by filtering ICMP echo request packets. If the computers inside the firewall do not receive the ICMP echo request packets, they will never send ICMP echo reply packets. Thus, computers outside the firewall will not be able to successfully ping computers inside the firewall. At the same time, the firewall will not prevent computers inside it from pinging computers outside the firewall.

After completing this lab, you will be able to:

- Configure a computer running Windows Server 2008 as a simple firewall
- Configure the Windows Server 2008 firewall to filter ICMP echo request packets

Materials Required

This lab will require the following:

- The network built at the end of Lab 6.2
- A computer named *SERVER1* running Windows Server 2008, Standard Edition with two NICs with Routing and Remote Access Service installed
- One NIC on the *SERVER1* computer configured with an IP address of 192.168.54.1 and a subnet mask of 255.255.255.0
- The other NIC on the *SERVER1* computer configured with an IP address of 172.16.1.1 and a subnet mask of 255.255.255.0
- Two computers running Windows XP Professional or Vista with NICs compatible with the hubs

- One of the Windows XP or Vista computers named *WORKSTATION1* and configured with an IP address of 192.168.54.2 and a default gateway of 192.168.54.1

- The other Windows XP or Vista computer named *WORKSTATION2* and configured with an IP address of 172.16.1.2 and a default gateway of 172.16.1.1

- Access to both Windows XP or Vista computers as the local administrator

- Two straight-through Cat 5 (or better) UTP cables

Estimated completion time: **30 minutes**

Activity

1. Connect one end of a cable to one of the hubs. Connect the other end of the cable to *WORKSTATION1*.

2. Repeat the previous step, connecting the other hub to *WORKSTATION2*.

3. Connect one end of a cable to one of the hubs. Connect the other end of the cable to one of the NICs in *SERVER1*.

4. Repeat the previous step, connecting the other hub to *SERVER1*. Now both *WORKSTATION1* and *WORKSTATION2* are connected to different hubs, and each hub is connected to one of the NICs on *SERVER1*.

5. Log on to *WORKSTATION1* as an administrator. The Windows desktop appears.

6. Click **Start**, point to **All Programs**, point to **Accessories**, and then click **Command Prompt**. (In Windows Vista, click **Start**, type **cmd** in the Start Search text box, and then press **Enter**.) A command prompt window opens.

7. Type **ping 172.16.1.2** and press **Enter** to confirm that *WORKSTATION1* can successfully ping *WORKSTATION2*.

8. Now you will configure *SERVER1* as a firewall.

9. Log on to *SERVER1* as the Administrator. The Windows Server 2008 desktop appears.

10. On the Windows Server 2008 computer, click **Start**, point to **Administrative Tools**, and then click **Windows Firewall with Advanced Security**.

11. Right-click **Inbound Rules** and click **New Rule**.

12. Select **Custom** and click **Next**.

13. Select **All Programs** and click **Next**.

14. Under Protocol Type, select **ICMPv4** and click **Next**.

15. Confirm that this rule applies to any local and remote IP addresses and click **Next**.

16. Select **Block the connection**, click **Next**, and click **Next** again.

17. Name the rule **Ping Block** and click **Finish**.

18. The computer will now drop ICMP echo request packets sent to *WORKSTATION2*.

19. In the command prompt window on *WORKSTATION1*, type **ping 172.16.1.2** and press **Enter**. The computer indicates four times that it is unable to reach the destination host.

20. Log off each computer.

Certification Objectives

Objectives for the Network+ Exam:

- Install, configure and differentiate between common network devices: hub, repeater, modem, NIC, media converters, basic switch, bridge, wireless access point, basic router, basic firewall, basic DHCP server

Review Questions

1. Which of the following could serve as firewalls? (Choose all that apply.)

   a. a modem

   b. a Windows Server 2008 computer

   c. a hub

   d. a Linux server

2. True or False? A firewall can run a routing protocol like a router.

3. What is the highest level of the OSI model in which a firewall can operate?

   a. Data Link

   b. Network

   c. Transport

   d. Application

4. A gateway connects two different types of networks, two different types of communications protocols, or two different computer architectures. Which of the following is *not* considered a gateway?

   a. a router connecting a Token Ring

   b. a computer translating application data from TCP/IP to IPX/SPX

   c. a computer translating voice signals into data and transmitting it over a TCP/IP network

   d. a file and print server communicating with clients using both TCP/IP and IPX/SPX

5. You have configured a device that runs the OSPF routing protocol, but whose primary purpose is to prevent unwanted Internet traffic from reaching your company's LAN. Which of the following is true about this device?

   a. It is a router because it runs a routing protocol.

   b. It is a router because its primary purpose is to control traffic.

   c. It is a firewall because it runs a routing protocol.

   d. It is a firewall because its primary purpose is to control traffic.

6. Which of the following statements about a bridge is false?

   a. Without IP addressing information, a bridge will not be seen with the Tracert command.

   b. Bridges require no Layer 3 addressing.

   c. Bridges decide which packets to forward based on their Layer 3 headers.

   d. Bridges operate at the Data Link layer.

CHAPTER SEVEN

WANs and Remote Connectivity

Labs included in this chapter

- Lab 7.1 Pricing WAN Services
- Lab 7.2 Connecting to an Internet Service Provider in Windows Server 2008
- Lab 7.3 Configuring a Remote Access Server
- Lab 7.4 Creating a VPN with the Point-to-Point Tunneling Protocol
- Lab 7.5 Configuring Remote Desktop Services (Terminal Services) on Windows Server 2008

Net+ Exam Objectives

Objective	Lab
Categorize WAN technology types and properties	7.1, 7.2, 7.3
Explain common logical network topologies and their characteristics	7.4
Given a scenario, select the appropriate command-line interface tool and interpret the output to verify functionality	7.2
Explain the methods of network access security	7.3, 7.4, 7.5

Lab 7.1 Pricing WAN Services

Objectives

In this lab, you will price several options for WAN services. Many organizations use multiple types of WAN links for redundancy and to eliminate single points of failure on the network. For example, an organization might use T-1s to connect its two largest remote offices to its central office, and it might use ISDN lines as backups in case either T-1 fails. To connect its smaller offices to the central office, an organization might use ISDN lines as the primary link and a dial-up modem as the backup link. Many organizations will also have a backup link for their Internet connection.

You can use these services to connect an organization to the Internet, as well as to connect offices in one location to offices in another. The pricing of Internet services is often more complicated, as you must purchase both a WAN link and Internet access itself. Depending on the type of WAN link, however, many WAN service providers offer both the WAN connection and the Internet access. Many telephone companies, for example, install a T-1 and provide Internet access with the T-1 service.

WAN topologies can also have a huge impact on price. The star, partial-mesh, and full-mesh WAN topologies are used most commonly. Independent of the cost of the actual WAN, the star topology is the cheapest. A star topology consists of one link from a central office to each satellite office. For each new office you add, you need to add only one new link. However, a star topology offers no redundancy in case of a link failure. In a partial-mesh topology, some (but not all) of the satellite offices are interconnected. If one link fails, there is often (but not always) a backup link. The price of adding an office rises depending on the number of satellite offices and on the degree to which they are linked. In a full-mesh topology, all offices are connected to each other. The price of adding an office increases with the number of offices. With a large number of offices, a full-mesh WAN topology costs many times what a star topology for the same number of offices would cost. Other WAN topologies, such as the bus and ring topologies, do not scale well and are rarely used for WANs with more than a handful of locations.

After completing this lab, you will be able to:

- Compare WAN links in terms of cost and speed
- Compare WAN topologies in terms of price and redundancy
- Identify WAN hardware components

Materials Required

This lab will require the following:

- Pencil and paper
- If some of the services discussed in this lab are not offered in your area, use representative pricing provided by your instructor for those services

Estimated completion time: **60–90 minutes**

Activity

1. Check the Web site of a local Internet service provider or telephone company, or call and speak to a representative about the cost and availability of high-speed Internet links for businesses. Identify the name of the organization you called or researched.

2. Explain that you are doing research for a school project on the pricing of Internet links. Give your name, the name of the networking class you are taking, and the name of your school.

3. For T-1 service, ask if the service is available in your area. If the service is available, ask if there are any geographic restrictions on the service. For instance, some services might not be available in all areas because the necessary infrastructure has not yet been built. Record the geographic availability of the service.

4. If the service is available, ask for the bandwidth of the service and record it. T-1 service should be available in most urban areas. If T-1 service is not available, go to Step 8.

5. Ask for the monthly cost of the service. Make sure to ask if you would be billed a flat fee, or whether your bill would change depending on how much you used the service. Record the monthly costs.

6. Ask if any additional equipment is required for the service and if the company provides it. Additionally, ask if the hardware charge is a flat fee or a monthly charge. If necessary, ask for the typical price of the additional equipment. Record the cost of additional equipment expected.

7. Ask about any initial setup fees that you might be charged. Typical setup fees include the installation of the T-1 line itself. Record the cost of the setup fees.

8. Repeat Step 3 through Step 7, this time referencing Digital Subscriber Line (DSL).

9. Repeat Step 3 through Step 7, this time referencing 128-Kbps partial T-1 or ISDN.

10. Repeat Step 3 through Step 7, this time referencing a Public Switched Telephone Network (PSTN) connection with a modem.

11. For each service, calculate the cost of any setup and installation fees and the cost of equipment required (excluding monthly charges for hardware). Record the setup, installation, and equipment costs.

12. For each service, calculate the cost of two years of monthly service, including any monthly charges for hardware. If the service is billed based on usage, estimate the cost based on medium usage. Record the cost of two years of service.

13. For each service, compare the costs calculated in Step 11 and Step 12.

14. Now you will examine the effects of different WAN topologies on WAN pricing. Calculate the cost of T-1 service connecting each office in Figure 7-1 in the star topology shown. Use the two-year monthly service fees you calculated in Step 12.

15. Calculate the cost of T-1 service connecting each office in Figure 7-2 in the partial-mesh topology shown. Use the two-year monthly service fees you calculated in Step 12.

16. Calculate the cost of T-1 service connecting each office in Figure 7-3 in the full-mesh topology shown. Use the two-year monthly service fees you calculated in Step 12.

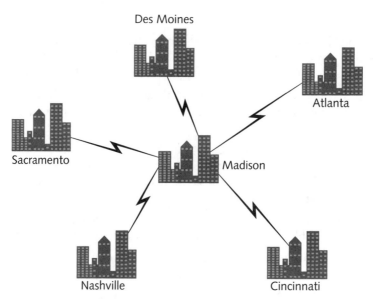

Figure 7-1 Star WAN topology

Courtesy Course Technology/Cengage Learning

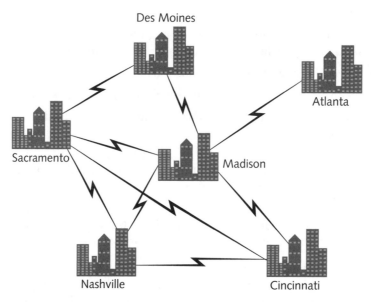

Figure 7-2 Partial-mesh WAN topology

Courtesy Course Technology/Cengage Learning

Certification Objectives

Objectives for the Network+ Exam:

- Categorize WAN technology types and properties: *Type*: frame relay, E1/T1, ADSL, SDSL, VDSL, cable modem, satellite, E3/T3, OC-x, wireless, ATM, SONET, MPLS,

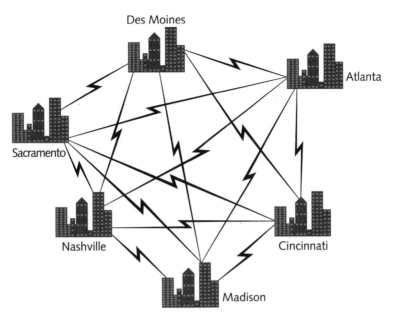

Figure 7-3 Full-mesh WAN topology

Courtesy Course Technology/Cengage Learning

ISDN BRI, ISDN PRI, POTS, PSTN; *Properties*: circuit switch, packet switch, speed, transmission media, distance

Review Questions

1. Which of the following best describes the function of a CSU?

   a. It transmits several signals over a single channel.

   b. It separates a single channel into multiple channels.

   c. It terminates a digital signal and ensures connection integrity.

   d. It converts the digital signal used by connectivity devices into the digital signal sent through the cabling.

2. Which of the following WAN topologies is the least expensive to build?

   a. star-wired ring

   b. full-mesh

   c. partial-mesh

   d. star

3. Which of the following WAN topologies gives the most redundancy?

   a. bus

   b. partial-mesh

   c. full-mesh

   d. star

4. What is the maximum number of channels that a single T-1 can contain?

    a. 12

    b. 24

    c. 48

    d. 64

5. What is the maximum throughput of a T-3 line?

    a. 1.544 Mbps

    b. 45 Mbps

    c. 672 Mbps

    d. 275 Mbps

6. What does DSL use to achieve higher throughput than PSTN over the same lines?

    a. full duplexing

    b. data modulation

    c. message switching

    d. framing

7. Which of the following WAN links is most reliable?

    a. DSL

    b. PSTN

    c. ISDN

    d. SONET

8. Which of the following is the most expensive type of connection to install and lease?

    a. DSL

    b. ISDN

    c. T-1

    d. T-3

Lab 7.2 Connecting to an Internet Service Provider in Windows Server 2008

Objectives

In this lab, you will make a connection to an ISP. Although higher-speed connections such as DSL or cable allow many people to connect more quickly to the Internet, dial-up connections to the Internet are still common in some areas. Dial-up access using the Public Switched Telephone Network (PSTN), also known as the plain old telephone service (POTS), is still used in many rural areas that do not yet have access to high-speed alternatives. In your work as a networking professional, you will find it valuable to understand how to configure and troubleshoot dial-up connections because some of your rural clients will rely on such connections for network access.

In many small networks, many or all users need at least occasional access to the Internet. Sharing a single Internet connection is cheaper and easier to configure than giving users their own modems and ISP accounts. Using Internet Connection Sharing (ICS), you can configure one modem on one computer and the rest of the office can connect through that computer. ICS will automatically configure the server to give DHCP addresses to workstations. Furthermore, you can configure the ICS server to dial the ISP connection whenever a workstation requests information on the Internet. However, a dial-up connection can quickly become congested as you add users so, if possible, most businesses will choose a high-speed connection option.

Additionally, ICS will automatically configure Network Address Translation (NAT) for the ISP connection. NAT allows an ICS server and any workstation using the ICS server to connect to the Internet to appear to the ISP as one IP address. Otherwise, you would need to arrange with the ISP for each workstation to have its own IP address. This would require additional configuration, as well as additional expense in many cases.

After completing this lab, you will be able to:

- Configure a dial-up connection to an ISP

- Share a dial-up Internet connection with a workstation

Materials Required

This lab will require the following:

- A computer running Windows Server 2008, Standard Edition named *SERVER1* with a NIC configured with an IP address of 192.168.54.1 and a subnet mask of 255.255.255.0; no secondary IP addresses must be configured for this NIC

- Routing and Remote Access disabled on *SERVER1*

- A modem installed and configured on *SERVER1*, without any location or Internet connection information configured

- Access to an analog outside phone line, or a digital-to-analog converter (to prevent the digital phone lines from ruining the modems)

- If dialing an additional number, such as 9, is required to access the outside line, knowledge of the number

- The phone number of an ISP's dial-up pool, and a user name and password for a valid account that does not require any advanced settings

- A computer running Windows XP Professional or Vista named *WORKSTATION1* with a NIC, and configured to receive an IP address through DHCP

- Administrative access to both computers

- Both computers connected to an Ethernet hub with straight-through Cat 5 (or better) UTP cables

Estimated completion time: 30 minutes

Activity

1. Plug the RJ-11 connector on one end of the phone cable into the modem attached to *SERVER1*. Plug the other end into the wall jack for the phone line.

2. Log on to *SERVER1* as the Administrator. The Windows Server 2008 desktop appears.

3. Click **Start**, click **Control Panel**, double-click **Network and Sharing Center**, and click **Set up a connection or network**. The Set up a connection or network window opens.

4. When you're asked to select a connection or network, make sure that the **Connect to the Internet** option is selected, and click **Next**.

5. Next you are asked how you want to connect to the Internet. If necessary, click the **Dial-up** option.

6. Enter **Netplus Lab** in the Connection name text box. Click **Next**.

7. Enter the phone number of the ISP in the Dial-up phone number text box. Include any additional digits needed, such as a 1, the area code, or any numbers (often a 9) required to use an outside phone line. Click **Next**.

8. If necessary, select the **Anyone's use** option. Click **Next**.

9. Enter the user name in the User name text box, and enter the account's password in the Password and Confirm password text boxes. Click **Next**. The window indicates that you have successfully completed it and summarizes the options that you have selected.

10. Click **Finish**. The New Connection window closes, and the Connect Netplus Lab dialog box opens. (If the Connect Netplus Lab dialog box does not open, click **Start**, click **Control Panel**, double-click **Network and Sharing Center**, click **Manage network connections**, and then click **Netplus Lab**.)

11. If necessary, click **Properties**. The Netplus Lab Properties dialog box opens.

12. Click the **Advanced** tab. The Advanced tab of the Netplus Lab Properties dialog box opens.

13. Click the **Allow other network users to connect through this computer's Internet connection** check box to place a check mark in it. The "Establish a dial-up connection whenever a computer on my network attempts to access the Internet" check box also becomes checked. See Figure 7-4.

14. If the Home networking connection drop-down box is present, select **Local Area Connection**. If not, go to the next step. (The Home networking connection drop-down box will only be available if the computer has more than one network card.)

15. Click **OK**. A dialog box might open, indicating that when Internet Connection Sharing is enabled, the NIC will be automatically configured with an IP address of 192.168.0.1 and that it might lose contact with other devices on the network.

16. Click **Yes**. The Netplus Lab Properties dialog box reopens. (If the dialog box does not reopen, click **Start**, click **Control Panel**, double-click **Network and Sharing Center**, click **Manage network connections**, and then click **Netplus Lab**.)

17. On *WORKSTATION1*, press **Ctrl+Alt+Del** to display the Log On to Windows dialog box. Log on as an administrator. The Windows desktop appears.

18. Click **Start**, point to **All Programs**, point to **Accessories**, and click **Command Prompt**. (In Windows Vista, click **Start**, type **cmd** in the Start Search text box, and then press **Enter**.) A command prompt window opens.

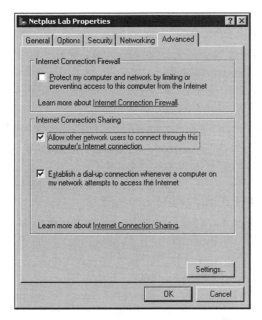

Figure 7-4   Netplus Lab Properties dialog box

Courtesy Course Technology/Cengage Learning

19. Type **ipconfig / renew** and press **Enter**. The computer obtains a new IP address from the server. Record the new IP address.

20. Click **Start**, and then click **Internet Explorer**. Internet Explorer opens.

21. In the Address bar, type **www.microsoft.com** and press **Enter**. The modem attached to *SERVER1* dials the ISP connection, and the Microsoft home page opens.

22. Log off both computers.

Certification Objectives

Objectives for the Network+ Exam:

- Categorize WAN technology types and properties: *Type*: frame relay, E1/T1, ADSL, SDSL, VDSL, cable modem, satellite, E3/T3, OC-x, wireless, ATM, SONET, MPLS, ISDN BRI, ISDN PRI, POTS, PSTN; *Properties*: circuit switch, packet switch, speed, transmission media, distance

- Given a scenario, select the appropriate command line interface tool and interpret the output to verify functionality: Traceroute, Ipconfig, Ifconfig, Ping, Arp ping, Arp, Nslookup, Hostname, Dig, Mtr, Route, Nbtstat, Netstat

Review Questions

1. What are two differences between PPP and SLIP?

   a. SLIP can handle only asynchronous transmission, whereas PPP can handle both asynchronous and synchronous transmission.

b. SLIP encapsulates traffic according to its original Network layer protocol, whereas PPP masks SLIP traffic as IP-based data.

c. SLIP cannot carry Network layer protocols other than TCP/IP, whereas PPP can carry any Network layer protocol.

d. SLIP is compatible with only NetWare servers, whereas PPP is compatible with both NetWare and Windows computers.

2. Which of the following is one primary difference between PPP and PPTP?

a. PPP can handle only asynchronous transmission, whereas PPTP can handle both asynchronous and synchronous transmission.

b. PPP encapsulates traffic according to its original Network layer protocol, whereas PPTP masks PPP traffic as IP-based data.

c. PPP cannot carry Network layer protocols other than TCP/IP, whereas PPTP can carry any Network layer protocol.

d. PPP is compatible with only NetWare servers, whereas PPTP is compatible with both NetWare and Windows computers.

3. Which of the following is the most secure remote access protocol?

a. SLIP

b. PPP

c. RAS

d. PPTP

4. Which of the following best describes the asynchronous communications method?

a. Data that is transmitted and received by nodes must conform to a timing scheme.

b. Data that is transmitted and received by nodes does not have to conform to any timing scheme.

c. Data that is transmitted and received by nodes is subject to resequencing by each connectivity device through which it passes.

d. Data that is transmitted and received by nodes requires an additional sequencing bit to ensure that data is reassembled in the proper order.

5. If your ISP uses DHCP to assign TCP/IP information to a dial-up connection, which of the following must you still specify in your connection parameters?

a. the type of server into which you are dialing

b. your workstation's IP address

c. the network's DHCP server address

d. the network's subnet mask

Lab 7.3 Configuring a Remote Access Server

Objectives

In this lab, you will create a remote access server (RAS) and connect to it from a client. With a remote access server, users may access network resources from home or on the road.

A salesperson, for example, might be on the road a large percentage of the time and have no network access besides her dial-up connection. By dialing into a dial-up server with Routing and Remote Access Service (RRAS), a remote user can check e-mail, share files, and use the network just as if she were locally connected to the network.

In Windows Server 2008, keep in mind that you need to specifically enable a user to dial in remotely to a Windows Server 2008 computer. Even if the server has a modem and is configured to accept incoming calls, it may reject a call if a user does not have dial-in permission.

After completing this lab, you will be able to:

- Configure RRAS to allow a Windows Server 2008 computer to accept dial-up connections

Materials Required

This lab will require the following:

- A computer running Windows Server 2008, Standard Edition named *SERVER1* in the NETPLUS workgroup, with ICS disabled and Routing and Remote Access installed but not activated
- Two NICs on *SERVER1*, one configured with an IP address of 192.168.54.1 and a subnet mask of 255.255.255.0 and the other configured with an IP address of 172.16.1.1 and a subnet mask of 255.255.255.0
- A shared folder on *SERVER1* named NETPLUS containing at least one text file
- A computer running Windows XP Professional or Vista named *WORKSTATION1*
- Administrative access to both computers
- A user account named netplus configured on *SERVER1* with the rights needed to dial in to the server
- Modems installed and configured on both machines
- Access to two outside analog phone lines in the same or different locations or to two digital-to-analog converters (to prevent digital phone lines from ruining the modems)
- Knowledge of the telephone number of the phone line to which the Windows Server 2008 computer is attached
- Two phone cords with RJ-11 connectors on both ends that are long enough to reach the wall outlet

Estimated completion time: **60 minutes**

Activity

1. Connect one end of a phone cord to the back of the modem installed on *SERVER1*, and connect the other end to the wall outlet.

2. Repeat the previous step with the Windows XP or Vista computer.

3. Log on to *SERVER1* as the Administrator. The Windows Server 2008 desktop appears.

4. Click **Start**, point to **Administrative Tools**, and then click **Routing and Remote Access**. The Routing and Remote Access dialog box opens.

5. Right-click the **SERVER1 (local)** icon in the left pane of the dialog box. From the shortcut menu, click **Configure and Enable Routing and Remote Access**. The Routing and Remote Access Server Setup Wizard opens.

6. Click **Next**. The wizard asks you for information on how to configure the Routing and Remote Access Service.

7. If necessary, select the **Remote access (dial-up or VPN)** option. Click **Next**.

8. Click the **Dial-up** check box to select it. Click **Next**. The wizard shows you information about the interfaces to which dial-up users will connect.

9. Make sure that **Local Area Connection** is highlighted, and click **Next**. The wizard asks you to choose how IP addresses will be assigned to remote clients. Figure 7-5 shows you an example of this dialog box in the Routing and Remote Access Server Setup Wizard.

10. Make sure that the **Automatically** option button is selected, and click **Next**. The wizard asks you how you would like to configure authentication.

11. Make sure that the **No, use Routing and Remote Access to authenticate connection requests** option is selected, and click **Next**. The computer indicates that you have completed the wizard.

12. Click **Finish**. A dialog box opens indicating that to support the relaying of DHCP messages from remote access clients; you must configure the DHCP Relay Agent.

13. Click **OK**. Message boxes appear indicating that the service is initializing. The Routing and Remote Access Server Setup Wizard closes. Log on to *WORKSTATION1* as an administrator. The Windows desktop appears.

14. On *WORKSTATION1*, click **Start**, point to **All Programs**, point to **Accessories**, point to **Communications**, and click **New Connection Wizard**. The New Connection

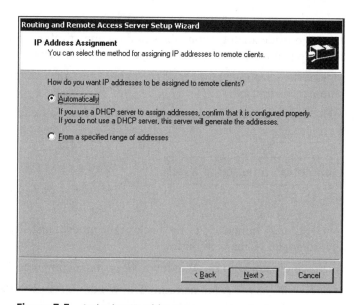

Figure 7-5   Assigning IP addresses to remote clients

Courtesy Course Technology/Cengage Learning

Wizard opens, and the Location Information dialog box opens on top of it. (In Windows Vista, click **Start**, click **Control Panel**, click **Network and Internet**, click **Network and Sharing Center**, and click **Set up a connection or network**. Select **Set up a dial-up connection** and click **Next**.) If the Location Information dialog box does not open, go to Step 17.

15. Select your country from the drop-down menu. Enter your area code in the "What area code (or city code) are you in now?" text box. If you need to enter a number to specify a carrier code or access an outside line, enter them in the appropriate text boxes. Click **OK**. The Location Information dialog box closes, and the Phone and Modem Options dialog box opens.

16. Click **OK**. The Phone and Modem Options dialog box closes, leaving the New Connection Wizard open.

If you are using Windows XP, follow these steps:

17. Click **Next**. The wizard asks what type of connection you would like to configure.

18. Select the **Connect to the network at my workplace** option. Click **Next**. The wizard asks how you would like to connect.

19. Select the **Dial-up connection** option and click **Next**. The wizard asks you to specify a name for the connection. Enter **Netplus Lab** in the Company Name box. Click **Next**. The wizard asks you for the phone number for the connection.

20. Enter the phone number of *SERVER1* in the Phone number text box. Click **Next**. The wizard asks you whether the account should be configured for all accounts or only this account.

21. Make sure that **Anyone's use** is selected and click **Next**. The computer indicates that you have completed the wizard.

22. Click **Finish**. The New Connection Wizard closes.

If you are using Windows Vista, follow these steps:

23. Enter the phone number of *SERVER1* in the **Dial-up phone number** text box.

24. Enter the appropriate user name and password to connect to *SERVER1*.

25. Enter **Netplus Lab** in the Connection name text box.

26. Make sure that **Allow other people to use this connection** is selected and click **Create**.

27. Click **Start**, right-click **Network**, and click **Properties**. Click **Manage network connections** (In Windows XP, click **Start**, point to **All Programs**, point to **Accessories**, point to **Communications**, and click **Network Connections**.) The Network Connections dialog box opens.

28. Right-click the **Netplus Lab** icon and select **Connect** from the shortcut menu.

29. In the User name text box, enter **netplus**. In the Password text box, enter the password for this account given to you by your instructor. Click **Connect**. The modem connects to the remote access server.

30. A dialog box indicating that you have connected successfully opens. Click **OK**. You have successfully logged on to the remote access server.

31. Click **Start**, and then click **Computer** (**My Computer** in Windows XP).

32. On the menu bar, click **Tools**, and then click **Map Network Drive**. The Map Network Drive dialog box opens.

33. In the Folder text box, enter **\\192.168.54.1\NETPLUS**. Click **Connect using a different user name**. The Connect As dialog box opens.

34. Type **Administrator** in the User name text box, and enter the password for the Administrator account on *SERVER1* in the Password text box. Click **OK**. The Connect As dialog box closes.

35. Click **Finish**. The Map Network Drive dialog box opens briefly, indicating that the computer is attempting to map the network drive. After it closes, an icon for the mapped network drive appears underneath Network Drives in the My Computer window.

36. Double-click the icon for the mapped network drive. A folder containing the name of at least one text file appears.

37. Double-click the text file. The text file opens.

38. Close the text file and log off both computers.

Certification Objectives

Objectives for the Network+ Exam:

- Categorize WAN technology types and properties: *Type*: frame relay, E1/T1, ADSL, SDSL, VDSL, cable modem, satellite, E3/T3, OC-x, wireless, ATM, SONET, MPLS, ISDN BRI, ISDN PRI, POTS, PSTN; *Properties*: circuit switch, packet switch, speed, transmission media, distance

- Explain the methods of network access security: *Filtering*: ACL, MAC filtering, IP filtering, tunneling and encryption, SSL VPN, VPN, L2TP, PPTP, IPSEC, remote access, RAS, RDP, PPPoE, PPP, VNC, ICA

Review Questions

1. Which of the following best describes a modem's function?

   a. to encapsulate Data Link layer protocols as Network layer protocols before transmitting data over the PSTN

   b. to separate data into frames as it is transmitted from the computer to the PSTN, and then strip data from frames as it is received from the PSTN

   c. to encrypt data as it is transmitted from the computer to the PSTN, and then decrypt data as it is received from the PSTN

   d. to convert a source computer's digital pulses into analog signals for the PSTN, and then convert analog signals back into digital pulses for the destination computer

2. What is another common term for *Public Switched Telephone Network*?

   a. plain old telephone service

   b. basic rate telephone service

   c. limited access telephone service

   d. transcontinental public telephone service

3. Which of the following types of dial-up connections would result in the best performance from the client's perspective?

   a. a PPP dial-up connection to an RRAS server that allowed the client to launch an application from the RRAS server

   b. a PPTP dial-up connection to an RRAS server that allowed the client to launch an application from another server on the LAN

   c. a SLIP dial-up connection to an RRAS server that allowed the client to log on to an application server on the LAN and run an application from that application server

   d. a PPTP dial-up connection to an RRAS server that allowed the client to log on to a Citrix terminal server and use ICA to run an application

4. What does RAS stand for?

   a. remote authentication service

   b. remote access server

   c. remote accounting service

   d. remote addressing server

5. Why do most remote clients (for example, those that dial in to an RRAS server) use DHCP and not static IP addressing?

   a. because using DHCP allows more efficient use of a limited number of IP addresses

   b. because using DHCP ensures that the client is authorized to access the network

   c. because using DHCP ensures that the client is assigned a valid IP address

   d. because using DHCP allows the client to use the same IP address each time he or she dials in to the LAN

Lab 7.4 Creating a VPN with the Point-to-Point Tunneling Protocol

Objectives

Although a remote access server allows users to dial in and use network resources, dialing in to a remote access server can be quite expensive if many of the users have to dial long distance. One way to reduce the cost of using a remote access server is to create a virtual private network (VPN). In a VPN, users connect to the remote access server over an encrypted channel through a public network, typically the Internet. Remote users have the same access that they had when dialing in directly to the remote access server. However, instead of paying long-distance fees per minute, an organization pays for its users' Internet connections and the Internet connectivity of its remote access server.

A VPN can be thought of as an imaginary cable, which is connected from one end of the VPN to the other end. In many types of VPNs, a virtual network interface is created on both ends of the VPN, just as if they were directly linked by the same cable even though the two endpoints might be across the Internet. Each virtual network interface has an IP address just as a normal interface does. However, this IP address is associated with a logical NIC and not a physical NIC. For this reason, an IP address like this is often called a virtual IP address.

In this lab, you will create a VPN using the Point-to-Point Tunneling Protocol (PPTP). PPTP creates virtual NICs on the server and client. Traffic between each virtual NIC is encrypted so that a malicious user with a protocol analyzer cannot view the contents. Although there may be many network devices between the client and the server, the PPTP tunnel makes the client and server seem to be attached to the same hub.

Other protocols, including IPSec, can also be used to carry VPN traffic. VPNs run on a wide variety of hardware, including servers with several different operating systems, routers, firewalls, and dedicated VPN hardware such as Cisco's ASA 5500 Series devices. As VPN traffic requires additional processing and can use a lot of CPU time, many devices will off-load processing of VPN traffic onto a special chip or module.

After completing this lab, you will be able to:

- Configure a VPN with PPTP between a client computer and a Windows Server 2008 computer

Materials Required

This lab will require the following:

- A computer running Windows Server 2008, Standard Edition named *SERVER1* with two NICs, one configured with an IP address of 192.168.54.1 and a subnet mask of 255.255.255.0 and the other configured with an IP address of 172.16.1.1 and a subnet mask of 255.255.255.0
- Routing and Remote Access disabled on the Windows Server 2008 computer
- A shared folder on *SERVER1* containing at least one text file
- A computer running Windows XP Professional or Vista named *WORKSTATION1* with a NIC configured with an IP address of 192.168.54.2 and a subnet mask of 255.255.255.0
- Each NIC on both computers connected with straight-through Cat 5 (or better) UTP cables to a single hub
- Administrative access to both computers
- An account on *SERVER1* with a known password and sufficient rights to connect to *SERVER1*

Estimated completion time: **30 minutes**

Activity

1. Log on to *SERVER1* as the Administrator. The Windows Server 2008 desktop appears.

2. Click **Start**, point to **Administrative Tools**, and then click **Routing and Remote Access**. The Routing and Remote Access dialog box opens.

3. In the left pane of the dialog box, right-click **SERVER1 (local)**. From the shortcut menu, select **Configure and Enable Routing and Remote Access**. The Routing and Remote Access Server Setup Wizard opens.

4. Click **Next**. The wizard displays configuration options for the Routing and Remote Access Service.

5. Select the **Virtual private network (VPN) access and NAT** option. Click **Next**. The wizard asks you to select at least one interface that connects this server to the Internet.

6. Select **Local Area Connection** and click **Next**. The wizard asks you to select options for IP address assignment.

7. If necessary, select the **Automatically** option and click **Next**. The wizard asks you to select options for managing multiple remote access servers.

8. If necessary, select **No, use Routing and Remote Access to authenticate connection requests** and click **Next**. The wizard indicates that you have finished.

9. Click **Finish**. A Routing and Remote Access dialog box might open, indicating that you must make further configuration changes to support the relay of DHCP messages. If not, go to Step 11.

10. Click **OK**. A dialog box opens, indicating that the Routing and Remote Access Service is starting. The dialog box closes, and the tree underneath SERVER1 (local) has expanded.

11. Right-click **Ports** on the tree underneath SERVER1 (local), and select **Properties** from the shortcut menu. The Ports Properties dialog box opens. See Figure 7-6.

12. Click **WAN Miniport (PPTP)** to select it. Click **Configure**. The Configure Device – WAN Miniport (PPTP) dialog box opens.

13. Click the **Demand-dial routing connections (inbound and outbound)** check box to remove the check. Click **OK** twice.

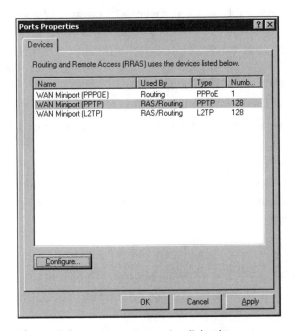

Figure 7-6   The Ports Properties dialog box

Courtesy Course Technology/Cengage Learning

14. Right-click **SERVER1 (local)**. From the shortcut menu, point to **All Tasks**, and then click **Restart**. The Routing and Remote Access Service restarts.

15. Log on to *WORKSTATION1* as an administrator. The Windows desktop appears.

16. Click **Start**, and then click **Control Panel**. The Control Panel window opens.

If you're using Windows XP, do the following steps:

17. Click the **Network and Internet Connections** category.

18. Click the **Set up or change your Internet connection** icon. The Internet Properties dialog box opens with the Connections tab displayed.

19. Click **Setup**. The New Connection Wizard opens. If no location information has been configured previously, the Location Information dialog box opens on top of it. If the Location Information dialog box does not open, go to Step 21.

20. Enter the area code. Click **OK** to close the Location Information dialog box.

21. In the New Connection Wizard, click **Next**. The wizard asks you to select network connection types.

22. Select **Connect to the network at my workplace**, and click **Next**. The wizard asks you to select the type of connection.

23. Select **Virtual Private Network connection**, and then click **Next**. The wizard asks you to enter a company name.

24. Enter **NetPlus** in the Company Name box. Click **Next**. The wizard asks you to configure settings for dialing the initial connection to the Internet or other public network. If the wizard instead asks for the name or IP address of the VPN server, go to Step 26.

25. Select the **Do not dial the initial connection** option button. Click **Next**. The wizard instead asks for the name or IP address of the VPN server.

26. Enter **192.168.54.1** in the Host name or IP address text box. Click **Next**. The wizard asks who will be using the connection. If necessary, select **Anyone's use** and click **Next**. The wizard indicates that you have finished.

27. Click **Finish**. The New Connection Wizard closes.

28. Click the **Network Connections** icon. The Network Connections window opens.

29. Double-click the **NetPlus** icon.

30. Enter the user name and password for the account that can connect to *SERVER1* in the User name and Password text boxes. Click **Connect**. The Connecting NetPlus dialog box opens, indicating that the computer is being registered on the network.

31. Skip to Step 38.

If you're using Windows Vista, do the following steps:

32. Click **Network and Internet** and then click **Network and Sharing Center**.

33. Click **Set up a connection or network**. The Set up a connection or network window opens.

34. Scroll down and select **Connect to a workplace** and click **Next**.

35. Click on **Use my Internet connection (VPN)**.

36. Enter **192.168.54.1** as the Internet address and **NetPlus** as the Destination name and click **Next.**

37. Enter the user name and password for the account that can connect to *SERVER1* in the User name and Password text boxes. Click **Connect.** The Connecting NetPlus dialog box opens, indicating that the computer is being registered on the network.

38. Click **Start**, point to **All Programs**, point to **Accessories**, and then click **Command Prompt**. (In Windows Vista, click **Start**, type **cmd** in the Start Search text box, and then press **Enter**.) A command prompt window opens.

39. Type **ipconfig** and press **Enter**. The computer displays the IP address for each NIC on the computer, including the virtual NIC. (Note that the virtual NIC is named PPP adapter NetPlus.) What is the IP address of the virtual interface?

40. On *SERVER1*, click **Start**, point to **All Programs**, click **Accessories**, and then click **Command Prompt**. A command prompt window opens.

41. Type **ipconfig** and press **Enter**. The computer displays the IP address for each NIC on the computer, including the virtual NIC for the VPN. Note that the name of the virtual NIC is PPP Adapter RAS Server (Dial In) Interface. What is the IP address of the virtual interface on *SERVER1*?

42. On *WORKSTATION1*, click **Start**, and then click **My Computer**.

43. On the menu bar, click **Tools**, and then click **Map Network Drive**. The Map Network Drive dialog box opens.

44. In the Folder text box, enter **\\192.168.54.1\NETPLUS**. Click **Connect using a different user name**. The Connect As dialog box opens.

45. Type **Administrator** in the User name text box, and enter the password for the Administrator account in the Password text box. Click **OK**. The Connect As dialog box closes.

46. Click **Finish**. The Map Network Drive dialog box opens briefly, indicating that the computer is attempting to map the network drive. After it closes, an icon for the mapped network drive appears underneath Network Drives in the My Computer window.

47. Double-click the icon for the mapped network drive. A folder containing the name of at least one text file appears.

48. Double-click the text file. The text file opens.

49. Close the text file and log off both computers.

Certification Objectives

Objectives for the Network+ Exam:

- Explain common logical network topologies and their characteristics: peer to peer, client/server, VPN, VLAN

- Explain the methods of network access security: *Filtering*: ACL, MAC filtering, IP filtering, tunneling and encryption, SSL VPN, VPN, L2TP, PPTP, IPSEC, remote access, RAS, RDP, PPPoE, PPP, VNC, ICA

Review Questions

1. What is one reason an organization might employ a VPN rather than simply allow users to dial directly in to their remote access server?

   a. VPNs always provide better performance than direct-dial connections.

   b. VPNs allow more users to connect to the LAN simultaneously.

   c. VPNs are less expensive for connecting a large number of remote users.

   d. VPNs prevent the need for firewalls between access servers and the Internet.

2. In this lab, you connected a workstation to a server using a VPN. Which of the following is true about the VPN connection you created in this lab?

   a. It uses physical IP addresses.

   b. It uses virtual IP addresses on the workstation end.

   c. It uses virtual IP addresses on both ends.

   d. It requires a modem for connection.

3. Which of the following transmission methods is most apt to be used by VPN clients?

   a. PSTN

   b. T-1

   c. frame relay

   d. SONET

4. What does the "T" in PPTP stand for?

   a. Tunneling

   b. Transmission

   c. Transport

   d. Telecommunications

5. Which of the following protocol suites could be used to transmit data over a VPN that relies on PPTP? (Choose all that apply.)

   a. IPX/SPX

   b. TCP/IP

   c. NetBEUI

   d. AppleTalk

Lab 7.5 Configuring Remote Desktop Services (Terminal Services) on Windows Server 2008

Objectives

The primary remote administration tool for Windows Server 2008 is Remote Desktop Services (Terminal Services). Terminal Services allows a network administrator to log on to a remote Windows Server 2008 computer almost as if the network administrator were at the console. This can be invaluable for administration. For instance, suppose that a problem with a particular server occurs while you are at home. Without some means of accessing the computer remotely, you must go to the computer to fix the problem. With Terminal Services, however, you can connect to the computer remotely and fix the problem without ever leaving home.

By default, Terminal Services on Windows Server 2008 is configured in Remote Administration mode. You can also configure it in Application Server mode. Application Server mode allows users to log on to the server and run applications. This has several advantages. First, network administrators can manage applications from one location. Otherwise, each application must be managed for each user's computer. Second, Terminal Services allows a network administrator to take over a particular user's session. This allows you to see exactly what the user sees. Finally, computers connecting to a computer running Terminal Services in Application Server mode, or a terminal server, may use a wide variety of hardware and operating systems. The terminal server does the bulk of the processing for applications run in Terminal Services. As a result, users may use older or less powerful computers.

One disadvantage of allowing users to connect to a terminal server is cost. Using Terminal Services in Application Server mode requires additional licensing, whereas running Terminal Services in Remote Administration mode does not. In this lab, you will activate temporary licensing for Terminal Services, which allows the use of Terminal Services for 120 days without the purchase of additional licensing. Additionally, managing applications on a terminal server is more complicated than managing the same applications on a user's desktop.

Finally, Windows XP or Vista allows users to log on to their computers through Remote Desktop. However, you may not have more than one user, local or remote, logged on to the same computer at the same time. Remote Desktop should not be confused with Remote Desktop Connection, the client used to connect to Terminal Services on remote Windows Server 2008 computers and Remote Desktop on remote Windows XP or Vista computers.

After completing this lab, you will be able to:

- Configure Terminal Services on Windows Server 2008

Materials Required

This lab will require the following:

- A computer running Windows Server 2008, Standard Edition named *SERVER1*, with a NIC configured with an IP address of 192.168.54.1 and a subnet mask of 255.255.255.0
- The server can be a member of a domain or a workgroup, although the steps will vary depending on your configuration
- Access to the Internet for *SERVER1* for activation of Terminal Server Licensing (and knowledge of any steps required to connect to the Internet), or prior activation of Terminal Server Licensing
- A computer named *WORKSTATION1* running Windows XP Professional (updated with SP3) or Vista, with a NIC configured with an IP address of 192.168.54.2 and a subnet mask of 255.255.255.0
- Administrative access to each computer
- Each computer connected to a hub with straight-through Cat 5 or better UTP cables

- Terminal Services and Terminal Services Licensing not installed on *SERVER1*
- Four ordinary user accounts with known passwords on *SERVER1*, each with suffi-cient permissions to log on interactively to *SERVER1* using Terminal Services

Estimated completion time: **45 minutes**

Activity

1. Log on to *SERVER1* as the Administrator. The Windows Server 2008 desktop appears.

2. Click **Start**, point to **Administrative Tools**, and then click **Server Manager**. The Server Manager window opens.

3. Select **Roles** and click **Add Roles**. The Add Roles Wizard opens. If the Before You Begin window opens, click **Next**.

4. On the Select Server Roles window, check the **Terminal Services** check box.

5. Click **Next**. The next window in the wizard provides some information on Terminal Server.

6. Click **Next** to open the Select Role Services window.

7. Check the **Terminal Server** and **TS Licensing** check boxes and click **Next**. If the server is a domain controller, a message will appear warning that Terminal Services is not recommended. Click **Install Terminal Server anyway (not recommended)**. The next window in the wizard recommends that you reinstall any applications for them to work properly on a Terminal Server. Click **Next**.

8. If you're running a Windows Vista client, select **Require Network Level Authentication** and click **Next**. The next window in the wizard is used to select the kind of client access licenses that will be used. If you're running Windows XP, select **Do not require Network Level Authentication**.

9. Select **Configure later** and click **Next**. Select the **Administrators** groups and click **Next**.

10. If necessary, select **This workgroup** or **This domain** and click **Next**. The next window summarizes your configuration choices.

11. Click **Install**. After several moments, the Add Roles Wizard indicates that you have successfully finished.

12. Click **Close**. The Add Roles Wizard dialog box opens, indicating that you must restart the computer.

13. Click **Yes**. The computer reboots. Log on as the Administrator and, when the installation of Terminal Services completes, click **Close** in the Installation Results window.

14. Now you will log on to *SERVER1* (from *WORKSTATION1*) while it is still configured in Remote Administration mode. Log on to *WORKSTATION1* as an administrator. The Windows desktop appears.

15. Click **Start**, point to **All Programs**, point to **Accessories**, and click **Remote Desktop Connection**. (In Windows Vista, click **Start**, click **All Programs**, click

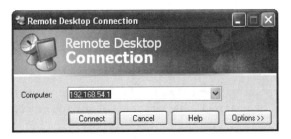

Figure 7-7   Remote Desktop Connection dialog box

Courtesy Course Technology/Cengage Learning

Accessories, and click **Remote Desktop Connection**.) The Remote Desktop Connection dialog box opens, as shown in Figure 7-7.

16. Enter **192.168.54.1** in the Computer text box. Click **Connect**. The Windows Security dialog box (Log On to Windows dialog box in Windows XP) opens for *SERVER1*. Log on to the remote computer as the Administrator. The Windows Server 2008 desktop appears.

17. Minimize the Remote Desktop Connection dialog box by clicking the horizontal line on the bar at the top of the screen.

18. Repeat Steps 14 through 17. Did Remote Desktop Connection allow you to open two sessions at the same time? If not, how was it prevented?

19. On *SERVER1*, press **Ctrl+Alt+Del** and log on to the computer as the Administrator. The Windows Server 2008 desktop appears.

20. Perform any steps that are necessary to obtain Internet access for *SERVER1*.

21. Click **Start**, point to **Administrative Tools**, point to **Terminal Services,** and click **TS Licensing Manager**. The TS Licensing Manager window opens, with an icon for *SERVER1* in the right pane of the window. In the Activation Status column, the activation status of *SERVER1* is Not activated.

22. If a dialog box opens indicating that no license servers can be found, click **OK**. Right-click **All servers** in the left pane of the window and click **Connect**. The Connect to License Server dialog box opens. Enter **SERVER1** and click **Connect**.

23. Right-click the SERVER1 icon. From the shortcut menu, select **Activate Server**. The Activate Server Wizard opens.

24. Click **Next**. The wizard asks you to select a connection method.

25. Make sure that **Automatic connection** is selected, and click **Next**. The wizard asks you for company information.

26. Fill in your name in the First name and Last name text boxes. Enter the name of your school in the Company text box, and select your country from the Country or Region drop-down menu. Click **Next**. The wizard asks you to fill in optional information, including your e-mail address.

27. Click **Next**. A dialog box opens briefly indicating that the computer is looking for the Microsoft activation server. Then the computer indicates that you have completed the Activate Server Wizard.

28. Click the **Start Install Licenses Wizard now** check box to remove the check from it. Click **Finish**. The wizard closes, and the activation status of the SERVER1 icon is now Activated. Close the TS Licensing Manager window.

29. If necessary, reattach *SERVER1* to the lab network.

30. Click **Start**, point to **Administrative Tools**, point to **Terminal Services**, and then click **Terminal Services Configuration**. The Terminal Services Configuration window opens.

31. In the left pane of the window, click the **Terminal Services Configuration** folder. Icons for server settings appear in the right pane of the window.

32. Now you will configure the server so that users can log on to multiple sessions. Right-click the **Restrict each user to a single session** icon. From the shortcut menu, click **Properties**. Uncheck **Restrict each user to a single session** and click **OK**. The shortcut menu closes.

33. On *WORKSTATION1*, repeat Steps 14 through 17. Repeat three more times, logging on each time as a different ordinary user.

34. On *SERVER1*, click **Start**, point to **Administrative Tools**, point to **Terminal Services**, and click **Terminal Services Manager**. The right pane of the window shows all the users currently logged on to the server and their sessions.

35. Right-click one of the sessions and click **Disconnect** from the shortcut menu. A Terminal Services Manager dialog box opens, indicating that each selected session will be disconnected.

36. Click **OK**. The session is disconnected, and the text underneath the Session heading reads Disconnected.

37. Repeat Steps 35 and 36 for each of the remaining sessions.

38. On *WORKSTATION1*, check to see if any of the sessions are open.

39. Log off both computers.

Certification Objectives

Objectives for the Network+ Exam:

- Explain the methods of network access security: *Filtering*: ACL, MAC filtering, IP filtering, tunneling and encryption, SSL VPN, VPN, L2TP, PPTP, IPSEC, remote access, RAS, RDP, PPPoE, PPP, VNC, ICA

Review Questions

1. Which of the following are reasons you might implement Terminal Services instead of a remote access server? (Choose all that apply.)

   a. no modems required with Terminal Services

   b. central configuration and control of applications on the Terminal Server

   c. no modems requirevd on clients

   d. no need to configure security on the Terminal Server

2. What is the difference between configuring a Windows Server 2008 computer to accept Remote Desktop Connection and configuring it to run Terminal Services?

   a. Remote Desktop Connection requires additional licensing.

   b. Terminal Services requires each client to have a modem.

   c. Terminal Services allows no more than two simultaneous connections.

   d. Terminal Services allows more than two simultaneous connections.

3. What is one way a network administrator can effectively troubleshoot a user's problem in a Terminal Services session that can't be done with a remote access server?

   a. by speaking with the user over the phone

   b. by examining the Terminal Server's error logs

   c. by taking over the user's session temporarily

   d. by rebooting the server

4. Which of the following is a potential disadvantage of Terminal Services?

   a. It requires additional licensing.

   b. It requires the client to be running Windows XP (SP3).

   c. It requires the client to have a high-speed connection such as a T-1.

   d. It requires the server to have a minimum of 1 GB of RAM.

5. True or False? You cannot log on to a Windows XP computer using a Remote Desktop connection.

CHAPTER EIGHT

WIRELESS NETWORKING

Labs included in this chapter

- Lab 8.1 Adding a Windows Client to a Wireless Network
- Lab 8.2 Adding a Linux Client to a Wireless Network
- Lab 8.3 Installing a Wireless Router
- Lab 8.4 Investigating Wireless Access Points

Net+ Exam Objectives

Objective	Lab
Compare the characteristics of wireless communication standards	8.4
Install, configure, and differentiate between common network devices	8.3, 8.4
Implement a basic wireless network	8.1, 8.2, 8.3
Identify common security threats and mitigation techniques	8.3

Lab 8.1 Adding a Windows Client to a Wireless Network

Objectives

In this lab, you will add a host to a wireless network. Wireless networks allow a user to connect to the network without cabling. This makes it possible to use a networked computer in a cafeteria, outdoors, in a coffee shop, and in many other places.

However, wireless networks come with a number of disadvantages. They do not have the throughput that some wired networks provide. Throughput also varies depending on reception, and good reception might not be possible from all locations. Wireless signals are affected by sources of electronic noise, including the weather, fluorescent lights, and microwave ovens. Finally, wireless networks might not be as secure as cabled networks. An unsecured wireless access point might mean that anyone with a wireless card in the next building or in the parking lot could gain access to your network resources.

After completing this lab, you will be able to:

- Add a client to a wireless network

Materials Required

This lab will require the following:

- A computer (ideally a laptop) named *WORKSTATION1* running Windows XP Professional or Vista with a wireless network card configured so that Windows manages wireless settings (instead of using the network card's client software to manage wireless settings)

- A wireless access point named "netplus" (or another name supplied by your instructor) configured with an IP address of 192.168.1.1 and a subnet mask of 255.255.255.0

- The wireless access point configured to give out DHCP addresses between 192.168.1.2 and 192.168.1.254 (or some portion of that range) and a subnet mask of 255.255.255.0

- Any additional settings needed to connect the Windows XP or Vista computer to this wireless access point

Estimated completion time: **25 minutes**

Activity

In Windows XP:

1. Log on to *WORKSTATION1* as an administrator. The Windows desktop appears.

2. Click **Start**, point to **All Programs**, point to **Accessories**, point to **Communications**, and click **Network Connections**. The Network Connections window opens.

3. Right-click **Wireless Network Connection**, and then select **Properties** from the shortcut menu that appears. The Wireless Network Connection Properties window opens.

4. Click the **Wireless Networks** tab. A list of available wireless networks appears under Available networks.

5. If you see the name of the wireless network, select it and go to Step 9. If you do not see the name of the wireless network, go to Step 6.

6. Click **Add** under Preferred networks. The Wireless network properties dialog box opens.

7. Enter **netplus** (or the name of the wireless access point) in the Network name (SSID) text box. Configure any additional settings as indicated by your instructor. Figure 8-1 shows the Wireless network properties dialog box.

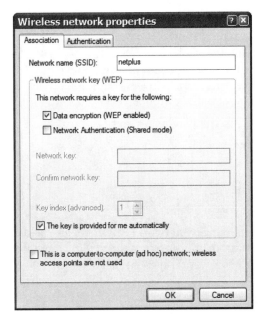

Figure 8-1   The Wireless network properties dialog box

Courtesy Course Technology/Cengage Learning

8. Click **OK**. The Wireless network properties dialog box closes, and the name of the wireless access point appears under Available networks.

9. Click **OK** to close the Wireless Network Connection Properties window.

In Windows Vista:

1. Log on to *WORKSTATION1* as an administrator. The Windows desktop appears.

2. Click **Start**, right-click **Network**, and click **Properties**. The Network and Sharing Center window opens.

3. Click **Connect to a network**. A list of available wireless networks appears.

4. If you see the name of the wireless network, select it and go to Step 7. If you do not see the name of the wireless network, go to Step 5.

5. Click **Set up a connection or network** and click **Manually connect to a wireless network**.

6. Enter **netplus** (or the name of the wireless access point) in the Network name (SSID) text box. Configure any additional settings as indicated by your instructor and click **Next**.

7. After you've connected to the network, close any open windows.

In either version of Windows:

1. Now you can test your connectivity to the wireless network. Click **Start**, point to **All Programs**, point to **Accessories**, and then click **Command Prompt**. (In Windows Vista, click **Start**, type **cmd** in the Start Search text box, and then press **Enter**.) A command prompt window opens.

2. Type **ping 192.168.1.1** and press **Enter**. The computer indicates that it has received four replies.

3. If the Windows computer is a laptop, type **ping -t 192.168.1.1** and press **Enter**. The Ping command begins running continuously, and will not stop until you end it. Pick up the laptop and walk away from the wireless access point. How far can you walk away from the wireless access point before the computer indicates that it is unable to reach 192.168.1.1?

4. Press **Ctrl+C** to stop the Ping command.

5. Log off the computer.

Certification Objectives

Objectives for the Network+ Exam:

- Implement a basic wireless network: install client; access point placement; install access point: configure appropriate encryption, configure channels and frequencies, set ESSID and beacon; verify installation

Review Questions

1. In which of the following ways does a wireless LAN differ from an Ethernet LAN?

    a. A wireless LAN requires additional protocols in the TCP/IP suite.

    b. A wireless LAN uses completely different protocols than an Ethernet LAN.

    c. A wireless LAN uses different techniques at the Physical layer to transmit data.

    d. A wireless LAN uses different techniques at the Data Link layer to transmit frames.

2. Which of the following are potential disadvantages of wireless LANs as compared with cabled LANs? (Choose all that apply.)

    a. Controlling access to a wireless LAN is more difficult.

    b. Issues such as the location of buildings and the weather can affect connectivity to a wireless LAN.

    c. The additional protocols required by wireless LANs create additional overhead.

    d. Signal strength can be affected by many sources of electronic noise.

3. How is a wireless NIC different from a NIC that requires a cable?

    a. A wireless NIC contains an antenna.

    b. A wireless NIC contains a chip, which does additional processing at higher levels of the OSI model.

    c. A wireless NIC requires an external power source.

    d. A wireless NIC requires an external antenna.

4. You have been hired as a network consultant by the East Coast Savings bank. East Coast Savings would like to implement a wireless LAN, but with high standards of security. What sort of restrictions would you recommend placing on the wireless LAN?

   a. Wireless LAN users have the same access as users attached to the Ethernet network.

   b. Wireless LAN users may surf the Web, but may not access the rest of the bank's network.

   c. Wireless LAN users may surf the Web, but may not access the rest of the bank's network without special security software.

   d. Wireless LAN users must use their own wireless ISP.

5. Why is a wireless signal susceptible to noise?

   a. Wireless NICs are usually poorly made.

   b. Wireless transmissions cannot be shielded like transmissions along an Ethernet cable.

   c. Wireless NICs do not support the network protocols necessary for error correction.

   d. Wireless NICs rely on the upper levels of the OSI model for error correction.

Lab 8.2 Adding a Linux Client to a Wireless Network

Objectives

In this lab, you will add a Linux host to a wireless network using the Network Manager tool. The Network Manager service can be accessed and configured through an applet in the GNOME environment. This makes connecting to a wireless network relatively easy, like in Windows, and only involves a small number of steps. Without the graphical network manager, the connection would have to be manually configured at the command line.

After completing this lab, you will be able to:

- Add a Linux client to a wireless network

Materials Required

This lab will require the following:

- A computer (ideally a laptop) running a current version of Fedora Linux, with a wireless network card, the GNOME desktop environment, and Network Manager installed

- A wireless access point named "netplus" (or another name supplied by your instructor) configured with an IP address of 192.168.1.1 and a subnet mask of 255.255.255.0

- The wireless access point configured to give out DHCP addresses between 192.168.1.2 and 192.168.1.254 (or some portion of that range) and a subnet mask of 255.255.255.0

- Any additional settings needed to connect the Linux computer to this wireless access point

Estimated completion time: **30 minutes**

Activity

1. Power on the computer and log on as root. The Fedora desktop appears.

2. If the Network Manager is not already active, you can start it by opening a terminal and typing **sudo /sbin/service NetworkManager start**.

3. Once the system has had a few minutes to discover any available wireless networks, click the Network Manager applet in the system tray to view them.

4. Select the wireless network named netplus by clicking it. If netplus has been set up with a password, you can enter it now to connect.

5. Test your wireless connection by moving back to the terminal and typing **ping 192.168.1.1** and pressing **Enter**. The computer indicates that it has received four replies.

6. Close any open applications and log off the computer.

Certification Objectives

Objectives for the Network+ Exam:

- Implement a basic wireless network: install client; access point placement; install access point: configure appropriate encryption, configure channels and frequencies, set ESSID and beacon; verify installation

Review Questions

1. What is the administrator's default account called in Linux?

    a. Admin

    b. Administrator

    c. default

    d. root

2. Where is the Network Manager service located?

    a. /user

    b. /sbin/services

    c. /etc/NetworkManager

    d. /Network/Manager

3. Describe how you could use Network Manager to switch between networks.

4. What Linux command is used to test network connections?

    a. root

    b. sudo

    c. ping

    d. start

Lab 8.3 Installing a Wireless Router

Objectives

In this lab, you will set up a basic unsecured wireless router. Later, in Lab 12.5, you will also implement some essential security features on the router. A wireless router is often used at home or with small peer-to-peer networks to allow several computers to wirelessly connect to an ISP and share an Internet connection. The router can also provide additional features such as functioning as a firewall or a DHCP server.

After completing this lab, you will be able to:

- Set up a wireless router

Materials Required

This lab will require the following:

- A computer (ideally a laptop) running Windows XP Professional or Vista with a wireless network card
- An unconfigured wireless router with setup CD or user's manual
- A Cat 5 (or better) network cable

Estimated completion time: **30 minutes**

Activity

1. If your router comes with a setup CD/DVD, run the setup program on your Windows XP/Vista computer. Follow the instructions in the manual on how to disconnect the Internet connection from your Windows computer and connect it to the router.

2. Physically connect your computer to a network port on the router using a Cat 5 (or better) straight-through cable. (Be sure to connect to one of the LAN ports on the router, not the Internet port.)

3. Plug in the router and turn it on.

4. Firmware on the router contains a configuration program that can usually be accessed using a Web browser. Determine the IP address of the router either by consulting the manual or by asking your instructor.

5. In your browser's Address bar, enter the IP address of the router (e.g., 192.168.1.1) and press **Enter**.

6. You might be required to sign in to the utility using a default password.

7. The main router configuration page should appear. The page will most likely have a pull-down menu with categories such as Setup, Wireless, and Security. Figure 8-2 shows the basic settings page for a Netgear wireless router.

8. For most situations, the default settings should work without any changes. However, the router should be secured by changing the default password, enabling wireless encryption (preferably WPA2), and so on. Securing a router is covered in Lab 12.5. The setup program should take you through the process of configuring your router.

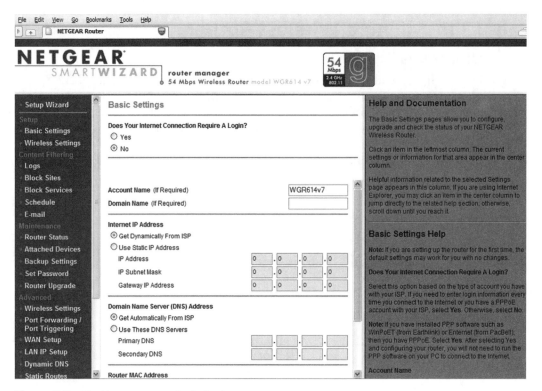

Figure 8-2 The Netgear router Basic Settings page

Courtesy Course Technology/Cengage Learning

9. Even if you're choosing not to secure your router, it's always a good idea to change your router's default password so other people cannot change the settings.

10. Spend some time examining the basic features of your router and then make the following changes:

- Enable DHCP
- Set the range of assigned addresses to begin at 192.168.1.100
- Change the Network Name (SSID) to "NETLAB"
- Set the Wireless Channel to "Auto"

11. After you've configured the router, you might have to reconnect your Internet connection so it correctly syncs up with the router.

12. Now shut down the Windows computer and disconnect the patch cable from the router.

13. Boot the Windows computer and use the steps in Lab 8.1 to wirelessly connect to the Internet.

14. When you're finished, close any open programs and log off the computer.

Certification Objectives

Objectives for the Network+ Exam:

- Install, configure, and differentiate between common network devices: hub, repeater, modem, NIC, media converters, basic switch, bridge, wireless access point, basic router, basic firewall, basic DHCP server
- Implement a basic wireless network: install client; access point placement; install access point: configure appropriate encryption, configure channels and frequencies, set ESSID and beacon; verify installation
- Identify common security threats and mitigation techniques: *Security threats*: DoS, viruses, worms, attackers, man in the middle, smurf, rogue access points, social engineering (phishing), mitigation techniques, policies and procedures, user training, patches and updates

Review Questions

1. How is a wireless router's configuration utility usually accessed?

   a. by flashing the RAM BIOS

   b. through a Web browser

   c. with the Windows Cfgrtr utility

   d. from the command line

2. Why is it a good idea to change your wireless router's password?

   a. so other people cannot change the router's settings

   b. so you won't forget it

   c. to make it the same as your login password

   d. the default password is most likely too complex

3. What type of connection is used to attach to the network port on a wireless router?

   a. none, it is wireless

   b. USB

   c. serial

   d. straight-through patch cable

Lab 8.4 Investigating Wireless Access Points

Objectives

In this lab, you will compare several wireless access points and choose the solution that best meets your needs. A wireless local area network (WLAN) connects computers through a wireless NIC to a device called a wireless access point (WAP or AP). WLANs use a variety of standards that offer different features such as range and throughput.

After completing this lab, you will be able to:

- Compare wireless access points in terms of price and features
- Identify wireless access point hardware

Materials Required

This lab will require the following:

- Pencil and paper
- A computer running Windows XP or Vista with Internet access
- An ordinary user account on the computer

Estimated completion time: **30 minutes**

Activity

1. Log on to the computer as an ordinary user. The Windows desktop appears.

2. Perform whatever steps are necessary for the computer to access the Internet. Start Internet Explorer (or another browser) and browse the Web sites of several distributors that sell networking equipment including wireless access points. Common manufacturers of wireless access points include Cisco/Linksys, D-Link, and 3Com.

3. Use these sites to find access points from at least two different manufacturers that meet the following criteria:

- 802.11g and 802.11n support
- Power over Ethernet (PoE)
- Ceiling mounted
- Plenum rated
- WPA2 encryption

4. On a separate piece of paper, record the make, model number, price, and a brief list of distinguishing features for each of the access points that you found.

5. Which access point is the best value?

6. Did you have any trouble finding information on the equipment?

7. When you're finished, log off the computer.

Certification Objectives

Objectives for the Network+ Exam:

- Compare the characteristics of wireless communication standards: *802.11 a/b/g/n*: speeds, distance, channels, frequency; *authentication and encryption*: WPA, WEP, RADIUS, TKIP

- Install, configure and differentiate between common network devices: hub, repeater, modem, NIC, media converters, basic switch, bridge, wireless access point, basic router, basic firewall, basic DHCP server

Review Questions

1. Which wireless networking standard is faster?

   a. 802.11a

   b. 802.11b

   c. 802.11g

   d. 802.11n

2. What feature will eliminate the need for a separate electrical outlet for your WAP?

   a. PoE

   b. WPA

   c. WPA2

   d. 802.11n

3. Why is plenum-rated cable often a requirement for ceiling-mounted access points?

   a. Ceiling-mounted APs are more than 7 feet off the ground.

   b. They work at higher speeds.

   c. They need to operate at higher temperatures.

   d. In the case of a fire, they do not give off toxic fumes.

NETWORKING OPERATING SYSTEMS

Labs included in this chapter

- Lab 9.1 Creating a New Domain Tree
- Lab 9.2 Delegating Administrative Rights
- Lab 9.3 Remotely Managing a Computer with Active Directory
- Lab 9.4 Starting and Stopping a Linux Server
- Lab 9.5 Connecting a Windows Client Using Samba
- Lab 9.6 Remotely Managing Linux Servers

Net+ Exam Objectives

Objective	Lab
Explain common logical network topologies and their characteristics	9.1
Explain issues that affect device security	9.2
Explain the methods of network access security	9.2, 9.3

Lab 9.1 Creating a New Domain Tree

Objectives

In Windows Server 2008, Active Directory allows you to manage computers and users throughout an organization. An Active Directory implementation is usually called a forest. Each forest consists of one or more domain trees. Each domain tree (often just called a tree) contains one or more domains arranged in a hierarchical manner. Each domain tree typically corresponds to an organization. For example, child domains inside the domain tree might correspond to the Sales, Marketing, and Manufacturing departments. If a forest consists of more than one domain tree, the other domain trees might correspond to related, but separate, organizations that nonetheless need to share resources. For instance, a conglomerate might own several companies that share only a handful of network resources. Each of these companies might correspond to a different domain tree within the forest.

When creating a new forest, you might create superfuntoys.com as the first domain tree in the forest. You might then create the following child domains for each location: cleveland.superfuntoys.com, milwaukee.superfuntoys.com, shanghai.superfuntoys.com, and so on. Each child domain might have additional child domains. Each department in each location might have its own child domain: marketing.cleveland.superfuntoys.com, manufacturing.cleveland.superfuntoys.com, accounting.cleveland.superfuntoys.com, and so on. The forest might contain another tree for a sister company, educationalsuperfuntoys.com, which would have its own child domains: toledo.educationalsuperfuntoys.com, berlin.educationalsuperfuntoys.com, boston.educationalsuperfuntoys.com, and so on. You can then configure each child domain so that its users and computers can use the network resources that they need in the rest of the tree and configure each tree so that its users and computers can use the resources they need in the other tree. As you might expect, an Active Directory forest can quickly become complicated, and you should carefully plan any Active Directory forest before you create it.

Active Directory requires DNS. If DNS is not configured properly or is not functioning properly, Active Directory will not work properly. When you first create a domain tree, however, Windows offers you the opportunity to configure the DNS server for the new domain tree.

After completing this lab, you will be able to:

- Create a new domain tree
- Create a new forest
- Add a client computer to the domain

Materials Required

This lab will require the following:

- A computer running Windows Server 2008, Standard Edition named *SERVER1* and configured with an IP address of 192.168.54.1 and a subnet mask of 255.255.255.0, configured to use 192.168.54.1 as its preferred DNS server and not configured as a domain controller
- A computer running Windows XP Professional or Vista named *WORKSTATION1*, configured with an IP address of 192.168.54.3 and a subnet mask of 255.255.255.0 and using 192.168.54.1 as its preferred DNS server

- Both computers connected to a hub with straight-through Cat 5 (or better) UTP cables
- Access to both computers as an administrator
- The Windows Server 2008 installation CD/DVD

Estimated completion time: **40 minutes**

Activity

1. Log on to *SERVER1* as the Administrator.

2. Click **Start**, and then click **Run**. The Run dialog box opens.

3. Type **dcpromo** and press **Enter**. If Terminal Services is installed on the computer, the Active Directory Domain Services Installation Wizard dialog box opens. Click **OK** to close it. The Active Directory Installation Wizard opens.

4. Click **Next**. The wizard describes some of the limitations that older versions of Windows will have with Windows Server 2008.

5. Click **Next**. The wizard asks what sort of domain you would like to create.

6. Make sure the **Create a new domain in a new forest** option is selected and click **Next**.

7. Type **netpluslab.net**. Figure 9-1 shows the Active Directory Domain Services Installation Wizard. Click **Next**.

8. After several moments, the wizard asks you to select the forest functional level. Because you are only using Server 2008, select Windows Server 2008 and click **Next**.

9. The wizard then asks you to select additional options for the domain controller. Make sure DNS server is selected and click **Next**. If the Static IP assignment message box appears, click **Yes, the computer will use a dynamically assigned IP address**. (In this case, this refers to the IPv6 address on your machine, and will not affect the lab.) If the Active Directory Domain Services Installation Wizard message box appears, click **Yes**.

10. The wizard asks you to specify the location of database and log files for Active Directory. Select the defaults by clicking **Next**.

11. The wizard asks you to select an administrator password for Directory Services Restore Mode.

12. Enter the password **Passw0rd** (or another password selected by your instructor) in the Password and the Confirm password text boxes. Click **Next**. The wizard summarizes the options you have selected.

13. Click **Next**. If prompted, insert the Windows Server 2008 installation CD/DVD into the CD/DVD-ROM drive and click **OK**. A dialog box opens, indicating that the wizard is configuring Active Directory. This might take several minutes, so do not click buttons or press keys until it has completed. After a few minutes, the computer indicates that you have completed the Active Directory Installation Wizard.

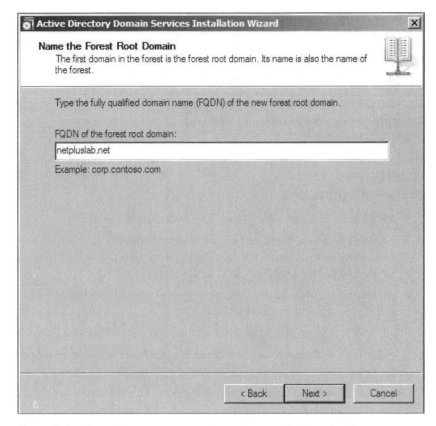

Figure 9-1 The Active Directory Domain Services Installation Wizard

Courtesy Course Technology/Cengage Learning

14. Click **Finish**. A dialog box opens, indicating that you must reboot the server before the configuration changes you made can become active.

15. Click **Restart Now**. The server reboots.

16. After the server reboots, press **Ctrl+Alt+Del** and log on as the Administrator. (Now the account is for the Administrator for the netpluslab.net domain.) The Windows Server 2008 desktop appears.

17. Click **Start** and then click **Command Prompt**. A command prompt window opens.

18. Now you will verify that the Active Directory Installation Wizard has configured DNS. Type **ipconfig /all** and press **Enter**. The computer displays detailed information about its IP configuration, including its IP address and the DNS servers it uses. What is the IP address used by this computer, and what are the DNS servers now used by this server?

19. Now you will confirm that the computer has added an entry for itself in DNS. Type **nslookup server1.netpluslab.net** and press **Enter**. What is the IP address for server1.netpluslab.net? Does it match the IP address for this computer that you saw in the previous step?

20. Log on to *WORKSTATION1* as an administrator. The Windows desktop appears.

21. In Windows XP, click **Start**, right-click **My Computer**, and click **Properties**. The System Properties window opens. Click the **Computer Name** tab.

22. In Windows Vista, click **Start**, right-click **Computer**, click **Properties**, and click **Change settings**. If a UAC dialog box opens, click **Continue**.

23. Click **Network ID**. The Network Identification Wizard opens.

24. Click **Next**. The wizard asks how you want to use the computer.

25. In Windows XP only, make sure the **This computer is part of a business network, and I use it to connect to other computers at work** option button is selected.

26. Click **Next**. The wizard asks what sort of network you use. Make sure the **My company uses a network with a domain** option button is selected and click **Next**. The wizard summarizes information required to add the computer to a domain.

27. Click **Next**. The wizard asks for account information.

28. In the User name text box, enter **Administrator**. Because the wizard is requesting account information for the new domain you have just created, in the Password text box, enter the password for this account on *SERVER1* (as this account is now the Administrator account for the netpluslab.net domain). In the Domain text box, enter **NETPLUSLAB.NET**. Click **Next**. The wizard asks you for information concerning the domain to which the computer itself belongs.

29. Enter **WORKSTATION1** in the Computer name text box if it hasn't already been filled in for you. Enter **NETPLUSLAB.NET** in the Computer domain text box. Click **Next**. The Domain User Name and Password dialog box opens.

30. In the User name text box, enter **Administrator**. In the Password text box, enter the password for the Administrator account on *SERVER1*. In the Domain text box, enter **NETPLUSLAB.NET**. Click **OK**. The wizard asks if you would like to configure a user account on this computer.

31. In Windows XP, click the **Do not add a user at this time** option button. In Windows Vista, click the **Do not add a domain user account** option button. You will add more users in later labs. Click **Next**. The wizard indicates that you have finished.

32. Click **Finish**. In Windows XP, the Computer Name Changes dialog box opens, indicating that you must restart the computer before the changes you made will take effect. Click **OK**.

33. Click **OK**. A dialog box opens, asking if you want to reboot the computer now.

34. Click **Yes or Restart Now**. The computer reboots.

35. After the computer has finished rebooting, log on to the **NETPLUSLAB** domain as the domain Administrator. The Windows desktop appears. You have now added *WORKSTATION1* to the netpluslab.net domain.

36. Log off both computers.

Certification Objectives

Objectives for the Network+ Exam:

- Explain common logical network topologies and their characteristics: peer to peer, client/server, VPN, VLAN

Review Questions

1. Which of the following services, if stopped, would prevent Active Directory from working properly?

   a. DHCP

   b. XNS

   c. HTTP

   d. DNS

2. You are creating a new Active Directory for a car company. The car company is owned by a holding company that also owns an auto parts company, and both companies need to share some network resources but remain independent of each other. How would you design Active Directory to do this?

   a. Put each company in separate forests.

   b. Put each company in separate domains in separate forests.

   c. Put each company in separate domains in the same forest.

   d. Put each company in the same domain.

3. True or False? Active Directory can also be used by computers running Windows Server 2008 that are in a workgroup instead of a domain.

4. A company has offices in four cities on four different continents. In which of the following ways could you organize Active Directory for this company? (Choose all that apply.)

   a. by creating a different forest for each office

   b. by creating a different tree for each office in the same forest

   c. by creating domains for each office in the same forest in the same domain tree

   d. by creating different workgroups for each office in the same domain

5. True or False? Windows Server 2008 requires the NTFS file system for many of its security features to operate properly.

6. In this lab, you created a domain controller. Which of the following is true about the number of domain controllers you should create for a domain?

   a. One domain controller is sufficient to handle the load.

   b. Create no more than two domain controllers per domain, or client workstations will become confused.

   c. Create at least two domain controllers, so that the domain database will still be available if one domain controller fails.

   d. Create three domain controllers, so that if two domain controllers disagree the third can break the tie.

Lab 9.2 Delegating Administrative Rights

Objectives

One of the advantages of a directory service such as Microsoft's Active Directory is that it allows the network administrator granular control over users and network resources. The administrator can make sure that users can access the network resources they need, while at the same time preventing them from accessing network resources they should not be able to access. This also allows the network administrator to delegate specific tasks to certain users without delegating any more authority than is needed.

For instance, in large organizations, resetting passwords, creating user accounts, and other relatively straightforward parts of network administration can take up a lot of time. This can prevent the network administrator from concentrating on larger issues of network design and maintenance. In some cases, it's more efficient to have a user in each department reset passwords and create user accounts specifically for that department, but only for that department. The network administrator is then free to spend time on more important issues. A department might also prefer to have control over its own resources. In large organizations, network administration might be divided between two or more groups.

One tool you can use to subdivide a domain is the organizational unit. An organizational unit is a group of users or network resources, such as printers. Organizational units can be used to enforce policies, including the delegation of administrative rights. For instance, a company might have a different organizational unit for each department. Dividing a domain into organizational units is simpler and usually more convenient than dividing a domain into multiple child domains.

Keep in mind that Active Directory can be quite complex, and it is often possible to find multiple ways to solve a particular problem. Although the simplest way to solve a problem might not be the best way, keeping your Active Directory installation as simple as possible will make it easier to administer over the long term.

After completing this lab, you will be able to:

- Create user accounts in Windows Server 2008
- Create organizational units in Windows Server 2008
- Delegate network administration roles as needed in Windows Server 2008

Materials Required

This lab will require the following:

- The network configured at the end of Lab 9.1
- No organizational units named Accounting or Manufacturing in Active Directory
- Access to *SERVER1* as the Administrator for the netpluslab.net domain
- Local logon for all users configured in the Domain Controller Security Policy (configured by an instructor, if necessary)

Estimated completion time: **40 minutes**

Activity

1. Log on to *SERVER1* as Administrator in the netpluslab.net domain. The Windows Server 2008 desktop appears.

2. Click **Start**, point to **Administrative Tools**, click **Active Directory Users and Computers**, and click **OK**. The Active Directory Users and Computers window

opens. If necessary, click the **plus sign (+)** next to netpluslab.net to expand the tree below it.

3. Right-click **netpluslab.net** in the tree in the left pane. In the shortcut menu, point to **New**, and then click **Organizational Unit**. The New Object – Organizational Unit dialog box opens.

4. Type **Accounting** in the Name text box and click **OK**. An Accounting icon appears below netpluslab.net in the tree.

5. Repeat Steps 3 and 4, creating an organizational unit named **Manufacturing**. Figure 9-2 shows the addition of a new organizational unit.

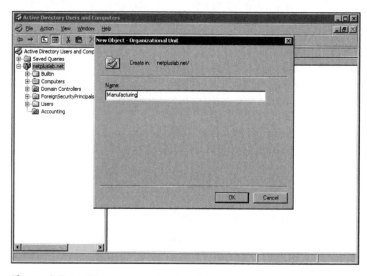

Figure 9-2   Adding an organizational unit

Courtesy Course Technology/Cengage Learning

6. Right-click the icon for the **Accounting** object. From the shortcut menu, point to **New**, and then click **User**. The New Object – User dialog box opens.

7. In the Full name and User logon name text boxes, enter **accounting-admin**. Click **Next**.

8. In both the Password and the Confirm password text boxes, type a password at least eight characters long that contains at least one number and a mixture of upper- and lowercase letters. Record or memorize this password.

9. Click the **User must change password at next logon** check box to remove the check mark. Click **Next**. The dialog box summarizes the account information.

10. Click **Finish** to close the dialog box. Click **Accounting** in the left pane and note that an icon for the accounting-admin account appears in the right pane. (If an Active Directory dialog box opens indicating that Windows cannot set the password because it does not meet the minimum password policy requirements, click **OK**. Then click **Back**. Change the password, click **Next**, and then click **Finish**.)

11. Right-click the **accounting-admin** object, and select **Add to a group** from the shortcut menu.

12. Now you will add the accounting-admin user to the Server Operators group. By default, users in the Server Operators group are able to log on to the domain controller, but ordinary users are not. In the "Enter the object names to select" text box, type **Server Operators**. Click **OK**. The Active Directory dialog box opens, indicating that the addition was successful. Click **OK**.

13. Repeat Steps 6 through 12 to create a user named **accountant** and add it to the Server Operators group. Record the password for this account.

14. Right-click the **Manufacturing** object. On the shortcut menu, point to **New**, and then click **User**. The New Object – User dialog box opens. Repeat Steps 6 through 10, creating a user account named **manufacturer**.

15. Right-click the **Accounting** object and select **Delegate Control** from the shortcut menu. The Delegation of Control Wizard opens.

16. Click **Next**. The wizard offers you the option of selecting users or groups.

17. Click **Add**. The Select Users, Computers, or Groups window opens. In the "Enter the object names to select" text box, type **accounting-admin** and click **OK**. The name of the user appears in the Selected users and groups box.

18. Click **Next**. The wizard lists a series of tasks you could delegate.

19. Place a check in the **Create, delete, and manage user accounts** check box. Click **Next**. The wizard summarizes the options you have chosen.

20. Click **Finish**. The wizard closes. You have now delegated control over user accounts in the Accounting organizational unit to the accounting-admin user. This user will not have rights over other parts of Active Directory, including the Manufacturing organizational unit.

21. Log off *SERVER1*.

22. Log on to *SERVER1* as the **accounting-admin** user. The Windows Server 2008 desktop appears.

23. Click **Start**, point to **Administrative Tools**, and then click **Active Directory Users and Computers**. If a UAC dialog box opens, enter the password for the accounting-admin user and click **OK**. The Active Directory Users and Computers window opens.

24. If the tree below netpluslab.net (in the left pane of the window) has not been expanded already, click the **plus sign (+)** next to netpluslab.net. Then click the icon for the **Accounting** object. Icons for user names appear in the right pane of the window.

25. Right-click the **accountant** user icon, and select **Reset Password**. The Reset Password dialog box opens.

26. Enter a new password in the New password and Confirm password text boxes. Click **OK**. A dialog box opens, indicating that the password for the accountant account has been changed.

27. Click **OK**.

28. Repeat Steps 6 through 10 for the Accounting object, creating a user named **bills**. Make sure to record the password.

29. Now you will verify that the accounting-admin account has no rights to other parts of Active Directory. Click the icon for the **Manufacturing** object. The icon for the manufacturer user appears.

30. Right-click the icon for the **manufacturer** user in the right pane of the window. From the shortcut menu, select **Reset Password**. The Reset Password dialog box opens.

31. Enter the new password in the New password and Confirm password text boxes. Click **OK**. A dialog box opens, indicating that Windows could not complete the password change and that access is denied. Click **OK**.

32. Right-click the **Manufacturing** icon in the left pane of the window. From the shortcut menu, note that you do not have the option to create a new user. Select **Delegate Control**. A dialog box opens, indicating that you do not have permission to write security information for this object.

33. Click **OK**. The dialog box closes.

34. On *WORKSTATION1*, log on to the netpluslab.net domain as the **bills** user you created in Step 28. The Windows desktop appears.

35. Log off both computers.

Certification Objectives

Objectives for the Network+ Exam:

- Explain issues that affect device security: physical security, restricting local and remote access, secure methods vs. unsecure methods: SSH, HTTPS, SNMPv3, SFTP, SCP, TELNET, HTTP, FTP, RSH, RCP, SNMPv1/2

- Explain the methods of network access security. *Filtering*: ACL, MAC filtering, IP filtering; *Tunneling and encryption*: SSL VPN, VPN, L2TP, PPTP, IPSEC; *Remote access*: RAS, RDP, PPPoE, PPP, VNC, ICA

Review Questions

1. What is an organizational unit?

   a. a department or division within an organization

   b. a container used to group users with similar permissions and rights

   c. a container used to group similar objects such as users or groups

   d. an organization

2. If a user is assigned Read permissions to a folder, what may he do with the folder's contents? (Choose all that apply.)

   a. View the listing of files in the folder.

   b. Launch executable files in the folder.

   c. Delete files in the folder.

   d. View the contents of files in the folder.

3. If a user is assigned Modify permissions to a folder, what may she do with the folder's contents? (Choose all that apply.)

   a. View the listing of files in the folder.

   b. Launch executable files in the folder.

   c. Delete files in the folder.

   d. View the contents of files in the folder.

4. Which of the following is a potential advantage of delegating user administration to another user? (Choose all that apply.)

   a. The network administrator can concentrate on more important network maintenance issues.

   b. One or more users in each department can handle user administration for their department.

   c. It allows large network administration departments to delegate tasks.

   d. It allows each user in a department to handle the administration of his own account.

5. By default, what permissions do users in the Everyone group have to a newly shared Windows Server 2008 folder?

   a. Read and Execute only

   b. List Folder Contents only

   c. Full Access

   d. By default, users have no rights to newly shared folders.

6. In this lab, you grouped users in the same department into organizational units, and then used the organizational units to delegate permissions within them. What is another approach you could have used to perform the same task?

   a. Group each department into separate forests.

   b. Group each department into separate domains in the same tree.

   c. Create a new forest for each department.

   d. Group each department into separate workgroups within the same tree.

Lab 9.3 Remotely Managing a Computer with Active Directory

Objectives

In addition to controlling users and groups, you can use Active Directory to help you manage remote computers. Through Active Directory, you can perform many of the functions on a remote computer that you can do when directly logged on to that computer. For example, you can start and stop services on the remote computer, look at system information, and browse the Event Viewer. The Event Viewer is where you can view information about error messages and other events that have occurred on the computer. If you need to administer a network with many users and many computers, this can save you significant time.

After completing this lab, you will be able to:

- Remotely manage Windows computers

Materials Required

This lab will require the following:

- The network built at the end of Lab 9.1 or 9.2

Estimated completion time: **40 minutes**

Activity

1. Log on to *SERVER1* as the Administrator for the netpluslab.net domain. The Windows Server 2008 desktop appears.

2. Click **Start**, point to **Administrative Tools**, and click **Computer Management**. The Computer Management window opens.

3. Click the **Disk Management** icon below Storage. How many hard disks are on the server, how large are they, and with what file system have they been configured?

4. Click the **Event Viewer** icon in the tree in the left pane of the window. A list of the event logs available appears in the right pane of the window.

5. In the left pane, expand **Event Viewer** and **Windows Logs**, and then double-click the **System** node. A list of events in the System event log appears in the right pane. Double-click the top event. The Event Properties window opens, showing detailed information about the event.

6. Click the down arrow on the right side of the window. The Event Viewer moves to the next event. Repeat a few times to see more events.

7. Close the Event Properties window by clicking **Close**.

8. Right-click **Computer Management (Local)** at the top of the tree in the left pane of the window. Select **Connect to another computer** from the shortcut menu. The Select Computer dialog box opens.

9. In the Another computer text box, type **WORKSTATION1** and click **OK**. The icon at the top of the left pane of the window changes to Computer Management (WORKSTATION1).

10. Click the **plus sign (+)** next to System Tools to expand the tree underneath it. Repeat this step with the Services and Applications icon. Figure 9-3 shows the Computer Management dialog box for *WORKSTATION1* as you manage the computer remotely.

11. Repeat Steps 4 through 7 to look at events on *WORKSTATION1*. Does *WORKSTATION1* have as many types of event logs as *SERVER1*?

12. Log on to *WORKSTATION1* as the Administrator of the NETPLUSLAB domain. The Windows desktop appears.

13. Click **Start**, and then click **Control Panel**. The Control Panel opens.

14. Click the **Performance and Maintenance (System and Maintenance** in Windows Vista) category.

15. Click the **Administrative Tools** icon.

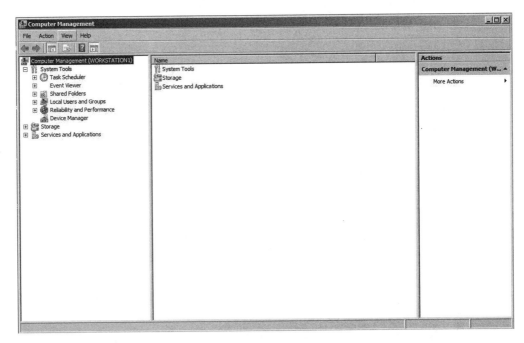

Figure 9-3   Managing *WORKSTATION1* remotely

Courtesy Course Technology/Cengage Learning

16. Double-click the **Services** icon. (In Windows Vista, if a UAC dialog box opens, click **Continue**.) The Services window opens.

17. Look for the Automatic Updates icon. Its status is "Started."

18. On *SERVER1*, click the **Services** icon in the left pane of the Computer Management window. A list of the services running on *WORKSTATION1* appears in the right pane of the window.

19. Right-click the **Automatic Updates** icon. From the shortcut menu, select **Stop**. A dialog box opens briefly, indicating that Windows is attempting to stop the service. The status disappears.

20. On *WORKSTATION1*, press **F5** to refresh the Services window. Look at the status of the Automatic Updates icon in the Services window. It is now blank, indicating that the service is not running.

21. Right-click the **Automatic Updates** icon in the Services window. From the shortcut menu, select **Start**. A dialog box opens briefly, indicating that Windows is attempting to start the service. The status changes to "Started."

22. Log off both computers.

Certification Objectives

Objectives for the Network+ Exam:

- Explain the methods of network access security. *Filtering*: ACL, MAC filtering, IP filtering; *Tunneling and encryption*: SSL VPN, VPN, L2TP, PPTP, IPSEC; *Remote access*: RAS, RDP, PPPoE, PPP, VNC, ICA

Review Questions

1. Which of the following is a potential advantage of being able to manage computers remotely?

   a. You will not need to log on to each individual computer.

   b. It eliminates the need for authentications.

   c. It uses less CPU time.

   d. It prevents security problems.

2. Which Windows Server 2008 utility would you use to find events that have happened on a particular server?

   a. Device Manager

   b. Disk Defragmenter

   c. Command Prompt

   d. Event Viewer

3. Why are you able to log on to the remote computer without supplying a user name and password?

   a. No user name or password is necessary.

   b. Active Directory handles authentication on the remote computer for you.

   a. Active Directory does not require authentication for remote computers.

   d. Your computer automatically supplies the user name and password without the help of Active Directory.

4. True or False? Only the domain administrator can manage remote computers.

5. When you select Services from the Administrative Tools menu on a Windows Server 2008 computer, what will you see?

   a. all services currently available on the Windows Server 2008 computer

   b. all services currently running on the Windows Server 2008 computer

   c. all services currently running on the Windows Server 2008 computer and its clients

   d. all services currently running on the Windows Server 2008 computer and other servers in the same domain

Lab 9.4 Starting and Stopping a Linux Server

Objectives

In this lab, you will stop and start a server running a current version of Fedora Linux. Although Linux is not identical to UNIX, the two have much in common, and managing a Linux server is much like managing a UNIX server. As a result, much of the material in this chapter also applies to UNIX.

Although most versions of Linux come with a GUI, it is not always installed. Instead, Linux servers are often managed through a text console. Stopping and restarting the server from a text console is a less-intuitive process than it is in Windows. Although this makes a

Linux server more difficult for a neophyte to administer than a Windows server, the lack of a GUI allows a Linux server to devote its processing power to the task of serving its users.

A Linux server typically has several different text consoles, which you can run at the same time. These consoles are often called virtual consoles because you can switch back and forth between them. You can always access a console (even from the GUI) through a keyboard shortcut.

In Linux, the init program is the master program that ultimately starts and stops all the programs on the server. It runs as a daemon, or a program that runs and performs its tasks in the background. The init program can also be used to change the runlevel of the computer. A runlevel is a state in which a particular group of software programs are to be run. In most versions of Linux, runlevel 3 is considered the normal state and all programs that should be started at boot are started. Runlevel 0 is used to shut down the computer, while runlevel 6 is used to reboot it. Runlevel 1 puts the computer in single user mode. Single user mode is a special state in which the computer operates with the absolute minimum number of programs running. It is typically used for maintenance. You can change the runlevel directly with the init command, or you can use the halt, reboot, or shutdown commands. Each of these commands ultimately calls the init command. If you use the shutdown command, you can tell the computer to reboot after a certain interval and send a warning message to users. This allows users to save their work and log off the computer before rebooting.

After completing this lab, you will be able to:

- Stop and restart a Linux computer
- Put a Linux computer into single user mode
- Switch back and forth between virtual consoles

Materials Required

This lab will require the following:

- A computer running a current version of Fedora Linux named *LINUX1. NETPLUSLAB.NET*, installed as a server with no firewall, GNOME Desktop Environment, Editors, Text-based Internet, Server Configuration Tools, Web Server, Mail Server, Windows File Server, Administration Tools, System Tools, and Printing Support package groups installed
- *LINUX1.NETPLUSLAB.NET* configured with an IP address of 192.168.54.5 and a subnet mask of 255.255.255.0
- The computer configured with a graphical login
- The computer initially powered off
- The root user's password

Estimated completion time: **30 minutes**

Activity

1. Power on the computer and log on as root. The Fedora desktop appears.

2. Now you will switch to one of the text consoles. Open a terminal by pressing **Ctrl+Alt+F1**. A text console appears, with the LINUX1 login prompt.

3. At the LINUX1 login prompt, type **root**. Press **Enter**. The Password prompt appears.

4. Type the password for the root account and press **Enter**. The computer displays the last login by the root account and displays the prompt.

5. Press **Alt+F2**. The computer switches to another virtual terminal, displaying the LINUX1 login prompt.

6. Press **Alt+F3**, **Alt+F4**, **Alt+F5**, and then **Alt+F6**. The computer cycles through each of its virtual terminals.

7. Press **Alt+F7**. The computer switches back to the Fedora desktop.

8. Open a terminal window. (For example, in Fedora 8, click the **Applications** menu, point to **System Tools**, and click **Terminal**.) A terminal window named root@ LINUX1:~ opens.

9. Type **init 1** and press **Enter**. The GUI closes, and in a text console the computer displays a message indicating that it is switching to single user mode. A prompt appears.

10. Type **init 6** and press **Enter**. The computer displays a message indicating that it is switching to runlevel 6, shuts down services, and reboots.

11. Log back on to the computer.

12. Open a terminal window and then open a second terminal window.

13. In either of the terminal windows, type **shutdown -h +2 The computer is shutting down for maintenance** and press **Enter**. The computer displays the text "The computer is shutting down for maintenance" and indicates that it is going to halt. Figure 9-4 shows a terminal window after the shutdown command has been run.

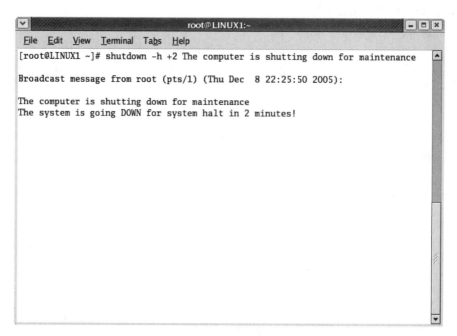

Figure 9-4 Shutting down the computer with the shutdown command

Courtesy Course Technology/Cengage Learning

14. Look in the other terminal window. The computer displays the warning message in that window, too. After a minute, the computer displays in both terminals the text "The system is going DOWN for system halt in 1 minute." After another minute, the computer powers itself off.

Certification Objectives

Objectives for the Network+ Exam:

- This lab does not directly map to an objective on the exam; however, it does teach a skill that is valuable to networking professionals

Review Questions

1. What is a daemon?

   a. any Linux GUI program that runs in the background

   b. a virus

   c. a Linux program that runs in the background and performs system services

   d. a Linux program that runs in the foreground and runs system services

2. What is the init program used for?

   a. to reboot the computer

   b. to halt the computer

   c. to change the runlevel of the computer

   d. to put the computer into single user mode

3. What is the advantage of running a Linux server without a GUI?

   a. The server can be managed more intuitively without a GUI.

   b. The server can devote more resources to serving users without a GUI.

   c. Server configuration can be performed without the use of a mouse or keyboard.

   d. The server can be rebooted without users logging off.

4. What is the purpose of the kernel?

   a. to change the computer's runlevel

   b. to store information about files and directories

   c. to load files into memory so that they can be accessed quickly

   d. to control access to system resources

5. What is the advantage of using the shutdown command instead of the init command to reboot the computer?

   a. You can announce the reboot with a broadcast message and allow users time to save their files and log off.

   b. You can automatically save the files of any user on the system and log them out.

   c. The shutdown command uses the init program, so there is no advantage.

   d. The shutdown command verifies that all users have logged off before proceeding.

Lab 9.5 Connecting a Windows Client Using Samba

Objectives

In this lab, you will connect a Windows XP or Vista client to a Linux server using Samba. Samba is a collection of programs that runs the Common Internet File System (CIFS) and NetBIOS on Linux. CIFS is also known as the Server Message Block (SMB) protocol. (The name Samba is an extension of the "SMB" acronym.) Windows clients use CIFS natively, so Samba allows Windows clients to log on to Linux servers without the installation of additional client software. Samba also allows Linux clients to connect to Windows servers.

To perform this lab, you will use a version of the vi editor. The vi (usually pronounced "vee eye") editor is a text-based editor that can be found in some form on virtually all Linux and UNIX computers. Although not nearly as intuitive as Notepad or Microsoft Word, it is useful for editing configuration files and programs and contains some powerful features such as searching and text replacement based on pattern matching.

The vi editor has two primary modes: normal mode and insert mode. In normal mode, you can navigate through a document and run commands to delete or change existing text, but you cannot add text. In insert mode, you can add text. You can move the cursor through a document with the arrow keys or with a variety of keyboard shortcuts.

After completing this lab, you will be able to:

- Connect a Windows XP Professional or Vista client to a Linux server using Samba
- Connect a Linux computer to a Windows Server 2008 computer using Samba
- Use the vi text editor to edit configuration files

Materials Required

This lab will require the following:

- A computer running a current version of Fedora Linux named *LINUX1. NETPLUSLAB.NET*, configured with no firewall, and with the GNOME Desktop Environment and Windows File Server package groups installed.
- *LINUX1.NETPLUSLAB.NET* configured with an IP address of 192.168.54.5 and a subnet mask of 255.255.255.0
- The default /etc/samba/smb.conf file in place
- A user named netplus on *LINUX1.NETPLUSLAB.NET* with a known password and a known password for the root account
- A computer running Windows XP Professional or Vista named *WORKSTATION1* and configured with an IP address of 192.168.54.3
- *WORKSTATION1* configured as part of the NETPLUS workgroup
- A computer running Windows Server 2008, Standard Edition named *SERVER1* and configured with an IP address of 192.168.54.1
- *SERVER1* configured as a domain controller for the netpluslab.net domain, with a user account named linux with a known password and a shared folder named netplus containing one or more files
- Access to both *WORKSTATION1* and *SERVER1* as an administrator
- All three computers connected to a hub with Cat 5 (or better) UTP cables

Activity

1. Log on to the Fedora machine as the netplus user. The Fedora desktop appears.

2. Open a terminal window and type **su –** and press **Enter**. The Password prompt appears.

3. Enter the password for the root account and press **Enter**. The prompt ends in a pound sign (#), indicating that you are logged on as the root user.

4. Type **mkdir /usr/netplus** and press **Enter**. The computer creates a directory named /usr/netplus, which you will share later.

5. Type **chmod a=rwxt /usr/netplus** and press **Enter**. The computer changes the permissions on the directory you just created. The changes in permissions will allow any user to create a file in the new directory, but they will only allow the user who created a file to modify or delete it.

6. Now you will configure Samba to share the new directory you created. Type **vi /etc/samba/smb.conf** and press **Enter**. The vi editor opens the file /etc/samba/smb.conf in the terminal window, and displays the name of the file at the bottom of the screen. The cursor blinks in the upper-left corner of the terminal window. Table 9-1 shows some of the most common keyboard commands in the vi editor.

Table 9-1   Keyboard commands in the vi editor

Keyboard shortcut	Meaning
j or ↓	Moves the cursor down
k or ↑	Moves the cursor up
h or ←	Moves the cursor to the left
l or →	Moves the cursor to the right
w	Moves the cursor to the beginning of the next word
i	Puts the vi editor in insert mode at the cursor
a	Puts the vi editor in insert mode after the cursor
A	Puts the vi editor in insert mode at the end of the line
ESC	Takes the vi editor from insert mode to normal mode
/pattern	Searches for *pattern* in the text of the file, where *pattern* is any combination of text or wildcard characters
G	Places the cursor at the end of the file
nG	Places the cursor at line *n*, where *n* is the number of the line
:w	Saves the file

(Continued)

Table 9-1 Keyboard commands in the vi editor (Continued)

Keyboard shortcut	Meaning
:q	Quits the vi editor
:wq	Saves the file and quits the vi editor
ZZ	Saves the file and quits the vi editor
:q!	Quits the vi editor without saving any changes
x	Deletes the character at the cursor
nx	Deletes n characters at the cursor, where n is the number of characters to be deleted
$	Places the cursor at the end of the line
0	Places the cursor at the beginning of the line
dd	Deletes the current line
dw	Deletes text from the cursor to the end of the word
$n$dw	Deletes text from the cursor through the next n words, where n is the number of words to be deleted
d$	Deletes text from the cursor until the end of the line

7. Type **G**. (Take care to type an uppercase G.) The vi editor places the cursor at the beginning of the last line in the file.

8. Type **i**. The vi editor enters insert mode. "INSERT" appears at the bottom of the terminal window.

9. Type **[netplus]** and press **Enter**. The vi editor inserts the line into the file and moves the cursor to the next blank line. This creates a share named netplus.

10. Type **path=/usr/netplus** and press **Enter**. The vi editor inserts the line into the file and moves the cursor to the next blank line. This makes the directory you created in Step 6 the location of the share named netplus.

11. Press **Esc**. The vi editor goes into normal mode.

12. Type **/workgroup = MYGROUP** and press **Enter**. The vi editor searches for the string "workgroup = MYGROUP" in the text file. If the computer does not find this line, scroll through the file manually looking for a line containing the text "workgroup =" that does not begin with a #. (The # character is a comment, and any line beginning with a # is not read by Samba.)

13. Press **w** twice. The cursor moves to the beginning of the word MYGROUP.

14. Type **d$**. The computer deletes all text from the cursor to the end of the line.

15. Press **a**. The vi editor goes into insert mode. "INSERT" appears at the bottom of the terminal window.

16. Type **NETPLUS**, then press **Esc**. The vi editor adds the text to the file, then goes back into normal mode. The entire line should read "workgroup = NETPLUS". Figure 9-5 shows the use of the vi editor.

17. Type **:w** and press **Enter**. The vi editor saves the file.

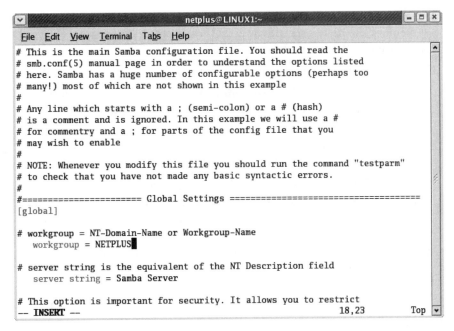

Figure 9-5   Using the vi editor

Courtesy Course Technology/Cengage Learning

18. Type **:q** and press **Enter**. The vi editor quits the file.

19. Type **testparm -s** and press **Enter**. This command checks the syntax of the Samba configuration file you just edited for errors. The computer displays the results of the configuration check and then a list of global Samba parameters. You might need to scroll upward to see the full command output.

20. Type **/etc/init.d/smb start** and press **Enter**. The computer displays a message indicating that it is starting the SMB and NMB services, and that both are OK.

21. Type **cp /etc/samba/smb.conf /usr/netplus** and press **Enter**. This copies the file into the shared directory you created in Step 6.

22. Type **smbpasswd -a netplus** and press **Enter**. The new SMB password prompt appears. Type a password and press **Enter**. Note that this password does not have to be the same as the current Fedora password for the netplus user. The Retype New SMB Password prompt appears. Type the password again and press **Enter**. The computer might display a message indicating that the "file /etc/samba/smbpasswd did not exist" but that it was able to successfully create the file and password.

23. Log on to *WORKSTATION1* as an administrator. The Windows desktop appears.

24. Click **Start**, and then click **My Computer**. (In Windows Vista, click **Computer**.) The My Computer or Computer window opens.

25. In Windows XP, click **Tools** on the menu bar, and then click **Map Network Drive**. In Windows Vista, click **Map Network Drive** on the toolbar. The Map Network Drive dialog box opens.

26. In the Folder text box, enter **\\192.168.54.5\netplus**. From the Drive drop-down menu, select **Z:** if it has not already been selected. If necessary, click the **Reconnect at logon** check box to remove the check mark.

27. Click **Connect using a different user name**. The Connect As dialog box opens.

28. In the User name text box, enter **netplus**. In the Password text box, enter the password for the netplus account that you created in Step 22. Click **OK**. The Connect As dialog box closes.

29. Click **Finish**. The Map Network Drive dialog box opens briefly and the Z: window opens with the contents of the newly shared folder, including the file smb.conf.

30. Now you will connect to *SERVER1*. In the terminal window on *SERVER1*, type **smbclient -W netpluslab.net -U Administrator //192.168.54.1/netplus** and press **Enter**. The Password prompt appears. Type the password for the Administrator and press **Enter**. The computer displays some information about the type of server it has connected to, and the prompt changes to smb: \>. Table 9-2 lists command-line options for the smbclient command. Note that the last option is usually the network resource to be used.

31. Type **ls** and press **Enter**. The computer displays the files in the remote share on *SERVER1*.

32. Log off all computers.

Table 9-2   Options for the smbclient command

Option	Meaning
-W *domain/workgroup*	Specifies the domain or workgroup of the remote computer
-U *username*	Specifies the user name on the remote server
-I *IP address*	Specifies the IP address of the remote server
-L *NetBIOS name*	Lists services available on the remote server named *name*
-n *NetBIOS name*	Overrides the default NetBIOS name used by Samba

Certification Objectives

Objectives for the Network+ Exam:

- This lab does not directly map to an objective on the exam; however, it does teach a skill that is valuable to networking professionals.

Review Questions

1. You are logged on to a Linux computer and you need to access files on a Windows server. What do you need to do to get access to those files?

   a. start Samba on the Linux server

   b. log on to the Windows server with the smbclient program

   c. share the files on the Windows server using the Linux File and Print Client

   d. use the syntax guide

2. In what mode of the vi editor can you add text to a document?

   a. text mode

   b. normal mode

   c. insert mode

   d. add mode

3. While editing a text file with the vi editor, what command would allow you to search for the word *password* within that text?

   a. /password

   b. find /password

   c. lookup password

   d. search /password

4. Which of the following is a network protocol used by Samba?

   a. IPX/SPX

   b. NetBIOS

   c. SNA

   d. NetBEUI

5. The chmod command allows you to change the permissions of a file or directory. What command would you use to view the permissions of a file?

   a. id

   b. ls -l

   c. vi

   d. checkpermissions

Lab 9.6 Remotely Managing Linux Servers

Objectives

Linux servers can be managed remotely much as they can be managed at the console, through a variety of tools. Almost all versions of Linux support Telnet servers. A Telnet server is a daemon that allows you to open a remote terminal session over a network. The Telnet client, usually just called Telnet, is available on most modern operating systems. However, the Telnet protocol does not use any encryption. As a result, Telnet is rapidly being replaced by the Secure Shell (SSH) protocol. The sshd daemon runs an SSH server, and the ssh program allows you to log on to an SSH server.

From a remote terminal window opened with the ssh program, you can do nearly anything that you can do on the system console. On a computer running the X Window software, you can also run any GUI program on the remote computer. X Window software is installed by default on most Linux computers, and can be installed on Windows computers as well. Remote terminal sessions run through either the ssh program or the Telnet program have only a few minor differences.

In this lab, you will use the Fedora GUI to configure a virtual NIC. A virtual NIC is treated just like a physical NIC by the operating system. Typically, a virtual NIC is added so that a computer can have an additional IP address; the virtual NIC is, therefore, referred to as a secondary IP address.

After completing this lab, you will be able to:

- Log on to a Linux computer remotely using SSH

- Configure a NIC on a Linux computer

Materials Required

This lab will require the following:

- A computer running a current version of Fedora Linux named *LINUX1. NETPLUSLAB.NET*, configured with no firewall, and with the GNOME Desktop Environment installed.

- *LINUX1.NETPLUSLAB.NET* configured with an IP address of 192.168.54.5 and a subnet mask of 255.255.255.0

- A computer running a current version of Fedora Linux named *LINUX2. NETPLUSLAB.NET*, configured with no firewall, and with the GNOME Desktop Environment installed.

- *LINUX2.NETPLUSLAB.NET* configured with an IP address of 192.168.54.7 and a subnet mask of 255.255.255.0

- A user named netplus and knowledge of the root password on both computers

- Both computers configured to allow X11 forwarding (this is the default)

- A computer running Windows XP Professional or Vista named *WORKSTATION1* and configured with an IP address of 192.168.54.3

- Cygwin 1.5.x (available at www.cygwin.com) installed on *WORKSTATION1*, with the openssh and openssl packages in the Net category and xorg-x11 packages (including X-startup-scripts, xorg-x11-base, xorg-x11-bin, xorg-x11-bin-dlls, xorg-x11-bin-lndir, xorg-x11-devel, xorg-x11-etc, xorg-x11-fenc, xorg-x11-fnts, xorg-x11-libs-data, xorg-x11-xwin, and xterm) in the X11 category installed in addition to the default packages

- All three computers connected to a hub with straight-through Cat 5 (or better) UTP cables

---

Estimated completion time: **40 minutes**

Activity

1. Log on to *LINUX2.NETPLUSLAB.NET* as the netplus user. The Fedora desktop appears.

2. Open a terminal window.

3. Type **ssh -X 192.168.54.5** and press **Enter**. (The –X option tells the ssh program to allow forwarding of GUI programs.) A message might appear indicating that the authenticity of the host cannot be established, followed by the text "Are you sure you want to continue connecting (yes/no)?". If so, type **yes** and press **Enter**. The computer asks for the password for the netplus account.

4. Type the password and press **Enter**. The prompt changes to [netplus@ LINUX1 net-plus]$, indicating that you are now logged on to *LINUX1.NETPLUSLAB.NET*.

5. Type **su -** and press **Enter**. The Password prompt appears. Type root's password and press **Enter**. The prompt now ends in a pound sign (#), indicating that you are logged on as the root user.

6. Type **ifconfig** and press **Enter**. The computer displays information about the network cards installed in it. In addition to the NIC in the computer (most likely named eth0 or eth1), the computer displays information about the lo NIC, or the loopback. This is a virtual (or software-only) NIC, primarily used for testing. A loopback NIC is configured by default on most devices that use TCP/IP. What are the names and IP addresses of the NICs on the computer?

7. Now you will add a virtual NIC to the computer. A virtual NIC exists in software only, but will be treated like a real NIC by the computer. Type **system-config-network-gui** and press **Enter**. The Network Configuration window opens, showing information about the NIC on *LINUX1.NETPLUSLAB.NET* in the Devices box at the bottom of the window. If the computer displays an error message indicating that it was unable to initialize the graphical environment, verify that you connected to the server using the -X flag in Step 3.

8. Click **New**. The Add New Device Type dialog box opens, showing types of devices that could be used to make a network connection.

9. If necessary, select **Ethernet connection**. Click **Forward**. The dialog box asks you to select an Ethernet card.

10. Click the name of the Ethernet card you recorded in Step 6. Click **Forward**. The dialog box asks you to configure network settings.

11. Click the **Statically set IP addresses** option button, if necessary. In the Address text box, enter **192.168.54.10**. In the Subnet mask text box, enter **255.255.255.0**. Click **Forward**. The dialog box summarizes the options you have chosen.

12. Click **Apply**. A new icon for the secondary IP address appears in the Network Configuration window.

13. Click the icon for the new secondary NIC to select it. Make sure that the **Profile** check box is selected. Click **Activate**. The Question dialog box opens, asking you if you want to make the changes necessary to activate the new virtual NIC.

14. Click **Yes**. The Information dialog box opens, indicating that you might want to restart the network or the computer.

15. Click **OK**. The system-config-network dialog box opens briefly, indicating that the computer is activating the virtual NIC.

16. Click **File** on the menu bar and then click **Quit**. The Network Configuration window closes.

17. Type **ifconfig** and press **Enter**. The computer displays information about the NICs on the computer. What is the name of the new interface on the computer?

18. Type **exit** and press **Enter**. Type **exit** and press **Enter** again to exit from *LINUX1. NETPLUSLAB.NET*. The prompt in the terminal window changes back to indicate that you are on *LINUX2.NETPLUSLAB.NET*.

19. Type **ifconfig** and press **Enter**. The computer indicates that the command cannot be found.

20. Now you will attempt to run the ifconfig command by typing the full path of the command. Type **/sbin/ifconfig** and press **Enter**. The computer displays information about the network cards on the computer. (The netplus user cannot find the ifconfig command without supplying the full pathname because the environment for the netplus user is different from that of the root user.)

21. Log on to *WORKSTATION1* as an administrator.

22. Click **Start**, point to **All Programs**, point to **Cygwin**, and then click **Cygwin Bash Shell**. A terminal window opens.

23. Type **startxwin.bat** and press **Enter**. This command starts the X Window software on *WORKSTATION1*, and opens a new terminal window named root@LINUX1. If a Windows Security Alert dialog box opens, click **Unblock**.

24. In the terminal window, type **ssh -X netplus@192.168.54.5** and press **Enter**. (The netplus@ tells the ssh program to use the netplus user when logging on to the remote server.) A message might appear indicating that the authenticity of the host cannot be established. If so, type **yes** and press **Enter**. The computer asks for the password for the netplus account.

25. Enter the password for the netplus account and press **Enter**. The prompt indicates that you have logged on to *LINUX1.NETPLUSLAB.NET*.

26. Type **su -** and press **Enter**. The Password prompt appears. Type root's password and press **Enter**. The prompt now ends with a pound sign (#), indicating that you are logged on as the root user.

27. Type **system-config-network-gui** and press **Enter**. The Network Configuration window opens, as shown in Figure 9-6.

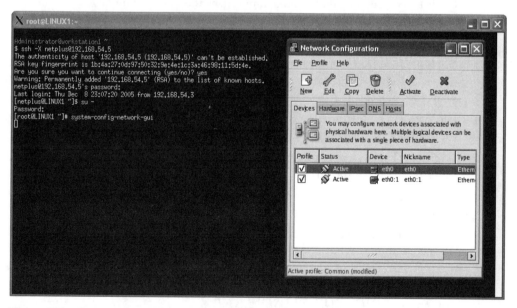

Figure 9-6   The Network Configuration window, as run from *WORKSTATION1*

Courtesy Course Technology/Cengage Learning

28. Click **File** on the menu bar and then click **Quit**. The Network Configuration window closes.

29. Type **exit** and press **Enter**. Type **exit** and press **Enter** again to exit the SSH session on *LINUX1.NETPLUSLAB.NET*.

30. Log off all computers.

Certification Objectives

Objectives for the Network+ Exam:

- This lab does not directly map to an objective on the exam; however, it does teach a skill that is valuable to networking professionals

Review Questions

1. What is the difference between the SSH protocol and the Telnet protocol?

   a. The Telnet protocol is encrypted.

   b. The Telnet protocol is faster than the SSH protocol.

   c. SSH is encrypted.

   d. SSH can only be used between Linux or UNIX servers.

2. Which of the following commands could you use to display a Linux computer's IP address?

   a. ipconfig

   b. ssh

   c. ipdisplay

   d. ifconfig

3. Why might a virtual NIC be configured on a Linux computer?

   a. because an additional IP address is needed for a Web server

   b. for the computer to act as a router between two networks

   c. for redundancy

   d. for load balancing

4. The ssh command allows you to open a remote terminal window on another computer. What is the major difference between working in an SSH session on a remote computer in another city, and working directly at the console of the remote computer?

   a. You cannot power cycle the remote computer.

   b. You cannot run GUI programs in the SSH session.

   c. You cannot run terminal programs such as top or ps while working in an SSH session.

   d. You cannot log on to other remote computers while working in an SSH session.

5. In this lab, how could you tell whether a terminal window was for the local computer or for an SSH session on a remote computer?

a. The prompt indicated the name of the remote computer.

b. There was no way to tell.

c. The prompt indicated the name of the program being run.

d. The computer beeped when you logged on to a remote computer.

In-Depth TCP/IP Networking

Labs included in this chapter

- Lab 10.1 Subnetting a Network
- Lab 10.2 Understanding the Purpose of the Default Gateway
- Lab 10.3 Understanding the TCP/IP Hosts File
- Lab 10.4 Setting Up an FTP Server
- Lab 10.5 Configuring a Mail Server

Net+ Exam Objectives

Objective	Lab
Explain the function of common networking protocols	10.4, 10.5
Identify the following address formats: IPv6, IPv4, MAC addressing	10.1
Given a scenario, evaluate the proper use of addressing technologies and addressing schemes	10.1, 10.3
Given a scenario, troubleshoot common connectivity issues and select an appropriate solution	10.1, 10.2
Given a scenario, select the appropriate command-line interface tool and interpret the output to verify functionality	10.1, 10.2
Explain issues that affect device security	10.1, 10.4

Lab 10.1 Subnetting a Network

Objectives

Subnetting allows you to divide a single network up into several smaller, separate networks. This might be done to enhance security, improve performance, or simplify network troubleshooting. Subnetting is accomplished by changing the subnet mask on each of the computers in a network. Because subnet masks are used to determine which part of an IP address corresponds to the network address, changing the subnet mask can also change the network address. In this lab, you will subnet a network by changing the subnet mask on the host computers.

After completing this lab, you will be able to:

- Subnet a network into several smaller networks

Materials Required

This lab will require the following:

- A computer running Windows XP Professional or Vista named *WORKSTATION1* and configured with an IP address of 192.168.54.3, a subnet mask of 255.255.255.0, and no default gateway

- A computer running Windows XP Professional or Vista named *WORKSTATION2* and configured with an IP address of 192.168.54.132, a subnet mask of 255.255.255.0, and no default gateway

- Administrative access to both computers

- Both computers connected to an Ethernet hub (not a router) with straight-through Cat 5 (or better) UTP cables

> Estimated completion time: **30 minutes**

Activity

1. Log on to *WORKSTATION1* as an administrator. The Windows desktop appears.

2. Click **Start**, point to **All Programs**, point to **Accessories**, and then click **Command Prompt**. (In Windows Vista, click **Start**, type **cmd** in the Start Search text box, and then press **Enter**.) A command prompt window opens.

3. At the command prompt, type **ping 192.168.54.132** and press **Enter**. The computer indicates that it has received four replies from the remote computer and is, therefore, on the same network.

4. Now you will change the subnet mask on one of the computers. On *WORKSTATION1*, click **Start**, point to **All Programs**, point to **Accessories**, point to **Communications**, and then click **Network Connections**. (In Windows Vista, click **Start**, right-click **Network**, click **Properties**, and click **Manage network connections**.) The Network Connections window opens.

5. Right-click **Local Area Connection**, and then click **Properties** from the shortcut menu. (In Windows Vista, if a UAC dialog box opens, click **Continue**.) The Local Area Connection Properties window opens.

6. Double-click **Internet Protocol (TCP/IP)**. (In Windows Vista, double-click **Internet Protocol Version 4 (TCP/IPv4)**.) The Internet Protocol (TCP/IP) Properties window opens.

7. Change the subnet mask from 255.255.255.0 to 255.255.255.240. This creates 16 new networks from your original Class C network.

8. Repeat Steps 4 through 7 on *WORKSTATION2* to also change its subnet mask.

9. Now use ping to test the connection between *WORKSTATION1* and *WORKSTATION2* (see Steps 2 and 3). The ping will not be successful because the computers are now on separate networks. *WORKSTATION1* is still on network 192.168.54.0, whereas *WORKSTATION2* has been moved to network 192.168.54.128.

10. Log off both computers.

Certification Objectives

Objectives for the Network+ Exam:

- Identify the following address formats: IPv6, IPv4, MAC addressing

- Given a scenario, evaluate the proper use of the following addressing technologies and addressing schemes: *Addressing technologies*: subnetting, classful vs. class-less (e.g., CIDR, supernetting), NAT, PAT, SNAT, public vs. private, DHCP (static, dynamic APIPA); *Addressing schemes*: unicast, multicast, broadcast

- Given a scenario, troubleshoot common connectivity issues and select an appropriate solution: *Physical issues*: cross talk, nearing crosstalk, near end crosstalk, attenuation, collisions, shorts, open impedance mismatch (echo), interference; *Logical issues*: port speed, port duplex mismatch, incorrect VLAN, incorrect IP address, wrong gateway, wrong DNS, wrong subnet mask; *Issues that should be identified but escalated*: switching loop, routing loop, route problems, proxy arp, broadcast storms; *Wireless issues*: interference (bleed, environmental factors), incorrect encryption, incorrect channel, incorrect frequency, ESSID mismatch, standard mismatch (802.11 a/b/g/n), distance, bounce, incorrect antenna placement

- Given a scenario, select the appropriate command line interface tool and interpret the output to verify functionality: Traceroute, Ipconfig, Ifconfig, Ping, Arp, Nslookup, Host, Dig, Mtr, Route, Nbtstat, Netstat

- Explain issues that affect device security: physical security; restricting local and remote access; secure methods vs. unsecure methods; SSH, HTTPS, SNMPv3, SFTP, SCP; TELNET, HTTP, FTP, RSH, RCP, SNMPv1/2

Review Questions

1. Why are *WORKSTATION1* and *WORKSTATION2* no longer able to communicate?

   a. They have different IP addresses.

   b. They are on different networks.

c. TCP/IP was uninstalled on *WORKSTATION2*.

d. The ping command can only be used once.

2. Which of the following is *not* an advantage of subnetting?

a. enhanced network security

b. more hosts per network

c. improved network performance

d. simplified network troubleshooting

3. How is subnetting accomplished?

a. by changing the subnet mask on the host computers

b. by changing the IP address on the host computers

c. by installing the subnet protocol

d. by installing a router running DHCP

4. What is the default subnet mask for a Class C network?

a. 255.0.0.0

b. 255.255.0.0

c. 255.255.255.0

d. 255.255.255.255

Lab 10.2 Understanding the Purpose of the Default Gateway

Objectives

To ensure that a computer knows where to send packets outside of its own network, you can configure a default gateway. The default gateway is a computer or router that knows where to send packets so that they will reach their destination. Often the default gateway appears in a computer's routing table as a route to 0.0.0.0 with a subnet mask of 0.0.0.0. The IP address 0.0.0.0 is a generic way to refer to all possible IP addresses.

For instance, suppose a small network has a single router that is attached to the Internet. Suppose also that each computer on the network has this Internet router configured as its default gateway. Each computer has a route in its routing table for the local network so it can send packets bound for local network resources to the appropriate computer. If the address of a network resource is not on the local network, each computer sends the packet to the Internet router. The Internet router knows where to send the packet so that it will reach its destination.

Often the Internet router's routing table will specify just a few local routes and a default route to an ISP router. It will send any packet with a destination address that is not in its routing table to the ISP router. The ISP router will usually have a large routing table containing information about destination networks on the Internet.

After completing this lab, you will be able to:

• Identify the purpose of a default gateway

• Configure a default gateway

Materials Required

This lab will require the following:

- A computer running Windows XP Professional or Vista named *WORKSTATION1* and configured with an IP address of 192.168.54.3, a subnet mask of 255.255.255.0, and no default gateway

- A computer running Windows XP Professional or Vista named *WORKSTATION2* and configured with an IP address of 192.168.54.4, a subnet mask of 255.255.255.0, and no default gateway

- Administrative access to both computers

- Both computers connected to an Ethernet hub with straight-through Cat 5 (or better) UTP cables

Estimated completion time: **30 minutes**

Activity

1. Log on to *WORKSTATION1* as an administrator. The Windows desktop appears.

2. Click **Start**, point to **All Programs**, point to **Accessories**, and then click **Command Prompt**. (In Windows Vista, click **Start**, type **cmd** in the Start Search text box, and then press **Enter**.) A command prompt window opens.

3. At the command prompt, type **ping 192.168.54.4** and press **Enter**. The computer indicates that it has received four replies from the remote computer.

4. Repeat Steps 1 through 3 on *WORKSTATION2*. However, ping the address **192.168.54.3** instead.

5. Now you will add a secondary IP address to one of the computers. On *WORKSTATION1*, click **Start**, point to **All Programs**, point to **Accessories**, point to **Communications**, and then click **Network Connections**. (In Windows Vista, click **Start**, right-click **Network**, click **Properties**, and click **Manage network connections**.) The Network Connections window opens.

6. Right-click **Local Area Connection**, and then click **Properties** from the shortcut menu. (In Windows Vista, if a UAC dialog box opens, click **Continue**.) The Local Area Connection Properties window opens.

7. Double-click **Internet Protocol (TCP/IP)**. (In Windows Vista, double-click **Internet Protocol Version 4 (TCP/IPv4)**.) The Internet Protocol (TCP/IP) Properties window opens.

8. Click **Advanced**. The Advanced TCP/IP Settings window opens.

9. Below the IP address text box, click **Add**. The TCP/IP Address window opens. In the IP address text box, type **172.16.1.1**. In the Subnet mask text box, type **255.255.255.0**.

10. Click **Add**. Click **OK** three times to finish configuring the secondary IP address.

11. In the command prompt window on *WORKSTATION2*, type **ping 172.16.1.1** and press **Enter**. The computer indicates that it is unable to reach the remote computer. *WORKSTATION2* does not know where to send packets destined for 172.16.1.1.

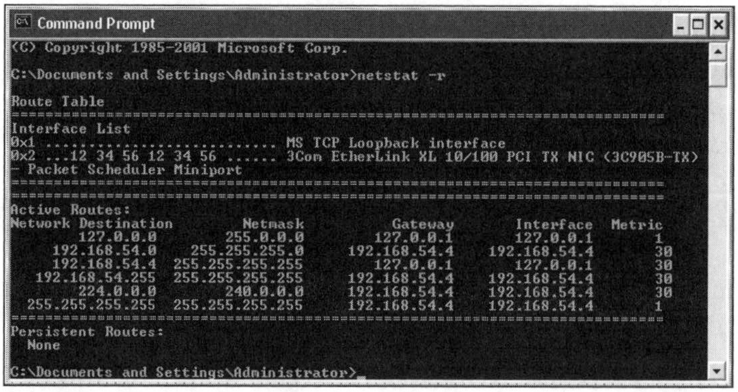

Figure 10-1 Output of the netstat –r command

Courtesy Course Technology/Cengage Learning

12. Type **netstat –r** and press **Enter** to display the routing table on *WORKSTATION2*. Record the destination addresses listed in the routing table. Figure 10-1 shows typical output of the netstat –r command in Windows XP. (The output in Windows Vista is slightly different.)

13. You will now add a default gateway to *WORKSTATION2*. Repeat Steps 5 through 7 on *WORKSTATION2* to open the Internet Protocol (TCP/IP) Properties window.

14. In the Default gateway text box, type **192.168.54.3**. This tells *WORKSTATION2* to send packets to 192.168.54.3 whenever it does not have another route for them. Click **OK** twice to exit.

15. At the command prompt on *WORKSTATION2*, type **ping 172.16.1.1**. The computer indicates that it has received four replies from *WORKSTATION1*.

16. Type **netstat –r** and press **Enter** to show the routing table again on *WORKSTATION2*. Compare this routing table with the one you saw in Step 12. Record the new destination addresses.

17. Log off both computers.

Certification Objectives

Objectives for the Network+ Exam:

- Given a scenario, troubleshoot common connectivity issues and select an appropriate solution: *Physical issues*: cross talk, nearing crosstalk, near end crosstalk, attenuation, collisions, shorts, open impedance mismatch (echo), interference; *Logical issues*: port speed, port duplex mismatch, incorrect VLAN, incorrect IP address, wrong gateway, wrong DNS, wrong subnet mask; *Issues that should be identified but escalated*: switching loop, routing loop, route problems, proxy arp, broadcast storms; *Wireless issues*: interference (bleed, environmental factors), incorrect encryption, incorrect channel, incorrect frequency, ESSID mismatch, standard mismatch (802.11 a/b/g/n), distance, bounce, incorrect antenna placement

- Given a scenario, select the appropriate command line interface tool and interpret the output to verify functionality: Traceroute, Ipconfig, Ifconfig, Ping, Arp, Nslookup, Host, Dig, Mtr, Route, Nbtstat, Netstat

Review Questions

1. What is the purpose of the default gateway?

    a. to assign IP addresses to clients as soon as they log on to the network

    b. to ensure that no two nodes on the same subnet have identical TCP/IP addresses

    c. to accept and relay packets from nodes on one network destined for nodes on another network

    d. to advertise the best, current routing paths between networks from one router to another

2. Which of the following is most likely to act as a default gateway?

    a. modem

    b. hub

    c. switch

    d. router

3. What type of information would the netstat –r command yield when typed at the command prompt of a networked client?

    a. a list of all routers to which that client might connect

    b. a list of the client's NIC adapter IP addresses

    c. the client's routing table

    d. the client's TCP/IP settings

4. What is the default subnet mask for a Class B network in the IP version 4 addressing scheme?

    a. 255.255.0.0

    b. 255.255.255.0

    c. 255.255.255.255

    d. 0.0.0.0

5. Which of the following utilities can show the route a packet traverses between its source node and destination node on a network?

    a. Ping

    b. Nbtstat

    c. Netstat

    d. Tracert

Lab 10.3 Understanding the TCP/IP Hosts File

Objectives

To use host names instead of IP addresses to reach remote computers, a computer must have some way to find the IP address that corresponds to each remote computer. One of the simplest ways to do this is to use the hosts file. The hosts file contains a list of IP addresses and the names of the computers at those addresses. When the computer recognizes the name of another computer in its hosts file, it uses the associated IP address when it tries to communicate with that computer.

Because it would be impossible to distribute hosts files to all the computers on the Internet, computers typically use the Domain Name System (DNS) to associate host names with IP addresses rather than using a copy of the hosts file. However, the hosts file is often useful as a temporary measure or when you cannot make a DNS entry. The hosts file can be useful, for example, when you want to make a DNS entry in a domain you do not control, or when you are using Network Address Translation (NAT). An IP address translated by NAT might not match the actual IP address of a computer, but a hosts entry forces the computer to use the appropriate IP address.

After completing this lab, you will be able to:

- Identify the purpose of the hosts file
- Modify a computer's hosts file
- Connect to another computer using its host name

Materials Required

This lab will require the following:

- A computer running Windows XP Professional or Vista named *WORKSTATION1* with an IP address of 192.168.54.3 and a subnet mask of 255.255.255.0
- Administrative access to the Windows computer
- A computer running a current version of Fedora Linux named *LINUX1. NETPLUSLAB.NET*, installed as a server with no firewall, and the GNOME Desktop Environment
- *LINUX1.NETPLUSLAB.NET* configured with an IP address of 192.168.54.5 and a subnet mask of 255.255.255.0
- A user named netplus on *LINUX1.NETPLUSLAB.NET* and the root password for *LINUX1.NETPLUSLAB.NET*
- Each computer connected to a hub with straight-through Cat 5 (or better) UTP cables

> Estimated completion time: **25 minutes**

Activity

1. Log on to *WORKSTATION1* as an administrator. The Windows desktop appears.
2. Click **Start**, point to **All Programs**, point to **Accessories**, and then click **Command Prompt**. (In Windows Vista, click **Start**, type **cmd** in the Start Search box, and then press **Enter**.) A command prompt window opens.
3. In the command prompt window, type **cd C:\windows\system32\drivers\etc** and press **Enter**. On a Windows XP or Vista computer, this directory contains the hosts file.

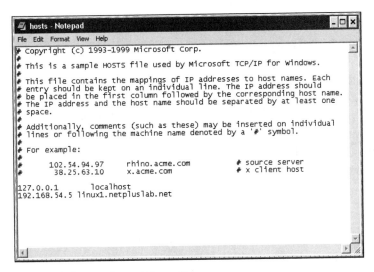

Figure 10-2   Windows XP hosts file

Courtesy Course Technology/Cengage Learning

4. To modify the hosts file, type **notepad hosts** and then press **Enter**. Notepad opens with the text of the hosts file. Note that many lines begin with a pound sign (#). These lines are comments and are ignored by the computer when it uses the hosts file.

5. At the bottom of the file, on a line by itself, type **192.168.54.5   linux1. netpluslab.net**. Click **File** on the menu bar, and then click **Save**. Figure 10-2 shows the Windows hosts file.

6. Click **File** on the menu bar, and then click **Exit**. Notepad closes.

7. At the command prompt, type **ping linux1.netpluslab.net**, and then press **Enter**. The computer indicates that it has received four replies from *LINUX1. NETPLUSLAB.NET*.

8. Log on to *LINUX1.NETPLUSLAB.NET* as the netplus user. The Fedora desktop appears.

9. Open a terminal window. At the prompt, type **su –** and press **Enter**. The Password prompt appears.

10. Type the root password for *LINUX1.NETPLUSLAB.NET* and press **Enter**. The prompt changes to end in #, indicating that you are now logged on as the root user.

11. Type **cd /etc** and press **Enter**.

12. Type **echo "192.168.54.3 workstation1.netpluslab.net" >> hosts** and press **Enter**. The computer appends the IP address and the host name between the quotation marks into the hosts file.

13. To see what the hosts file contains, type **cat hosts** and press **Enter**. The computer displays the contents of the hosts file.

14. Type **ping workstation1.netpluslab.net** and press **Enter**. The computer indicates that it is receiving replies from *WORKSTATION1*. Press **Ctrl+C** to stop the ping utility.

15. Log off both computers.

Certification Objectives

Objectives for the Network+ Exam:

- Given a scenario, evaluate the proper use of the following addressing technologies and addressing schemes: *Addressing technologies*: subnetting, classful vs. classless (e.g. CIDR, supernetting), NAT, PAT, SNAT, public vs. private, DHCP (static, dynamic APIPA); *Addressing schemes*: unicast, multicast, broadcast

Review Questions

1. What is the purpose of a host name?

   a. to uniquely identify a node on a network

   b. to associate a node with a particular domain

   c. to indicate which domain a node belongs to

   d. to identify the IP address of a host

2. What is the purpose of a hosts file?

   a. to help determine the best route for packets between gateways

   b. to make it easier for network administrators to remember a computer's IP address

   c. to map IP addresses to host names

   d. to indicate which hosts on a network are available to a client

3. What file on a Linux system holds information about host names and their IP addresses?

   a. /etc/hosts

   b. /bin/hosts

   c. /lib/users/hostfile

   d. /root/hostfile

4. Which of the following symbols indicates a comment in the hosts file?

   a. >

   b. >>

   c. :

   d. #

5. What is the alias of the computer whose host name is "C2" in the following hosts file?

160.12.122.13	C1C2.gameco.com	canasta
156.11.21.145	Comp2.gameco.com	chess
123.14.11.214	C2.gameco.com	checkers
44.112.133.15	CIC2.gameco.com	backgammon

   a. canasta

   b. chess

   c. checkers

   d. backgammon

Lab 10.4 Setting Up an FTP Server

Objectives

File Transfer Protocol (FTP) is an Application layer protocol used to send and receive files. The process requires both server and client software to function. In Lab 4.4 you learned how to use an FTP client to download files from an FTP server running on a remote host. In this lab, you will learn how to install and configure the FTP service in Windows Server 2008.

After completing this lab, you will be able to:

- Install the FTP service in IIS
- Set permissions so that certain users can connect to the FTP server and download files

Materials Required

This lab will require the following:

- A computer running Windows Server 2008, Standard Edition named *SERVER1*, configured as a domain controller for the netpluslab.net domain with an IP address of 192.168.54.1 and a subnet mask of 255.255.255.0
- Access to *SERVER1* as the Administrator
- A user account named netplus in the Domain Users group in the netpluslab.net domain
- A computer running Windows XP Professional or Vista named *WORKSTATION1*, configured with an IP address of 192.168.54.3 and a subnet mask of 255.255.255.0
- Both computers connected to a hub with Cat 5 (or better) UTP cables

Estimated completion time: **30 minutes**

Activity

1. Log on to *SERVER1* as the Administrator. The Windows Server 2008 desktop appears.
2. Click **Start** and click **Server Manager**. The Server Manager window opens.
3. Click **Roles**. If IIS is not yet installed, click **Add Roles** from the Roles Summary section in the right pane. The Add Roles Wizard opens.
4. If the Before You Begin window opens, click **Next** to continue.
5. Place a check mark in the **Web Server (IIS)** check box and click **Add Required Features** in the Add Roles Wizard dialog box that opens. Click **Next** and click **Next** again after reading through the description of IIS.
6. On the Select Role Services window, place a check mark in the **FTP Publishing Service** check box and click **Add Required Role Services** in the Add Roles Wizard dialog box that opens. Click **Next** to continue.
7. Click **Install** to confirm your installation selections and click **Close** after the installation is complete.

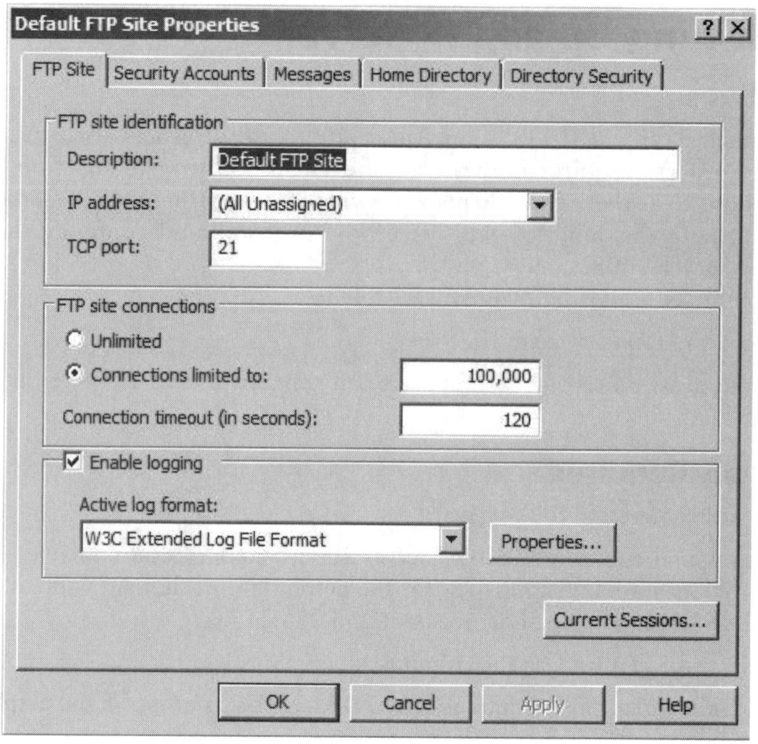

Figure 10-3   The Default FTP Site Properties window

Courtesy Course Technology/Cengage Learning

8. Now start the FTP service. Click **Start**, point to **Administrative Tools**, and click **Internet Information Services (IIS) 6.0 Manager**.

9. Double-click **SERVER1**, double-click **FTP Sites**, and right-click **Default FTP Site**. Click **Start**. If a message appears that says "Cannot change the state of the site," click **Yes**.

10. Right-click **Default FTP Site** and click **Properties**. The Default FTP Site Properties window opens, as shown in Figure 10-3.

11. Click the **Security Accounts** tab and select the **netplus** user for anonymous access. Click the **Browse** button, enter **netplus** as the user name, click **Check Names**, and click **OK**. Click the **Home Directory** tab and ensure that the local path to the ftproot directory is C:\inetpub\ftproot.

12. Click **OK** and close the Internet Information Services Manager.

13. Click **Start**, point to **All Programs**, click **Accessories**, and then click **Command Prompt**. A command prompt window opens.

14. In the command prompt window, type **echo** *your name* **> C:\Inetpub\ftproot \netplus.txt** and press **Enter**. (Substitute your name for *your name*.) This creates a file named netplus.txt containing your name in the C:\Inetpub\ftproot directory.

15. Use the skills you learned in Lab 4.4 to connect to the FTP server from the Windows client.

16. When you're finished, close any open windows and log off both computers.

Certification Objectives

Objectives for the Network+ Exam:

- Explain the function of common networking protocols: TCP, FTP, UDP, TCP/IP suite, DHCP, TFTP, DNS, HTTP(S), ARP, SIP (VoIP), RTP (VoIP), SSH, POP3, NTP, IMAP4, Telnet, SMTP, SNMP2/3, ICMP, IGMP, TLS
- Explain issues that affect device security: physical security; restricting local and remote access; secure methods vs. unsecure methods; SSH, HTTPS, SNMPv3, SFTP, SCP; TELNET, HTTP, FTP, RSH, RCP, SNMPv1/2

Review Questions

1. What is the default FTP directory in Windows Server 2008?

   a. C:\ftp\root

   b. C:\root\dir\ftp

   c. C:\ftproot\ftproot

   d. C:\Inetpub\ftproot

2. The FTP protocol functions at which layer?

   a. Application

   b. Transport

   c. Internetwork

   d. Network Interface

3. Using FTP to upload or download data requires both server and _____ software.

   a. session

   b. client

   c. IIS

   d. remote host

4. General access to an FTP server is referred to as what kind of access?

   a. root

   b. anonymous

   b. limited

   d. privileged

Lab 10.5 Configuring a Mail Server

Objectives

E-mail is one of the most important applications on the majority of business networks. E-mail is sent from a user's computer to its destination using the Simple Mail Transfer Protocol (SMTP). A wide variety of programs run SMTP. In this lab, you will configure one such program, Sendmail. Sendmail is used primarily on Linux and UNIX computers.

A computer running SMTP looks at the domain name in the e-mail address and performs a DNS lookup to find the mail exchanger, or MX, record for the domain. The MX record is the domain name of the e-mail server where e-mail for that domain must be sent. For instance, the netpluslab.net domain might have an MX record of linux1.netpluslab.net. This tells other computers running SMTP that any e-mail sent to e-mail addresses in the netpluslab.net domain (such as netplus@netpluslab.net) should be sent to the server linux1.netpluslab.net. As you might expect, DNS must be properly configured for SMTP to work correctly and for e-mail to be delivered. A domain might have multiple MX records with different priorities, which allows for load balancing or for a backup server to collect e-mail in case the primary server fails.

After an e-mail has been delivered to its final destination, the user must collect it. E-mail programs employ a variety of methods to collect e-mail. Some popular protocols used for collecting e-mail include POP3 and IMAP. In this lab, you will configure the Outlook Express program to use POP3 to collect e-mail. Typically, settings for receiving mail are given to users by their network administrators.

After completing this lab, you will be able to:

- Configure an e-mail server

Materials Required

This lab will require the following:

- A computer running Windows Server 2008, Standard Edition named *SERVER1*, configured as a domain controller for the netpluslab.net domain and with an IP address of 192.168.54.1 and a subnet mask of 255.255.255.0

- A user named netplus configured in the netpluslab.net domain

- A computer running Windows XP Professional or Vista named *WORKSTATION1* configured with an IP address of 192.168.54.3 and a subnet mask of 255.255.255.0

- A computer running a current version of Fedora Linux named *LINUX1. NETPLUSLAB.NET*, installed as a server with no firewall, and the GNOME Desktop Environment; in addition to the Mail Server package, Dovecot IMAP needs to be installed

- *LINUX1.NETPLUSLAB.NET* configured with an IP address of 192.168.54.5 and a subnet mask of 255.255.255.0

- A user named netplus on *LINUX1.NETPLUSLAB.NET*

- *LINUX1.NETPLUSLAB.NET* configured to use 192.168.54.1 as its DNS server; the file /etc/resolv.conf should contain the line "nameserver 192.168.54.1"

- The DNS server on *SERVER1* configured and running, with a domain named netpluslab.net

- Forward and reverse DNS entries for *LINUX1.NETPLUSLAB.NET* at 192.168.54.5 and for *WORKSTATION1.NETPLUSLAB.NET* at 192.168.54.3

- All three computers configured to use 192.168.54.1 for DNS resolution

- A line in the /etc/hosts file on *LINUX1.NETPLUSLAB.NET* for 192.168.54.5 containing the text "192.168.54.5 linux1.netpluslab.net"

- The default /etc/mail/sendmail.mc and /etc/dovecot.conf files on *LINUX1.NETPLUSLAB.NET*

- No e-mail accounts configured in Windows Mail or Outlook Express on *WORKSTATION1*

Estimated completion time: **90–120 minutes**

Activity

1. Log on to *LINUX1.NETPLUSLAB.NET* as the netplus user. The Fedora desktop appears.

2. Open a terminal window and at the prompt, type **su –** and press **Enter**. The Password prompt appears. Type the root password and press **Enter**. The prompt now ends in a pound sign (#), indicating that you are logged on as the root user.

3. Next, you will configure the dovecot daemon to allow users to check for e-mail from this computer. Dovecot is one of a variety of programs that will deliver e-mail to users using POP3, IMAP3, and other protocols. Type **vi /etc/dovecot.conf** and press **Enter**. The vi editor opens the file /etc/dovecot.conf in normal mode.

4. Press **G**. The cursor moves to the last line of the file.

5. Press **i**. The vi editor enters insert mode.

6. Type **protocols = pop3** and press **Esc**. The vi editor enters normal mode.

7. Type **:wq** and press **Enter**. The vi editor saves the file and exits.

8. Type **/etc/init.d/dovecot start** and press **Enter**. The computer starts the Dovecot IMAP server.

9. Now you will configure the Sendmail program so that this computer can be used to send e-mail. Type **vi /etc/mail/sendmail.mc** and press **Enter**. The /etc/mail/sendmail.mc file opens.

10. Type **/127.0.0.1** and press **Enter**. The vi editor searches for the text 127.0.0.1. Type **/** and press **Enter**. The vi editor searches for the text from the previous search (127.0.0.1). Repeat until the vi editor places the cursor at the beginning of the IP address 127.0.0.1 in the line "DAEMON OPTIONS('Port=smtp,Addr=127.0.0.1, Name=MTA') dnl".

11. Press **0**. The cursor moves to the beginning of the line.

12. Press **i**. The vi editor goes into insert mode.

13. Type **dnl #** at the beginning of the line. This command tells the computer to ignore this line when the file is processed later in the lab. Press **Esc** to put the vi editor back into normal mode.

14. Type **/LOCAL_DOMAIN** and press **Enter**. The cursor moves to the start of a line containing the text LOCAL_DOMAIN.

15. Press **w** twice. The cursor moves to the beginning of the word "localhost.localdomain."

16. Type **d3w**. The computer deletes the text "localhost.localdomain."

17. Press **i**. The vi editor goes into insert mode. Type **netpluslab.net** and press **Esc**.

18. Type **:wq** and press **Enter**. The vi editor saves the file and then closes.

19. Type **cd /etc/mail** and press **Enter**. The computer changes your current working directory to /etc/mail.

20. Type **make** and press **Enter**. The computer processes the changes you have made in the sendmail.mc file and places them in the sendmail.cf file.

21. Type **/etc/init.d/sendmail restart** and press **Enter**. The computer restarts the Sendmail daemon with the configuration changes you have made.

22. Now you will configure DNS so that each computer on the network knows where to send e-mail. Log on to *SERVER1* as the Administrator. The Windows Server 2008 desktop appears.

23. Press **Start**, point to **Administrative Tools**, and then click **DNS**. The dnsmgmt window opens.

24. In the left pane of the window, click **SERVER1**. Icons appear in the right pane.

25. Double-click the **Forward Lookup Zones** icon in the right pane of the window. A list of domains appears. Double-click the **netpluslab.net** icon in the right pane.

26. Right-click **netpluslab.net** in the left pane, and click **New Mail Exchanger (MX)**. The New Resource Record dialog box opens.

27. In the "Fully qualified domain name (FQDN) of mail server" text box, enter **linux1. netpluslab.net**. See Figure 10-4.

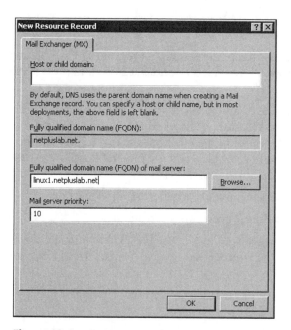

Figure 10-4   The New Resource Record dialog box

Courtesy Course Technology/Cengage Learning

28. Click **OK**. The New Resource Record dialog box closes. Right-click the **netpluslab. net** icon, and click **Reload**. The DNS dialog box opens, asking if you want to reload the domain.

29. Click **Yes**. The computer reloads the netpluslab.net domain.

In Windows Vista, follow these steps:

 1. Log on to *WORKSTATION1* as the netplus user. The Windows Vista desktop appears.

 2. Click **Start**, click **All Programs**, and then click **Windows Mail**. The Windows Mail program opens. If the Internet Connection Wizard opens (at the Your Name window), skip to Step 4.

 3. Click **Tools** on the menu bar, and then click **Accounts**. The Internet Accounts window opens. Click **Add**, click **E-mail Account**, and then click **Next**.

 4. In the Display name text box, enter **Net+ Lab**. Click **Next**. The next window asks for an e-mail address.

 5. In the E-mail address text box, enter **netplus@netpluslab.net**. Click **Next**. The next window asks for information about the e-mail servers you will use.

 6. In the Incoming mail (POP3 or IMAP) server text box, enter **linux1.netpluslab. net**. In the Outgoing mail (SMTP) server text box, enter **linux1.netpluslab.net**. Click **Next**. The next window asks you for information about the account you will use.

 7. In the E-mail username text box, enter **netplus**. In the Password text box, enter the password for the netplus account on *LINUX1.NETPLUSLAB.NET*. Click **Next**. The Congratulations window indicates that you have finished.

 8. Click **Finish**. The Internet Connection window closes. Click **Close** to close the Internet Accounts window.

 9. In the Windows Mail window, click **Create Mail**. The New Message window opens.

10. In the To text box, enter **netplus@netpluslab.net**. In the Subject text box, enter **Test Message**. In the bottom window, enter your name. Click **Send**. Windows Mail sends the message.

11. Click **Send/Receive**. The Windows Mail dialog box opens briefly as the program checks for e-mail.

12. In the tree in the left pane, click **Inbox**. In the upper-right pane, a message with the subject "Test Message" appears.

13. Double-click the message with the subject "Test Message" to open it in a new window.

14. Click **File** on the menu bar, and then click **Close** to close the Test Message window.

15. Click **File** on the menu bar, and then click **Exit**. Windows Mail closes.

16. Log off all three computers.

In Windows XP, follow these steps:

 1. Log on to *WORKSTATION1* as the netplus user. The Windows XP desktop appears.

 2. Click **Start** and then click **Outlook Express**. The Outlook Express window opens. If the Internet Connection Wizard does not open, click **Tools** on the menu

bar, and then click **Accounts**. The Internet Accounts window opens. Click **Add** and then click **Mail**.

3. In the Display name text box, enter **Net+ Lab**. Click **Next**. The next wizard window asks for an e-mail address.

4. In the E-mail address text box, enter **netplus@netpluslab.net**. Click **Next**. The next wizard window asks for information about the e-mail servers you will use.

5. In the Incoming mail (POP3, IMAP, or HTTP) server text box, enter **linux1. netpluslab.net**. In the Outgoing mail (SMTP) server text box, enter **linux1. netpluslab.net**. Click **Next**. Now the wizard asks for information about the account you will use.

6. In the Account name text box, enter **netplus**. In the Password text box, enter the password for the netplus account on *LINUX1.NETPLUSLAB.NET*. If necessary, uncheck the **Log on using Secure Password Authentication (SPA)** check box. Click **Next**. The next wizard window indicates that you have finished.

7. Click **Finish**. The Internet Connection Wizard closes.

8. In the Outlook Express window, click **Create Mail**. The New Message dialog box opens.

9. In the To text box, enter **netplus@netpluslab.net**. In the Subject text box, enter **Test Message**. In the bottom window, enter your name. Click **Send**. Outlook Express sends the message.

10. Click **Send/Recv**. The Outlook Express dialog box opens briefly as the program checks for e-mail.

11. In the tree in the left pane, click **Inbox**. In the upper-right pane, a message with the subject "Test Message" appears.

12. Double-click the message with the subject "Test Message." The message opens in the Test Message dialog box.

13. Click **File** on the menu bar, and then click **Close** to close the Test Message dialog box.

14. Click **File** on the menu bar, and then click **Exit**. Outlook Express closes.

15. Log off all three computers.

Certification Objectives

Objectives for the Network+ Exam:

- Explain the function of common networking protocols: TCP, FTP, UDP, TCP/IP suite, DHCP, TFTP, DNS, HTTP(S), ARP, SIP (VoIP), RTP (VoIP), SSH, POP3, NTP, IMAP4, Telnet, SMTP, SNMP2/3, ICMP, IGMP, TLS

Review Questions

1. Which of the following protocols is used to send e-mail?

   a. POP3

   b. SMTP

    c. IMAP

    d. SNMP

2. You are sending e-mail to your friend Bob, whose e-mail address is bob@otherdomain.com. What information does your SMTP server need to deliver this e-mail to Bob?

    a. It needs to look up the IP address of otherdomain.com.

    b. It needs to look up the IP address of the otherdomain.com POP3 server.

    c. It needs to use the MX record for the otherdomain.com domain to find the IP address of the appropriate IMAP server.

    d. It needs to use the MX record for the otherdomain.com domain to find the IP address of the appropriate SMTP server.

3. The DNS server on your network is not functioning properly. Which of the following is *not* a possible consequence of this?

    a. User e-mail programs inside your network are unable to find the IP address of your SMTP server.

    b. SMTP servers outside your network are unable to make TCP connections to your mail server.

    c. Your SMTP server is unable to find the IP addresses of remote mail servers.

    d. User e-mail programs inside your network are unable to find the IP address of your IMAP server.

4. Why is it important to secure and configure a mail server properly?

    a. A misconfigured or improperly secured mail server might not be able to deliver e-mail.

    b. A misconfigured or improperly secured mail server might be hijacked to send large amounts of unsolicited commercial e-mail.

    c. A misconfigured or improperly secured mail server might not be able to run SMTP.

    d. A misconfigured or improperly secured mail server might not allow clients to download their e-mail.

5. A user has been given an e-mail address of sally@otherorg.net. How is this user most likely to determine the settings she needs to receive e-mail?

    a. from the MX record for the otherorg.net domain

    b. by finding the IP address of the otherorg.net domain

    c. from the network administrator

    d. from other SMTP servers on the Internet

CHAPTER ELEVEN

VIDEO AND VOICE OVER IP

Labs included in this chapter

- Lab 11.1 Setting Up a Video Streaming Server

- Lab 11.2 Installing an SIP Proxy

- Lab 11.3 Installing an SIP Client

- Lab 11.4 Researching Open Source VoIP Solutions

Net+ Exam Objective

Objective	Lab
Explain different methods and rationales for network performance optimization	11.1, 11.2, 11.3

Lab 11.1 Setting Up a Video Streaming Server

Objectives

Streaming video is one of the more common applications of Video-over-IP. A video streaming server hosts a number of videos as stored files that can be viewed remotely from a client machine. Videos sent when requested are referred to as video-on-demand, whereas live streaming videos are those sent continuously regardless of whether they're requested. In this lab, you will set up a popular open source program (VLC) that is capable of functioning as both a video streaming server and a media player.

After completing this lab, you will be able to:

- Set up and configure a video streaming server
- Connect to a streaming video with a media player

Materials Required

This lab will require the following:

- A computer running Windows Server 2008, Standard Edition named *SERVER1*, configured with an IP address of 192.168.54.1 and a subnet mask of 255.255.255.0
- A computer running Windows XP Professional or Vista named *WORKSTATION1*, configured with an IP address of 192.168.54.2 and a subnet mask of 255.255.255.0
- VLC media player (*www.videolan.org*) downloaded and installed on both computers
- A video file suitable for streaming, such as DIVX or WMV, on *SERVER1*
- Some kind of portable media to transfer VLC installation and video files if the computers do not have a direct connection to the Internet
- Both computers connected to a hub with straight-through Cat 5 (or better) UTP cables
- Administrative access to all three computers

Estimated completion time: **30 minutes**

Activity

1. Log on to *SERVER1* as the Administrator. The Windows desktop appears.
2. Click **Start**, click **All Programs**, click **VideoLAN**, and click **VLC media player**. If the Privacy and Network Policies dialog box opens, click **OK**.
3. Click **Media** on the menu bar and click **Streaming**. The Open Media Window opens.
4. Click **Add**, choose the file you want to stream, and click **Open** to continue.
5. Select the **Network** tab.
6. Select **UDP** as the protocol and enter **192.168.54.2** as the address of the computer that will be receiving the video stream.
7. Note the port being used and then click **Stream**.

8. Click **OK** again to begin streaming.

9. Now run VLC on *WORKSTATION1*.

10. Click **File** from the pull-down menu and select **Open Network Stream**.

11. Make sure **UDP/RTP** is selected and that the same port is being used. Click **OK**.

12. After a short pause, the video should start streaming. When you're finished, exit all programs and log off both computers.

Certification Objectives

Objectives for the Network+ Exam:

- Explain different methods and rationales for network performance optimization:
  Methods: QoS, traffic shaping, load balancing, high availability, caching engines, fault tolerance; *Reasons*: latency sensitivity, high bandwidth applications, VoIP, video applications, uptime

Review Questions

1. A computer that is sending a video stream is referred to as a video streaming _____.

   a. hub

   b. server

   c. switch

   d. proxy

2. Which protocol is typically used to stream video?

   a. UDP

   b. TCP

   c. HTTP

   d. FTP

3. For a client to receive a video stream, both the server and client applications must use the same _____.

   a. gateway

   b. IP address

   c. port

   d. SIP

Lab 11.2 Installing an SIP Proxy

Objectives

SIP and H.323 are the two most common protocols used by VoIP communications. Although SIP does not have as many features as H.323, it is more popular with most VoIP venders because of its simplicity and lower overhead. SIP is an Application layer signaling protocol modeled on the HTTP protocol. In this lab, you will install and configure part of an IP PBX called an SIP Proxy or Proxy Server.

After completing this lab, you will be able to:

- Set up and install an SIP Proxy Server

Materials Required

This lab will require the following:

- A computer running Windows Server 2008, Standard Edition named *SERVER1,* configured with an IP address of 192.168.54.1 and a subnet mask of 255.255.255.0, with Internet access

- Access to the computer as the Administrator

- The latest .NET Framework downloaded from *www.microsoft.com* and installed on *SERVER1*

- The Windows Server 2008 installation CD/DVD (if necessary)

Estimated completion time: **25 minutes**

Activity

1. Log on to *SERVER1* as the Administrator. The Windows desktop appears.

2. Perform whatever steps are necessary for the computer to access the Internet.

3. Start Internet Explorer.

4. Go to **www.officesip.com**.

5. Select the **Download** tab on the left and download OfficeSIP Server 2.5 to your desktop. Open the OfficeSIP-Server-2.5.zip file and extract all files to your desktop.

6. Double-click on **Setup-2.5.exe**. If an Open File Security Warning dialog box opens, click **Run** to continue. The OfficeSIP Server Setup Wizard window opens.

7. Click **Next** to continue to the License Agreement.

8. Select the **I Agree** option button and click **Next**.

9. Keep the default officesip.local as a domain name and click **Next**.

10. Click **Next** after selecting the installation folder and click **Next** again to confirm your choices.

11. When the installation is complete, click **Close**.

12. To run OfficeSIP Server 2.5, click **Start**, click **All Programs**, click **OfficeSIP Server**, and click **Control Panel**.

13. Click **Connect** to log in and the OfficeSIP Server Control Panel should open, as shown in Figure 11-1.

14. Select the **Users** tab and click **Add** to add a new user.

15. Add the necessary user credentials to add a user named User1 and click **OK**.

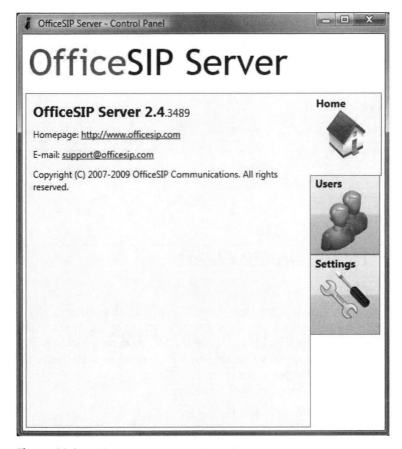

Figure 11-1   OfficeSIP Server Control Panel

Courtesy Course Technology/Cengage Learning

16. Add a second user named User2 and click **OK**.

17. Log off the computer unless you are progressing directly to Lab 11.3.

Certification Objectives

Objectives for the Network+ Exam:

- Explain different methods and rationales for network performance optimization: *Methods*: QoS, traffic shaping, load balancing, high availability, caching engines, fault tolerance; *Reasons*: latency sensitivity, high bandwidth applications, VoIP, video applications, uptime

Review Questions

1. Why is SIP a popular choice with VoIP venders?

   a. It has lower licensing costs.

   b. It is simpler with lower overhead.

   c. It is more fault tolerant and robust.

   d. It was the first standard developed.

2. SIP and H.323 are both examples of _____.

   a. protocols

   b. soft phones

   c. media gateways

   d. end devices

3. SIP functions at the _____ layer

   a. Transport

   b. Data Link

   c. Network

   b. Application

Lab 11.3 Installing an SIP Client

Objectives

An SIP client is any end-user device that initiates an SIP connection. This could include physical devices, such as IP telephones or PDAs, or software applications, such as soft phones or messaging programs. An SIP client can use the SIP protocol to send text, voice, or video to another client. In this lab, you will install an SIP client on two machines and have them communicate through the SIP server set up in Lab 11.2.

After completing this lab, you will be able to:

- Set up an SIP client application
- Communicate by voice with an SIP-based messaging application

Materials Required

This lab will require the following:

- A computer running Windows Server 2008, Standard Edition named *SERVER1,* configured with an IP address of 192.168.54.1 and a subnet mask of 255.255.255.0
- The installation of OfficeSIP Server 2.4 running on *SERVER1* from Lab 11.2
- A computer running Windows XP Professional or Vista named *WORKSTATION1,* configured with an IP address of 192.168.54.2 and a subnet mask of 255.255.255.0
- A second computer running Windows XP Professional or Vista named *WORKSTATION2,* configured with an IP address of 192.168.54.3 and a subnet mask of 255.255.255.0
- Working speakers and a microphone on both *WORKSTATION1* and *WORKSTATION2*
- The latest .NET Framework downloaded from *www.microsoft.com* and installed on *WORKSTATION1* and *WORKSTATION2*
- All three computers connected to a hub with straight-through Cat 5 (or better) UTP cables
- Administrative access to all three computers

Estimated completion time: **30 minutes**

Activity

1. Log on to *WORKSTATION1* as an administrator. The Windows desktop appears.
2. Perform whatever steps are necessary for the computer to access the Internet.
3. Start Internet Explorer.
4. Go to **www.officesip.com**.
5. Select the **Download** tab on the left, download OfficeSIP Messenger 1.9.0 to your desktop, and double-click the setup icon to begin installing the program.
6. The OfficeSIP Messenger Setup Wizard opens. Click **Next** to continue.
7. Select an installation folder and click **Next**.
8. Click **Next** to confirm the installation. If a UAC dialog box opens, click **Allow** to continue.
9. When the installation is complete, click **Close**.
10. Click **Start**, point to **All Programs**, and click **OfficeSIP Messenger** to run the program.
11. Log in with the credentials you created for User1 in Lab 11.2.
12. Repeat Steps 1 through 11 on *WORKSTATION2* and log in as User2.
13. Select the **Contacts** pull-down menu and click **Add Contacts**.
14. Add User1 as a contact, as shown in Figure 11-2.

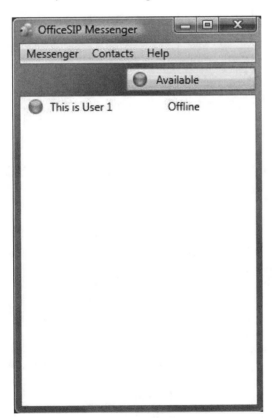

Figure 11-2   OfficeSIP Messenger Contacts

Courtesy Course Technology/Cengage Learning

15. From the **Contacts** pull-down menu, select **Start Audio Conversation**. If a Windows Security Alert warns you that the Windows firewall has blocked some features of this program, click **Unblock**.

16. If possible, have a partner answer the call from *WORKSTATION1*; otherwise, terminate the session and close any windows.

17. Log off all three computers.

Certification Objectives

Objectives for the Network+ Exam:

- Explain different methods and rationales for network performance optimization: *Methods*: QoS, traffic shaping, load balancing, high availability, caching engines, fault tolerance; *Reasons*: latency sensitivity, high bandwidth applications, VoIP, video applications, uptime

Review Questions

1. SIP clients _____.

   a. are daemons that run on an SIP server

   b. are end-user devices

   c. never initiate an SIP connection

   d. are used to redirect requests from user agents

2. True or False? Both hardware devices and software applications can be SIP clients.

Lab 11.4 Researching Open Source VoIP Solutions

Objectives

VoIP (Voice over IP) is quickly becoming common in the workplace because of its lower cost, enhanced features, and centralized management. The infrastructure for voice and data is often integrated to avoid the redundancy of having separate networks and private branch exchange (PBX) systems.

To access VoIP, users can run client applications called soft phones and place calls through their computers or, with specialized hardware, place calls through either analog or digital telephone handsets. These devices are often connected through an IP PBX, which may be a hardware system or an application running on a server.

One of the more common open source IP PBX applications is called Asterisk. In this lab, you will investigate some of the features available for a Windows version of Asterisk called AsteriskWin32.

After completing this lab, you will be able to:

- Identify some of the features available on an open source IP PBX

Materials Required

This lab will require the following:

- Pencil and paper
- A computer running Windows XP Professional or Vista with Internet access
- An ordinary user account on the computer

Estimated completion time: **20 minutes**

Activity

1. Press **Ctrl+Alt+Del** to display the Log On to Windows dialog box. Log on as an ordinary user. The Windows desktop appears.

2. Perform whatever steps are necessary for the computer to access the Internet.

3. Start Internet Explorer.

4. Go to **www.asterisk.org** and click on Learn More.

5. Record some of the protocols supported by Asterisk.

6. Explain the four key applications of Asterisk.

7. Record some of the operating systems that can run Asterisk.

8. There is also a Windows-based version of Asterisk called AsteriskWin32. Go to **http://asteriskwin32.com/** and click the **About** tab.

9. Does Asterisk require any additional hardware to connect soft phones?

10. Click the **Install & Notes** tab.

11. View the AsteriskWin32 Install videos on Installing, Configuring, Running, and SoftPhone Setup.

12. Close any open windows and log off both computers.

Certification Objectives

Objectives for the Network+ Exam:

- This lab does not directly map to an objective on the exam; however, it does teach concepts that are valuable to networking professionals.

Review Questions

1. Why is the infrastructure for voice and data often integrated into a single system?

    a. to improve security

    b. to adhere to local regulations

    c. to filter outgoing communications

    d. to avoid redundancy

2. Client applications for placing VoIP calls are called _____.

    a. soft phones

    b. digital phones

    c. analog phones

    d. IP phones

3. True or False? Analog telephones require additional hardware to be used with VoIP.

NETWORK SECURITY

Labs included in this chapter

- Lab 12.1 Auditing
- Lab 12.2 Checking for Vulnerable Software
- Lab 12.3 Implementing Network Address Restrictions on a Linux Server
- Lab 12.4 Plaintext Versus Encrypted Protocols
- Lab 12.5 Securing a Wireless Network

Net+ Exam Objectives

Objective	Lab
Explain the function of common networking protocols	12.4
Compare the characteristics of wireless communication standards	12.5
Given a scenario, troubleshoot common connectivity issues and select an appropriate solution	12.5
Explain the purpose of network scanners	12.4
Explain the function of hardware and software security devices	12.1, 12.2, 12.4
Explain the methods of network access security	12.1, 12.3, 12.5
Explain issues that affect device security	12.2, 12.4
Identify common security threats and mitigation techniques	12.1, 12.5

Lab 12.1 Auditing

Objectives

Although preventing security problems should be the first goal of network administrators, security problems cannot always be prevented. Fortunately, auditing can help you identify both security vulnerabilities and potential security breaches.

Auditing is the gathering and analysis of large amounts of network-related information, including data about logons, access attempts, system events, and so on. For instance, auditing can indicate when someone is repeatedly attempting and failing to log on to your domain controller, which could in turn indicate that someone is attempting to compromise your network. Auditing can also help you troubleshoot server problems, such as an unexpected failure.

Auditing is not limited to a network operating system; in most cases, you can configure firewalls, routers, and switches to compile, or log, information (on their own disks or to an external server) as well. Often this information can be useful in determining whether intruders have attempted to access devices on your network.

In Windows Server 2008 (and in most other network operating systems), auditing is not enabled by default because it can affect performance and use a large amount of disk space. Thus, to view the failed logon attempts in a Windows Server 2008 domain, you must first activate auditing for the domain. Then, you must activate auditing on the domain controller so that it will capture the logging.

After completing this lab, you will be able to:

- Enable auditing in Windows Server 2008
- Review information on audited events

Materials Required

This lab will require the following:

- A computer running Windows Server 2008, Enterprise Standard named *SERVER1*, configured as the domain controller for the netpluslab.net domain with an IP address of 192.168.54.1 and a subnet mask of 255.255.255.0
- Access as the Administrator to *SERVER1*
- A computer running Windows XP Professional or Vista named *WORKSTATION1*, configured as a member of the netpluslab.net domain and with an IP address of 192.168.54.3 and a subnet mask of 255.255.255.0
- A user account named netplus in the Domain Users group in the netpluslab.net domain
- Both computers connected to a hub with straight-through Cat 5 (or better) UTP cables

Estimated completion time: **40 minutes**

Activity

1. Log on to *SERVER1* as the Administrator. The Windows Server 2008 desktop appears.
2. Click **Start**, point to **Administrative Tools**, and click **Local Security Policy**. The Local Security Policy window opens.
3. Click **Local Policies** in the left pane. Icons for policies appear in the right pane.

4. In the right pane, double-click **Audit Policy**. Several icons whose names begin with "Audit" appear. As you'll see in the next few steps, you can double-click these icons to define and configure various policies.

5. Double-click **Audit account logon events**. The Audit account logon events Properties dialog box opens. This setting determines whether the computer will record every instance of a user logging on or off the domain.

6. If necessary, click to select the **Success** and **Failure** check boxes, and then click **OK**. Figure 12-1 shows the Audit account logon events Properties dialog box. You have now configured the computer to record every attempt by a user to log on, whether successful or unsuccessful.

7. Repeat Steps 5 and 6 for **Audit logon events**. (Note the distinction between "Audit account logon events" and "Audit logon events.") The Audit logon events settings determine whether the domain controller will record every instance of a user logging on or off a computer for which the domain controller performs authentication.

8. In the left pane, right-click **Security Settings** and click **Reload** on the shortcut menu. The computer updates the security policy for the domain with the changes that you have made.

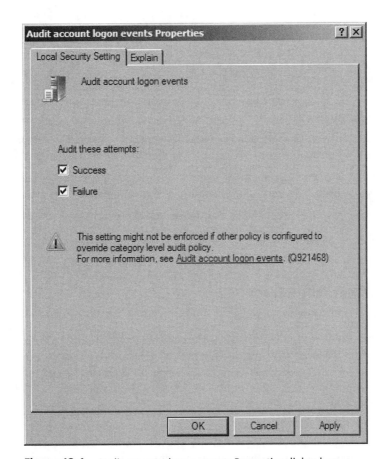

Figure 12-1   Audit account logon events Properties dialog box

Courtesy Course Technology/Cengage Learning

9. For auditing events to be captured, you must specifically enable logging on the domain controller itself. Otherwise, the domain controller will not know that it is supposed to capture audit events and will discard them. Click **Start**, point to **Administrative Tools**, and then click **Group Policy Management**. Double-click **Group Policy Management, Forest: netpluslab, Domains, netpluslab.net**, and **Domain Controllers**, and then right-click **Default Domain Controllers Policy** and click **Edit**. The Default Domain Controller Security Settings window opens.

10. In the tree in the left pane, click **Local Policies**. A list of icons appears in the right pane. Double-click **Audit Policy**. Policies appear in the right pane.

11. Double-click **Audit account logon events**. The Audit account logon events Properties dialog box opens.

12. Make sure that the **Define these policy settings, Success**, and **Failure** check boxes are all checked, and then click **OK**.

13. Repeat Steps 11 and 12 for **Audit logon events**.

14. Right-click **Security Settings**, and then click **Reload**. The computer reloads security policies for the domain controller.

15. Attempt to log on to *WORKSTATION1* using an invalid password.

16. An error message appears, indicating that the logon attempt failed. Click **OK**.

17. Repeat Steps 15 and 16.

18. Log on as the netplus user with the correct password. The Windows desktop appears.

19. On *SERVER1*, click **Start**, point to **Administrative Tools**, and click **Event Viewer**. The Event Viewer window opens.

20. In the left pane, expand **Windows Logs** (if necessary) and click **Security**. A list of security events appears in the middle pane, including all successful and failed logon attempts.

21. Double-click a **Failure Audit** icon. The Event Properties dialog box opens. The dialog box gives information about a failed logon attempt.

22. Repeat the previous step with a **Success Audit** icon.

23. Log off both computers.

Certification Objectives

Objectives for the Network+ Exam:

- Explain the function of hardware and software security devices: network-based firewall, host-based firewall, IDS, IPS, VPN concentrator
- Explain the methods of network access security: *Filtering*: ACL, MAC filtering, IP filtering, tunneling and encryption, SSL VPN, VPN, L2TP, PPTP, IPSEC, remote access, RAS, RDP, PPPoE, PPP, VNC, ICA
- Identify common security threats and mitigation techniques: *Security threats*: DoS, viruses, worms, attackers, man in the middle, smurf, rogue access points, social engineering (phishing); *Mitigation techniques*: policies and procedures, user training, patches and updates

Review Questions

1. Which of the following best describes authentication?

   a. the process of verifying the precise spelling of a user name

   b. the process of accepting and matching a user name with unique account information, such as a password

   c. the process of replicating user logon information from one domain controller to the others on a network

   d. the process of tracking a user's logon habits and collecting that information in an audit log

2. How does knowing about failed logon attempts help a network administrator's security efforts?

   a. The information could help her determine whether stricter password requirements need to be implemented.

   b. The information could help her refine the NOS schema.

   c. The information could help her determine whether an unauthorized user is attempting to log on with that user name.

   d. The information could help her predict the likelihood of future security breaches.

3. Which of the following tools allows you to view security events that have occurred on a Windows Server 2008 computer?

   a. Event Viewer

   b. Authentication Log

   c. Domain Security Policy

   d. Domain Controller Security Policy

4. In the context of Windows networking, why must failed logon attempts be recorded by a domain controller instead of by any random server on the network?

   a. Only a domain controller will have the resources necessary to record and hold the volume of information that auditing requires.

   b. Domain controllers contain a complete set of Windows Server 2008 computer administrative tools, whereas other servers do not.

   c. Domain controllers typically provide Web and remote access, enabling a network administrator to remotely audit events on a network.

   d. Domain controllers authenticate users.

5. As a network administrator, what should you do if you notice that a user account has experienced multiple failed logon attempts?

   a. Revoke the user's logon privileges.

   b. Change the user's password.

   c. Contact the user to find out whether she is having trouble logging on.

   d. Limit the times of day during which that user account may log on.

Lab 12.2 Checking for Vulnerable Software

Objectives

Software patches can reverse potentially dangerous vulnerabilities on a network. However, network administrators commonly compromise their networks' security by running unpatched software. For instance, in 2003 several worms, including the MSBlast and Sobig. F worms, infected hundreds of thousands of computers even though software patches that could fix the vulnerabilities were available. Many administrators simply did not know that they needed to patch their software.

In this lab, you will run a utility that can determine which service packs or hot fixes you need to apply on a Windows Server 2008 computer.

After completing this lab, you will be able to:

- Scan a Windows Server 2008 computer to identify whether it is operating with vulnerable software

Materials Required

This lab will require the following:

- A computer running Windows Server 2008, Standard Edition with Internet access and with Internet Information Services (IIS) installed
- Microsoft Baseline Security Analyzer 2.1 (currently available from *www.microsoft.com/technet/security/tools/mbsahome.mspx*) installed on the Windows Server 2008 computer
- At least one missing security update for the computer; the missing security update should be minor or the computer should be protected by a firewall
- Access as the Administrator to the Windows Server 2008 computer

Estimated completion time: **30 minutes**

Activity

1. Log on to the Windows Server 2008 computer as the Administrator. The Windows Server 2008 desktop appears.

2. Establish a connection to the Internet.

3. Click **Start**, point to **All Programs**, and click **Microsoft Baseline Security Analyzer 2.1**. The Microsoft Baseline Security Analyzer opens.

4. Click **Scan a computer**. The computer asks you to choose a computer to scan for security vulnerabilities.

5. Make sure that the name of the local computer is selected in the Computer name drop-down box, and that the **Check for Windows administrative vulnerabilities**, **Check for weak passwords**, **Check for IIS administrative vulnerabilities**, and **Check for security updates** check boxes are checked. Uncheck the **Check for SQL administrative vulnerabilities** check box. Click **Start Scan**. The computer downloads security information from Microsoft and

checks for security vulnerabilities. This might take several minutes. The computer then displays the results, as shown in Figure 12-2.

6. At the top of the report is a summary of the security status of the computer. What is the security assessment for your computer?

7. Scroll down to the Security Update Scan Results section. The program displays a red X for any items that present a serious security risk, a green check mark for any items that do not present a security vulnerability, a blue *i* in a white circle for any informational items, a yellow X for any items that should be changed, and a blue star for any items that could be changed. Some types of items might not be present. Which critical security updates, if any, should you install on your computer?

8. Scroll down to the Vulnerabilities section under Windows Scan Results. What is the status of Automatic Updates on your computer? Do any items represent a serious security risk?

9. For one of the items with a red or yellow X, click **Result details**. Internet Explorer opens to a page describing the security problem. Read the page and close Internet Explorer.

10. For the item you selected in the previous step, click **How to correct this**. Internet Explorer opens with instructions to correct the problem. Read the page and close Internet Explorer.

11. Log off the computer.

Figure 12-2 Microsoft Baseline Security Analyzer

Courtesy Course Technology/Cengage Learning

Certification Objectives

Objectives for the Network+ Exam:

- Explain the function of hardware and software security devices: network-based firewall, host-based firewall, IDS, IPS, VPN concentrator
- Explain issues that affect device security: physical security, restricting local and remote access, secure methods vs. unsecure methods, SSH, HTTPS, SNMPv3, SFTP, SCP, TELNET, HTTP, FTP, RSH, RCP, SNMPv1/2

Review Questions

1. Which of the following security risks can potentially be addressed by applying a new patch to a software program?

    a. social engineering

    b. insecure data transmissions between a Web client and Web server

    c. IP spoofing

    d. RF emission over a wireless network

2. Which of the following methods of accessing files over the Internet is the most secure?

    a. HTTP

    b. HTTPS

    c. TFTP

    d. FTP

3. Which of the following types of software can be patched to improve their security? (Choose all that apply.)

    a. router OS

    b. Web browser

    c. e-mail client

    d. database program

    e. workstation OS

4. Which of the following types of transmission media is the most secure?

    a. fiber-optic cable

    b. infrared wireless

    c. shielded twisted-pair cable

    d. coaxial cable

5. Which of the following network enhancements can introduce new security risks? (Choose all that apply.)

    a. adding remote access for users who travel

    b. adding time-of-day restrictions for logons

    c. modifying a tape backup rotation scheme

    d. providing Web access to a server's data files

    e. upgrading the processors on every server

Lab 12.3 Implementing Network Address Restrictions on a Linux Server

Objectives

Most NOSs have some mechanism that ensures that users can only log on from certain Network layer or Data Link layer addresses. The potential advantage to requiring users to log on from only certain machines is that you can prevent them from logging on to the network from any workstation but their own. This can help you keep a closer eye on users, as well as entirely prevent users from accessing certain networks. The disadvantage is that this requires more maintenance. If a user changes machines, you have to reconfigure the network address restrictions.

Additionally, some network devices can restrict access by Network layer or Data Link layer addresses. For instance, some switches allow you to configure ports so that only certain MAC addresses can pass traffic through those ports. If a user attempts to plug another machine with another MAC address into the same port, the switch will not allow it to pass traffic and the computer will be unable to use the network.

On a Linux or UNIX server, the most common mechanism for configuring network address restrictions is the use of TCP wrappers. TCP wrappers are used by a variety of programs to determine whether they should accept network traffic from a particular address. Firewall software such as iptables on Linux is also commonly used.

A careful intruder can circumvent this sort of protection. For instance, an intruder can manually configure both IP addresses and MAC addresses on a computer, or he can attack a computer with packets containing bogus IP addresses. This is often called spoofing. However, good network security policies should make it difficult or impossible to use bogus addresses from outside a network. In this case, an intruder would need to place a machine physically on the network to circumvent address restrictions.

After completing this lab, you will be able to:

- Configure network address restrictions on a Linux server

Materials Required

This lab will require the following:

- A computer running a current version of Fedora Linux named *LINUX1. NETPLUSLAB.NET*, configured with the firewall disabled, with SELinux disabled, and with the GNOME Desktop Environment

- *LINUX1.NETPLUSLAB.NET* configured with an IP address of 192.168.54.5 and a subnet mask of 255.255.255.0

- The default /etc/samba/smb.conf file in place

- A user named netplus on *LINUX1.NETPLUSLAB.NET* with a known password and a known password for the root account

- A computer running Windows XP Professional or Vista named *WORKSTATION1,* configured with an IP address of 192.168.54.3 and a subnet mask of 255.255.255.0

- Cygwin 1.7.x (available at *www.cygwin.com*) installed on *WORKSTATION1*, with the openssh and openssl packages in the Net category installed in addition to the default packages

- Access to *WORKSTATION1* as an administrator

- Both computers connected to a hub with straight-through Cat 5 (or better) UTP cables

Estimated completion time: 35 minutes

Activity

1. Log on to *LINUX1.NETPLUSLAB.NET* as the netplus user. The Fedora desktop appears.

2. Open a terminal window. The netplus@LINUX1:~ prompt appears.

3. Type **su -** and press **Enter**. The Password prompt appears.

4. Enter the password for the root account and press **Enter**. The prompt ends in a pound sign (#), indicating that you are logged on as the root user.

5. Type **echo "sshd: ALL" >>/etc/hosts.deny** and press **Enter**. The computer appends the text "sshd: ALL" to the file /etc/hosts.deny. This tells TCP wrappers to prohibit computers from any IP address from logging on to *LINUX1.NETPLUSLAB.NET*.

6. Type **cat /var/run/sshd.pid** and press **Enter**. The computer displays the PID for the running sshd daemon. Record this number.

7. Type **kill -HUP** followed by the PID number you recorded in Step 6, and then press **Enter**. The computer restarts the sshd daemon.

8. Log on to *WORKSTATION1* as an administrator. The Windows desktop appears.

9. Click **Start**, point to **All Programs**, point to **Cygwin**, and click **Cygwin Bash Shell**. A terminal window opens.

10. In the terminal window, type **ssh netplus@192.168.54.5** and press **Enter**. As shown in Figure 12-3, the computer displays the error message "ssh_ exchange_identification: Connection closed by remote host."

Figure 12-3   An SSH login prevented by TCP wrappers

Courtesy Course Technology/Cengage Learning

11. Now you will configure *LINUX1.NETPLUSLAB.NET* to accept SSH connections from *WORKSTATION1*. In the terminal window on *LINUX1.NETPLUSLAB.NET*, type `echo "sshd: 192.168.54.3" >>/etc/hosts.allow` and press **Enter**. The computer appends the text "sshd: 192.168.54.3" to the end of the file /etc/hosts.allow.

12. Repeat Steps 6 and 7 to restart the sshd daemon.

13. In the terminal window on *WORKSTATION1*, type `ssh netplus@192.168.54.5` and press **Enter**. If a message appears indicating that the authenticity of the connection cannot be confirmed, type **yes** and press **Enter**. The netplus@192.168.54.5's password: prompt appears.

14. Type the password for the netplus account and press **Enter**. The prompt changes, indicating that you have logged on to the remote server.

15. Log off both computers.

Certification Objectives

Objectives for the Network+ Exam:

- Explain the methods of network access security: *Filtering*: ACL, MAC filtering, IP filtering, tunneling and encryption, SSL VPN, VPN, L2TP, PPTP, IPSEC, remote access, RAS, RDP, PPPoE, PPP, VNC, ICA

Review Questions

1. Which of the following is a potential weakness in using restrictions on either Network layer addresses or Data Link layer addresses to control access to a network or server?

    a. For a machine on the same network, both Network and Data Link layer addresses may be configured manually.

    b. For a machine on an external network, both Network and Data Link layer addresses may be configured manually.

    c. Network address restrictions typically require more maintenance.

    d. Network layer addresses may be configured manually, whereas Data Link layer addresses may not.

2. Which files on a Linux server are used to configure TCP wrappers? (Choose all that apply.)

    a. /etc/hosts

    b. /etc/hosts.allow

    c. /etc/hosts.deny

    d. /etc/tcpwrappers

3. Which of the following network security methods provides the greatest resistance to unauthorized external file access on a server?

    a. a central computer room that is accessible only to authorized personnel through hand scanning

    b. an NOS that is configured to allow logons only during the hours of 8:00 a.m. to 5:00 p.m.

   c. an NOS that requires users' computers to have an address that matches one belonging to their LAN segment to log on to the server

   d. a proxy server that disguises transmissions issued from clients on a private LAN

4. What is the best defense against social engineering?

   a. a strong security policy and educating users

   b. employing Kerberos authentication for all users

   c. configuring a firewall to accept transmissions only from certain IP addresses

   d. limiting the ports on a server through which client communication may take place

5. In which of the following situations would it be most beneficial for a network administrator to employ network address restrictions on a TCP/IP-based network (that does not use DHCP) to improve security?

   a. A salesperson accesses a company's network via a dial-up connection to upload sales data every night.

   b. A corporate executive frequently travels to a company's various locations and requires access to confidential information on the server.

   c. A new employee is working on tutorials in temporary quarters until her office can be completely furnished.

   d. A contractor works on a project from a cubicle specially designated and furnished for use by consultants.

Lab 12.4 Plaintext Versus Encrypted Protocols

Objectives

Most of the older communications programs still in use, such as FTP or Telnet, use plaintext. Using such a program to administer a server or a network device can make it easy for an intruder to steal account information using a protocol analyzer.

In this lab, you will use a protocol analyzer to examine the dangers of using plaintext protocols. An administrator who carelessly uses a plaintext protocol such as FTP or Telnet to manage a server might compromise its security. An intruder with a protocol analyzer can easily find the password and use it to log on to the server. Once intruders have compromised a server, they often install a protocol analyzer to find account names and passwords, which they can use to compromise other servers. Use of encrypted protocols such as SSH instead of FTP or Telnet makes compromise of account information more difficult.

It is important to keep in mind that, although a protocol analyzer is an important and valuable tool for network administrators, using a protocol analyzer to obtain the passwords of users or to eavesdrop on their communications without their consent is unethical and illegal. In addition, you should always have clear and specific consent before using a protocol analyzer. This is especially true on a network that is not yours, such as a customer network. On networks that you manage, you should determine whether use of a protocol analyzer is permissible before using one. In some high-security environments, such as a financial or military institution, you might be prohibited from using a protocol analyzer at all. In other environments, you should make sure that you have explicit permission to use a protocol analyzer when necessary.

After completing this lab, you will be able to:

- Describe the difference between encrypted and unencrypted network protocols

Materials Required

This lab will require the following:

- A computer running Windows Server 2008, Standard Edition named *SERVER1,* configured with an IP address of 192.168.54.1 and a subnet mask of 255.255.255.0
- IIS and the File Transfer Protocol (FTP) Publishing Service installed and running on *SERVER1*
- A computer running Windows Server 2008, Standard Edition named *SERVER2,* configured with an IP address of 192.168.54.2 and a subnet mask of 255.255.255.0
- The Wireshark protocol analyzer (available from *www.wireshark.org*) and, if necessary, the WinPcap packet capture library (available from *winpcap.polito.it*) installed on *SERVER2*
- Access to *SERVER1* and *SERVER2* as the Administrator
- A computer running a current version of Fedora Linux *LINUX1.NETPLUSLAB. NET,* configured with the firewall disabled, with SELinux disabled, and with the GNOME Desktop Environment
- *LINUX1.NETPLUSLAB.NET,* configured with an IP address of 192.168.54.5 and a subnet mask of 255.255.255.0
- A computer running Windows XP Professional or Vista named *WORKSTATION1,* configured with an IP address of 192.168.54.3 and a subnet mask of 255.255.255.0
- A user named netplus on *LINUX1.NETPLUSLAB.NET* with a known password and a known password for the root account
- Cygwin 1.5.x (available at *www.cygwin.com*) installed on *WORKSTATION1*, with the openssh and openssl packages in the Net category installed in addition to the default packages
- Access to the Windows XP computer as the netplus user
- All four computers connected to a hub with straight-through Cat 5 (or better) UTP cables

Estimated completion time: **30 minutes**

Activity

1. Log on to *SERVER1* as the Administrator. The Windows Server 2008 desktop appears.

2. Click **Start**, point to **Administrative Tools**, and then click **Internet Information Services (IIS) 6.0 Manager**. The Internet Information Services (IIS) Manager window opens.

3. If necessary, click the **plus sign (+)** next to *SERVER1* (local computer) to expand the tree in the left pane. In the left pane, right-click **FTP Sites**. On the shortcut menu, click **Properties**. The FTP Sites Properties dialog box opens.

4. Click the **Security Accounts** tab. Options appear for configuring access to the FTP sites on *SERVER1*.

5. If necessary, click the **Allow anonymous connections** check box to remove the check. The IIS Manager dialog box might open, indicating that the option you have selected will result in the transmission of clear text passwords over the network.

6. If necessary, click **Yes** to close the IIS Manager dialog box. Click **OK** to close the FTP Sites Properties dialog box.

7. In the left pane, right-click **SERVER1 (local computer)**. On the shortcut menu, point to **All Tasks** and then click **Restart IIS**. The Stop/Start/Restart dialog box opens.

8. Make sure that **Restart Internet Services on SERVER1** is selected and click **OK**. A dialog box opens, indicating that Internet services are being shut down, and after a short wait, the Stop/Start/Restart dialog box closes.

9. Log on to *SERVER2* as the Administrator. The Windows Server 2008 desktop appears.

10. Click **Start**, point to **All Programs**, and click **Wireshark**. The Wireshark Network Analyzer window opens.

11. On the menu bar, click **Capture**, click **Interfaces**, and then click the **Options** button that corresponds to your network adapter. The Wireshark: Capture Options window opens.

12. In the Capture Filter text box, enter **host 192.168.54.3**. This configures Wireshark to capture only packets being sent from or to IP address 192.168.54.3. Click **Start**. Wireshark begins to capture any packets sent to or from 192.168.54.3.

13. Log on to *WORKSTATION1* as an administrator. The Windows desktop appears.

14. Click **Start**, point to **All Programs**, point to **Accessories**, and then click **Command Prompt**. A command prompt window opens.

15. Type **ftp 192.168.54.1** and press **Enter**. The FTP program prompts for the user name.

16. Type **netplus** and press **Enter**. The FTP program displays the Password prompt.

17. Type the password for the netplus account. The FTP program indicates that the netplus user has logged on.

18. Type **dir**. The computer displays any files that might be present in the root directory of the FTP server.

19. Type **quit** to exit the FTP program.

20. On *SERVER2*, click **Stop** in the Wireshark dialog box. Wireshark displays the captured packets.

21. In the Filter text box, type **ftp** and press **Enter**. The computer displays only those packets that have FTP in the Protocol field.

22. In the top pane, click the first packet. In the middle pane, click the **arrow** next to File Transfer Protocol (FTP). Detailed information about the FTP portion of the packet appears. (You might need to scroll down to see it all.) Click any **arrow** signs you see beneath File Transfer Protocol (FTP) so that more information appears beneath them.

23. In the top frame, click the first packet again. Using the ↓ key, scroll down through the list of packets. Look for a packet containing the text "Request: PASS" and a password. Figure 12-4 shows this packet. Does this password match the password you typed in Step 17?

24. Scroll through the remaining packets. Do you see everything that you typed when you were logged on to the FTP server?

25. Now you will use a protocol analyzer to view an encrypted SFTP session. In the Wireshark window on *SERVER2*, click **Capture** and then click **Start**. The Wireshark dialog box opens, asking if you would like to save the capture file.

26. Click **Continue without Saving**. The Wireshark: Capture Options dialog box opens. Notice that the Capture Filter text box still contains the text "host 192.168.54.3".

27. Click **OK**. Wireshark begins capturing packets again.

28. On *WORKSTATION1*, click **Start**, point to **All Programs**, point to **Cygwin**, and then click **Cygwin Bash Shell**. A terminal window named ~ opens.

29. Type **sftp netplus@192.168.54.5** and press **Enter**. The computer might indicate that the authenticity of the host cannot be established and ask if you would like to continue connecting. If so, type **yes**. The computer prompts for the netplus user's password.

30. Type the password for the netplus user account on *LINUX1.NETPLUSLAB.NET* and press **Enter**. The computer displays the sftp> prompt.

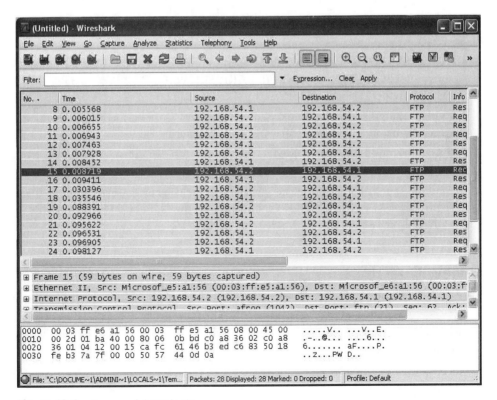

Figure 12-4   A successful FTP login

Courtesy Course Technology/Cengage Learning

31. Type **dir**. The computer displays the names of any files in the home directory of the netplus user on *LINUX1.NETPLUSLAB.NET*.

32. Type **quit**. The computer closes the SFTP connection.

33. On *SERVER2*, click **Stop** in the Wireshark dialog box. Wireshark displays the captured packets.

34. In the Filter text box, type **ssh** and press **Enter**. The computer displays only those packets that have SSHv2 in the Protocol field. (You type "ssh" instead of "sftp" in the Filter text box because the SFTP program uses the SSH protocol.)

35. In the top pane, click the first packet. In the middle pane, click the **arrow** next to SSH Protocol. Detailed information about the SSH portion of the packet appears. (You might need to scroll down to see it all.) Click any **arrow** signs you see beneath SSH Protocol so that more information appears beneath them.

36. In the top frame, click the first packet again. Using the ↓ key, scroll down through the list of packets. As you scroll through the packets, click any **arrow** signs you see beneath SSH Protocol. Do you see any of the text you typed when connected to *LINUX1. NETPLUSLAB.NET*?

37. Log off all the computers.

Certification Objectives

Objectives for the Network+ Exam:

- Explain the function of common networking protocols: TCP, FTP, UDP, TCP/IP suite, DHCP, TFTP, DNS, HTTP(S), ARP, SIP (VoIP), RTP (VoIP), SSH, POP3, NTP, IMAP4, Telnet, SMTP, SNMP2/3, ICMP, IGMP, TLS

- Explain the purpose of network scanners: packet sniffers, intrusion detection software, intrusion prevention software, port scanners

- Explain the function of hardware and software security devices: network-based firewall, host-based firewall, IDS, IPS, VPN concentrator

- Explain issues that affect device security: physical security, restricting local and remote access, secure methods vs. unsecure methods, SSH, HTTPS, SNMPv3, SFTP, SCP, TELNET, HTTP, FTP, RSH, RCP, SNMPv1/2

Review Questions

1. True or False? Encrypted protocols such as SSH do not send passwords over the network.

2. In which of the following situations would it be most beneficial for a network administrator to restrict the time of day during which the users can log on to the network to improve security?

   a. A salesperson accesses a company's network via a dial-up connection to upload sales data every night.

   b. Groups of customer service representatives access customer financial data during regular business hours.

    c. A corporate executive frequently travels to a company's various locations and requires access to confidential information on the server.

    d. A group of engineers is establishing an international office in a country several time zones away from the server's location.

3. The practice of falsifying an IP address is known as _____

    a. spoofing

    b. faking

    c. impersonating

    d. configuring a secondary IP address

4. Which of the following encryption methods is commonly used to secure transmissions over virtual private networks (VPNs)?

    a. Kerberos

    b. RAS

    c. PGP

    d. IPSec

5. If someone floods your gateway with so much traffic that it cannot respond to or accept valid traffic, what type of security breach has she caused?

    a. IP spoofing

    b. social engineering

    c. denial of service

    d. Trojan horse

Lab 12.5 Securing a Wireless Network

12

Objectives

Wireless routers are often used to connect a laptop to a small peer-to-peer or home network. Without adequate security, a wireless router can leave your network open to a wide range of threats. In this lab, you will learn how to implement some of the more common security features often found on wireless routers.

After completing this lab, you will be able to:

- Secure a wireless router

Materials Required

This lab will require the following:

- A computer (ideally a laptop) running Windows XP Professional or Vista with a wireless network card

- An unconfigured wireless router with the included setup CD or user's manual

Estimated completion time: **30 minutes**

Activity

1. Begin by installing an unsecured wireless router (see Lab 8.3).

2. Most wireless routers can be configured through a Web browser. Use a browser to open your router's configuration program; typically, this is done by accessing the router's configuration page at, for example, http://192.168.1.1.

3. Although configuration programs can vary from router to router, they are usually menu driven and fairly easy to navigate. Use the router's configuration pages to implement the following changes. When in doubt, consult the documentation included with the router.

4. Begin by updating the router's firmware either through the configuration program or from the manufacturer's Web site. This will help address any known security flaws with the router.

5. Set a strong password for the router itself. The default passwords for all common router models are available on the Internet; for example, the default password of many Linksys routers is "admin". With this information, an attacker can easily access the router's configuration program and disable any security features.

6. Change the name of the wireless network, or SSID (service set identifier), from the default name. The default SSID on most Linksys routers is "linksys".

7. Turn off SSID broadcasting so your network does not show up in a list of available networks. This will not stop determined attackers, but it will prevent the network from appearing as available to casual wireless users in your area.

8. Disable remote administration so your router can only be configured by a computer that is physically attached.

9. Enable some form of encryption such as WEP, WPA, or WPA2. WPA and especially WPA2 are strongly preferred because WEP encryption can be easily broken by knowledgeable attackers. However, using WEP encryption is preferable to using no encryption at all.

10. Use MAC filtering to create a list of computers that are allowed access to the network. This too will prevent casual users from accessing your network, but can be overcome by an advanced user employing a wireless sniffer.

11. Now connect to the router with your wireless computer and test your wireless connection by opening your browser and navigating to a site on the Internet.

12. When you're finished, reset the router to its factory defaults and log off your computer.

Certification Objectives

Objectives for the Network+ Exam:

- Compare the characteristics of wireless communication standards: *802.11 a/b/g/n*: speeds, distance, channels, frequency; *Authentication and encryption*: WPA, WEP, RADIUS, TKIP

- Given a scenario, troubleshoot common connectivity issues and select an appropriate solution: *Physical issues*: cross talk, nearing crosstalk, near end crosstalk, attenuation, collisions, shorts, open impedance mismatch (echo), interference; *Logical issues*:

port speed, port duplex mismatch, incorrect VLAN, incorrect IP address, wrong gateway, wrong DNS, wrong subnet mask; *Issues that should be identified but escalated*: switching loop, routing loop, route problems, proxy arp, broadcast storms; *Wireless issues*: interference (bleed, environmental factors), incorrect encryption, incorrect channel, incorrect frequency, ESSID mismatch, standard mismatch (802.11 a/b/g/n), distance, bounce, incorrect antenna placement

- Explain the methods of network access security: *Filtering*: ACL, MAC filtering, IP filtering, tunneling and encryption, SSL VPN, VPN, L2TP, PPTP, IPSEC, remote access, RAS, RDP, PPPoE, PPP, VNC, ICA

- Identify common security threats and mitigation techniques: *Security threats*: DoS, viruses, worms, attackers, man in the middle, smurf, rogue access points, social engineering (phishing); *Mitigation techniques*: policies and procedures, user training, patches and updates

Review Questions

1. What does SSID stand for?

   a. service set identifier

   b. security service Internet domain

   c. security station identification

   d. simple security Internet device

2. WEP, WPA, and WPA2 are all forms of wireless _____.

   a. access

   b. routers

   c. services

   d. encryption

3. You can limit access to certain computers with:

   a. encryption

   b. MAC filtering

   c. remote administration

   d. using a strong password

CHAPTER THIRTEEN

TROUBLESHOOTING NETWORK PROBLEMS

Labs included in this chapter

- Lab 13.1 Using the Ping Utility to Troubleshoot a TCP/IP Network
- Lab 13.2 Using the Traceroute Utility to Troubleshoot a TCP/IP Network
- Lab 13.3 Troubleshooting Client Logon Problems
- Lab 13.4 Troubleshooting Web Client Problems

Net+ Exam Objectives

Objective	Lab
Given a scenario, implement a network troubleshooting methodology	13.3, 13.4
Given a scenario, troubleshoot common connectivity issues and select an appropriate solution	13.4
Given a scenario, select the appropriate command-line interface tool and interpret the output to verify functionality	13.1, 13.2

Lab 13.1 Using the Ping Utility to Troubleshoot a TCP/IP Network

Objectives

The Ping utility (also known as the Ping command) is one of the basic tools used to check network connectivity in a TCP/IP network. Every operating system that supports TCP/IP also supports the Ping utility.

The Ping command works by sending an ICMP message to the target asking for a reply. If the message reaches the target, it sends an ICMP reply. This indicates that you have network connectivity between the computer where you used the Ping command and the computer you are trying to reach. Keep in mind, however, that the Ping utility does not tell you anything about network services running on the remote computer, nor does the Ping utility tell you anything about the type or number of hops that the ICMP messages took to reach a host.

When you use the Ping command to troubleshoot a connectivity problem, you should first verify that TCP/IP is working properly by pinging the loopback address (127.0.0.1) and the computer's own IP address. Then, you should ping each stop along the way to the remote host that you cannot reach to verify that you can reach each stop. For instance, if you cannot ping a router along the way to a remote host, this might indicate that the router is down and might explain why you cannot reach the remote host. (Note that some routers might block ICMP packets and prevent the Ping utility from working properly.)

After completing this lab, you will be able to:

- Use the Ping command to determine the source of problems in a TCP/IP network
- Isolate a problem by following a logical methodology

Materials Required

This lab will require the following:

- A computer running Windows Server 2008, Standard Edition named *SERVER1* with two NICs
- One NIC configured with an IP address of 192.168.54.1 and a subnet mask of 255.255.255.0, and the other NIC configured with an IP address of 172.16.1.1 and a subnet mask of 255.255.255.0
- Routing and Remote Access configured on *SERVER1* so that it acts as a router
- A hub named *HUB1* connected (with a straight-through Cat 5 or better UTP cable) to the NIC on *SERVER1* that was configured with an IP address of 192.168.54.1
- A hub named *HUB2* connected (with a straight-through Cat 5 or better UTP cable) to the NIC on *SERVER1* that was configured with an IP address of 172.16.1.1
- A computer running Windows XP Professional or Vista named *WORKSTATION1*, configured with an IP address of 192.168.54.2 and a subnet mask of 255.255.255.0, connected to *HUB1* with a straight-through Cat 5 (or better) UTP cable

- A computer running Windows XP Professional or Vista named *WORKSTATION2*, configured with an IP address of 172.16.1.2 and a subnet mask of 255.255.255.0, connected to *HUB2* with a straight-through Cat 5 (or better) UTP cable

- Administrative access to all three computers

Estimated completion time: **45 minutes**

Activity

1. Review the layout and IP addresses of the network in Figure 13-1.

2. Now you can determine if *WORKSTATION2* (which has an IP address of 172.16.1.2) is up and running. Review the following problem-isolation methodology. (Do not perform the steps yet; simply review them so that you have an overall view of how you will troubleshoot the network.)

- Log on to the *WORKSTATION1* computer. Ping the local computer's loopback address, 127.0.0.1, to ensure that TCP/IP is installed.

- Ping the local computer's IP address to ensure that the local computer's NIC is addressed and functioning properly.

- Ping the near side of the router to ensure that the connection between 192.168.54.2 and 192.168.54.1 is operating properly. The term *near side* refers to the router's NIC with an IP address on the same network as the local computer.

- Ping the far side of the router to ensure that the connection through the router is operating properly; specifically, this test ensures that the connection between 192.168.54.2 and 172.16.1.1 is functional. The term *far side* refers to the router's NIC that is on the path to a destination host with an IP address on a different network than the local computer.

- Ping a computer on the network segment on the far side of the router; in this situation, the computer on the far side of the router is the *WORKSTATION2* computer. This ensures connectivity all the way from *WORKSTATION1* at 192.168.54.2 to *WORKSTATION2* at 172.16.1.2.

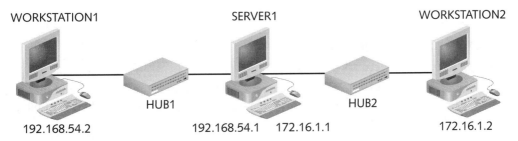

Figure 13-1   Network layout of Lab 13.1

Courtesy Course Technology/Cengage Learning

The following steps walk you through the procedure outlined in Step 2. For each ping test, the Ping command issues a message indicating either success or failure. If the Ping command returns an error at any step, you can assume that the problem lies with the connection at the particular step that produced the error.

3. Log on to *WORKSTATION1* as an administrator. The Windows desktop appears.

4. Click **Start**, point to **All Programs**, point to **Accessories**, and then click **Command Prompt**. (In Windows Vista, click **Start**, type **cmd** in the Start Search text box, and then press **Enter**.) A command prompt window opens.

5. To determine if the local computer's NIC is operating correctly, type **ping 127.0.0.1** and then press **Enter**. Was the Ping command successful?

6. To determine if TCP/IP is operating properly, type **ping 192.168.54.2** and then press **Enter**. Was the Ping command successful?

7. To determine if the connection to the near side of the router is operating properly, type **ping 192.168.54.1** and then press **Enter**. Was the Ping command successful?

8. To determine if the router is operating properly, type **ping 172.16.1.1** and then press **Enter**. Was the Ping command successful?

9. To determine if a computer on the network segment on the far side of the router is operating properly, type **ping 172.16.1.2** and then press **Enter**. Was the Ping command successful?

10. Cover the link lights on each hub with a piece of paper or another obstruction. If the link lights on each computer's NICs are visible, place a box or another obstruction in front of each NIC.

11. Have your instructor or lab partner unplug one of the cables from one of the NICs in the back of the router. This should be done so that you cannot identify which cable has been removed.

12. Without looking at the link lights on the NICs or the hubs, repeat Steps 7 through 9. Record the step that failed, and record the cable you think failed.

13. Remove the obstructions added in Step 10 and examine the link lights on the hubs and on the NICs. Which cable was unplugged?

14. Plug in the cable that was unplugged in Step 11.

15. If you have a lab partner, repeat Steps 10 through 14 with your lab partner.

16. Log off *WORKSTATION1*.

Certification Objectives

Objectives for the Network+ Exam:

- Given a scenario, select the appropriate command-line interface tool and interpret the output to verify functionality: Traceroute, Ipconfig, Ifconfig, Ping, Arp ping, Arp, Nslookup, Hostname, Dig, Mtr, Route, Nbtstat, Netstat

Review Questions

1. What would you ping to determine whether TCP/IP was functioning properly on your computer?

    a. the gateway address

    b. the near side of the router

    c. the loopback address

    d. the far side of the router

2. Which of the following responses to a Ping command issued on a Windows-based computer indicates that the ping test was successful?

    a. Packets: Sent = 4, Received = 4, Lost = 0 (0%)

    b. Packets: Sent = 0, Received = 0, Lost = 0 (0%)

    c. Packets: Sent = 0, Received = 0, Lost = 4 (100%)

    d. Packets: Sent = 4, Received = 4, Lost = 4 (100%)

3. When you issue a Ping command, what Application layer protocol sends a message to the destination host?

    a. ARP

    b. RARP

    c. SNMP

    d. ICMP

4. Suppose you were troubleshooting a network connectivity problem between a workstation on a private LAN and a server on the Internet. As part of a logical troubleshooting methodology, what address would you ping after determining that the TCP/IP stack on the workstation was functioning properly?

    a. the workstation's loopback address

    b. the workstation's default gateway

    c. the private LAN's Internet name server

    d. the Internet server you're trying to reach

5. In the scenario described in Question 4, as part of a logical troubleshooting methodology, what address would you ping second?

    a. the workstation's loopback address

    b. the workstation's default gateway

    c. the private LAN's Internet name server

    d. the Internet server

6. Which of the following is the loopback address in IP version 4 addressing?

    a. 127.0.0.1

    b. 1.1.1.1

    c. 127.0.0.0

    d. 10.0.0.0

7. What type of message would you receive if you were trying to ping *www.comptia.org* from a Windows XP computer and misspelled the host's name as *wwv.comptia.org* in the Ping command syntax?

a. Host wwv.comptia.org not responding

b. Ping request could not find host wwv.comptia.org. Please check the name and try again.

c. Reply from wwv.comptia.org: bytes= 0

d. Unknown host wwv.comptia.org

Lab 13.2 Using the Traceroute Utility to Troubleshoot a TCP/IP Network

Objectives

Another useful troubleshooting command in a TCP/IP network is the Traceroute command. The Traceroute command traces the path a packet travels as it goes over the network from a source to a destination node. This is particularly useful on large networks (including the Internet), as it can indicate at which hop along the route between two computers a problem exists. In smaller networks where you already know the network path, you can use the Ping command instead. Note that on the Internet, firewalls and packet filtering can restrict the usefulness of the Traceroute command (as well as the Ping command).

On Windows machines, the Traceroute command is known as Tracert. Both the Traceroute command and the Tracert command begin by sending a packet to the destination host with a TTL (Time to Live) value of one. When the packet reaches the first router along the way, the TTL expires and the router sends an ICMP message back to the computer running the command. The command uses this ICMP message to identify the first router along the path. The computer increases the TTL value by one and sends another packet to the destination host. When the packet reaches the next router, the TTL expires and the next router sends an ICMP message. The command continues to increase the TTL value until it either reaches the destination or until a maximum number of routers have been tested (usually 30 by default). Although each program uses the same basic technique, the implementation varies slightly. The UNIX Traceroute command sends UDP packets as test packets, whereas the Windows Tracert command sends ICMP packets.

After completing this lab, you will be able to:

- Use the Traceroute and Tracert commands to trace the path to a destination
- Interpret both successful and unsuccessful Traceroute responses

Materials Required

This lab will require the following:

- The lab setup built for Lab 13.1
- A computer running a current version of Fedora Linux named *LINUX1. NETPLUSLAB.NET*, configured with the firewall disabled, and with the GNOME Desktop Environment
- *LINUX1.NETPLUSLAB.NET*, configured with an IP address of 192.168.54.5 and a subnet mask of 255.255.255.0, connected to *HUB1* with a straight-through Cat 5 (or better) UTP cable

- Access to *LINUX1.NETPLUSLAB.NET* as the netplus user
- A computer running Windows XP Professional, Windows Vista, or Windows Server 2008 that is connected to the Internet

Estimated completion time: **35 minutes**

Activity

1. Log on to *WORKSTATION1* as an administrator. The Windows desktop appears.

2. Click **Start**, point to **All Programs**, point to **Accessories**, and then click **Command Prompt**. (In Windows Vista, click **Start**, type **cmd** in the Start Search text box, and then press **Enter**.) A command prompt window opens.

3. At the command prompt, type **tracert 172.16.1.2** and press **Enter.** The Tracert command traces the path from *WORKSTATION1* to *WORKSTATION2*, showing the number of each hop, three round-trip response times, and the name or IP address for each hop. (Note that you can also use a domain name, such as microsoft.com.) Figure 13-2 shows an example of the output of the Tracert command.

4. Remove the cable from the NIC attached to *WORKSTATION2*.

5. Type **tracert 172.16.1.2** and press **Enter**. Instead of recording two hops and stopping, the Tracert command continues. However, after the first hop, the response times are replaced by asterisks and the IP address is replaced by "Request timed out." This indicates that the Tracert command could not determine the path to the destination address after the first hop.

6. Replace the cable you removed from *WORKSTATION2* in Step 4.

7. Remove the cable from the NIC on *SERVER1* attached to *HUB1*.

8. Repeat Step 3. This time, the Tracert command exits with the message "Destination host unreachable."

9. Replace the cable you removed in Step 7.

Figure 13-2 Output of the Tracert command

Courtesy Course Technology/Cengage Learning

10. Log on to *LINUX1.NETPLUSLAB.NET* as the netplus user. The Fedora desktop appears.

11. Open a terminal window. Type **traceroute 172.16.1.2** and press **Enter**. The Traceroute command traces the path to *WORKSTATION2,* showing the number of each hop, three response times, and the name or IP address for each hop.

12. Remove the cable from the NIC attached to *WORKSTATION2.*

13. Repeat Step 11. How do the results differ from those in Step 11?

14. Replace the cable you removed in Step 12, and log off both computers.

15. On the Windows XP Professional, Windows Vista, or Windows Server 2008 computer connected to the Internet, repeat Steps 1 through 3. However, substitute the name of a Web site such as *www.cisco.com* or *www.google.com* for the IP address in Step 3. Note that firewalls and other security measures between this computer and the Web site, as well as the security configuration of the Web site itself, might prevent the Tracert command from working as expected. Repeat with several different Web sites.

Certification Objectives

Objectives for the Network+ Exam:

- Given a scenario, select the appropriate command-line interface tool and interpret the output to verify functionality: Traceroute, Ipconfig, Ifconfig, Ping, Arp ping, Arp, Nslookup, Hostname, Dig, Mtr, Route, Nbtstat, Netstat

Review Questions

1. Which of the following commands can reveal the number of hops a packet takes between a source and target node?

   a. ipconfig

   b. ping

   c. tracert

   d. ifconfig

2. Which of the following commands can indicate whether a host is unreachable?

   a. ping

   b. ipconfig

   c. ifconfig

   d. winipcfg

3. Which of the following commands would you use to determine the relative location of network congestion between your Windows workstation and an Internet host?

   a. netstat

   b. nbtstat

   c. tracert

   d. ipconfig

4. If you attempted the Tracert command on an Internet host and that host was not connected to the network, which of the following would the Tracert command's response contain?

   a. Destination host unreachable

   b. Unknown host

   c. Host not responding

   d. Request timed out

5. What does a hop represent in the context of a Traceroute command?

   a. an Internet client

   b. a modem, hub, switch, or router

   c. a router

   d. a carrier's POP

Lab 13.3 Troubleshooting Client Logon Problems

Objectives

In this lab, you will troubleshoot a scenario in which a user cannot log on to the server. From a user's perspective, when he cannot log on to the server, the network is unavailable, no matter what the reason. However, the ultimate cause of the problem might be anything from a hardware failure on the server to an expired password.

When troubleshooting problems, you should attempt to be as methodical as possible. You can start by determining the scope of the problem. Is only one user affected, or are all users affected? Then determine if the user's computer (or the users' computers, if multiple users are affected) and the server have physical connectivity. Do all the NICs seem to be working properly? Is the hub or switch functioning and is the network cabled properly? After establishing that physical connectivity is not the problem, determine whether the user's computer has network connectivity. Can you ping the server from the user's computer? After you have determined that network connectivity is not the problem, try to determine if the application is functioning properly.

Keep in mind that being able to log on to a computer does not necessarily indicate that the network is functioning properly. Windows computers cache passwords for user names, so that a user can still log on to a computer during a network outage.

In this lab, you will first verify that the network, the client computers, and the server are all functioning properly by logging on to two client computers. Then your instructor or another set of lab partners will do something to prevent at least one of the computers from logging on to the server. Your assignment will be to identify and solve the problem.

After completing this lab, you will be able to:

- Follow a logical troubleshooting methodology to determine the nature of client connectivity problems

- Identify a network problem by interpreting the results of diagnostic utilities such as Ping and Ipconfig

Materials Required

This lab will require the following:

- A computer named *SERVER1* running Windows Server 2008, Standard Edition, configured as a domain controller for the netpluslab.net domain, with an IP address of 192.168.54.1 and a subnet mask of 255.255.255.0

- The DHCP server running on *SERVER1* and configured to assign DHCP addresses in the range from 192.168.54.50 to 192.168.54.100, with a subnet mask of 255.255.255.0

- Access as the Administrator to the netpluslab.net domain and user accounts named client1 and client2 in the Domain Users group

- A shared folder named NETPLUS on *SERVER1*, configured so that the users in the Domain Users group have full control over the shared folder on the network

- Two computers running Windows XP Professional or Vista named *WORKSTATION1* and *WORKSTATION2*, each configured to receive DHCP addresses

- Both *WORKSTATION1* and *WORKSTATION2* configured as members of the netpluslab.net domain

- All three computers configured to use *SERVER1* as their DNS server

- No network protocols besides TCP/IP configured on any of the computers

- Each computer connected to a hub with straight-through Cat 5 (or better) UTP cables, as shown in Figure 13-3

- A faulty straight-through cable that is the same color of at least one of the working Cat 5 (or better) cables; a crossover cable may be substituted

- An instructor or classmate assigned to cause a problem in the network

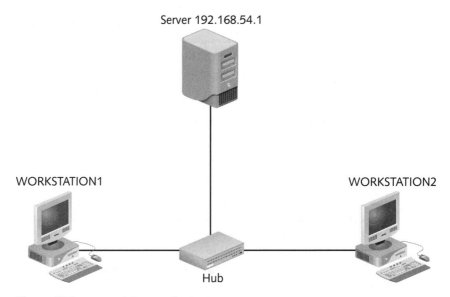

Figure 13-3   Network layout of Lab 13.3

Courtesy Course Technology/Cengage Learning

Estimated completion time: **60–90 minutes**

Activity

1. Log on to *WORKSTATION1* as client1. The Windows desktop appears.

2. Click **Start**, and then click **My Computer** (**Computer** in Windows Vista). The My Computer window opens.

3. Click **Tools** on the menu bar, and then click **Map Network Drive**. (In Windows Vista, click **Map network drive** on the toolbar.) The Map Network Drive dialog box opens.

4. Accept the default setting for the Drive drop-down menu, Z:. In the Folder text box, type **\\192.168.54.1\netplus** and click **Finish**. The computer maps the NETPLUS shared folder.

5. Return to My Computer or Computer. The netplus on '192.168.54.1' (Z:) icon now appears below the heading "Network Drives." (In Windows Vista, the netplus (\\server1) icon appears in the Network Location section.)

6. Repeat Steps 1 through 5 on *WORKSTATION2*, logging on as the client2 user. You have now verified that you can log on to *SERVER1* with both client computers.

7. Leave the room while your instructor or classmate causes a network problem by performing one of the actions listed in Table 13-1. After performing one of the actions, your instructor or classmate should log off all three computers.

8. When you return to the room, reboot both client computers.

9. Attempt to repeat Steps 1 through 5 on *WORKSTATION1*. You should be unable to browse to the NETPLUS folder. Attempt to solve the problem using the following steps. If you identify the problem before completing all the steps, proceed to Step 16.

Table 13-1: Possible actions to be performed by a classmate or instructor

Action	Instruction
Install faulty cable on *WORKSTATION1*	Replace the network cable connecting *WORKSTATION1* to the hub with the faulty network cable.
Install faulty cable on server	Replace the network cable connecting the Windows Server 2008 computer to the hub with the faulty network cable.
Disrupt cable connection	Pull the cable far enough out of *WORKSTATION1*'s NIC so that the link light turns off but not so far that it falls completely out of the NIC.
Reconfigure the IP address on *WORKSTATION1*	a. Log off *WORKSTATION1*, and then log back on as an administrator. The Windows desktop appears.
	b. Open the Network Connections window.
	c. Right-click **Local Area Connection** and click **Properties**. The Local Area Connection Properties window opens.

(Continued)

Table 13-1: **Possible actions to be performed by a classmate or instructor (*Continued*)**

Action	Instruction
	d. Double-click **Internet Protocol (TCP/IP)**. (In Windows Vista, double-click **Internet Protocol Version 4 (TCP/IPv4)**). The Internet Protocol (TCP/IP) Properties window opens.
	e. Click the **Use the following IP address** option button, if necessary. In the IP address text box, type **192.168.154.50**. In the Subnet mask text box, type **255.255.255.0**.
	f. Click **OK** twice (or click **OK**, and then click **Close**), and then close all open dialog boxes.
Reconfigure the IP address on *SERVER1*	a. Log off *SERVER1*, and then log back on as an administrator. The Windows Server 2008 desktop appears.
	b. Click **Start**, right-click **Network**, click **Properties**, and then click **Manage network connections**.
	c. Right-click **Local Area Connection** and click **Properties**. The Local Area Connection Properties window opens.
	d. Double-click **Internet Protocol Version 4 (TCP/IPv4)**. The Internet Protocol Version 4 (TCP/IPv4) Properties window opens.
	e. Click the **Use the following IP address** option button. In the IP address text box, type **192.168.54.11**. In the Subnet mask text box, type **255.255.255.0**.
	f. Click **OK** twice, and then close all open dialog boxes or windows.
Reconfigure the IP address on *WORKSTATION2*	a. Log off *WORKSTATION2*, and then log back on as an administrator. The Windows desktop appears.
	b. Open the Network Connections window.
	c. Right-click **Local Area Connection** and click **Properties**. The Local Area Connection Properties window opens.
	d. Double-click **Internet Protocol (TCP/IP)**. (In Windows Vista, double-click **Internet Protocol Version 4 (TCP/IPv4)**). The Internet Protocol (TCP/IP) Properties window opens.
	e. Click the **Use the following IP address** option button, if necessary. In the IP address text box, type **192.168.154.50**. In the Subnet mask text box, type **255.255.255.248**.
	f. Click **OK** twice (or click **OK**, and then click **Close**), and then close all open dialog boxes.

10. Begin to determine the scope of the problem by attempting to log on to *WORKSTATION2*. Repeat Steps 1 through 5. If you are able to log on and browse the NETPLUS folder, the problem is local to the *WORKSTATION1* computer and you may concentrate on potential problems that affect only *WORKSTATION1*. Otherwise, the problem is common to all clients and you should concentrate on potential problems that affect all clients.

11. To determine the state of physical connectivity in the network, check the status of the link lights on the hub and in the NICs for each computer.

12. To determine the state of network connectivity in the network, on *WORKSTATION1*, click **Start**, point to **All Programs**, point to **Accessories**, and click **Command Prompt**. (In Windows Vista, click **Start**, type **cmd** in the Start Search text box, and then press **Enter**.) A command prompt window opens. Type **ping 127.0.0.1** and then press **Enter**. Success indicates that the TCP/IP stack on *WORKSTATION1* is working. Depending on the scope of the problem, repeat this step for *WORKSTATION2*.

13. At the command prompt on *WORKSTATION1*, type **ping 192.168.54.1** and then press **Enter**. If the output indicates success, network connectivity exists between *WORKSTATION1* and the server. Depending on the scope of the problem, repeat this step for *WORKSTATION2*.

14. If there is no network connectivity, at the command prompt on *WORKSTATION1*, type **ipconfig** and then press **Enter**. IP addressing information displays on the computer. If this is correct, there might be a problem with the network configuration on the server. Depending on the scope of the problem, repeat for *WORKSTATION2*.

15. On *SERVER1*, repeat Steps 12 through 14. However, in Step 13, ping the IP addresses of the client computers.

16. By this time, you should have identified the problem. Fix it and repeat Steps 7 through 15, asking your instructor or classmate to perform another action listed in Table 13-1.

Certification Objectives

Objectives for the Network+ Exam:

- Given a scenario, implement the following network troubleshooting methodology: information gathering—identify symptoms and problems, identify the affected areas of the network, determine if anything has changed, establish the most probable cause, determine if escalation is necessary, create an action plan and solution identifying potential effects, implement and test the solution, identify the results and effects of the solution, document the solution and the entire process

Review Questions

1. Which of the following comes first in the series of steps recommended for a logical approach to network troubleshooting?

   a. Establish what has changed on the network.

   b. Implement a solution.

    c. Establish the symptoms.

    d. Identify the affected area.

2. If a client workstation has been assigned the wrong IP address, which of the following will be true?

    a. The client will be able to connect to other nodes on the LAN, but will not be able to connect through its default gateway to the Internet.

    b. The client will be able to ping the loopback address successfully, but will not be able to connect to other nodes on the LAN.

    c. The client will not be able to ping the loopback address successfully, nor will it be able to connect to other nodes on the LAN.

    d. The client will be able to connect to other nodes on its LAN segment, but will not be able to connect to nodes on other segments.

3. Which of the following commands will reveal TCP/IP addressing information on a Windows Server 2008 computer?

    a. ipconfig

    b. winipcfg

    c. ifconfig

    d. netipcfg

4. If the LED on a workstation's NIC is blinking green, which of the following is true?

    a. The workstation is connected to the network and successfully exchanging data over its connection.

    b. The workstation is connected to the network, but is not currently exchanging data over its connection.

    c. The workstation is connected to the network, but is experiencing errors when attempting to exchange data over the network.

    d. The workstation is not successfully connected to the network.

5. Of the following troubleshooting actions, which one would come first in a logical troubleshooting methodology?

    a. Replace a faulty memory chip on a server.

    b. Determine whether a problem is limited to a segment or affects the whole network.

    c. Summarize your solution in a troubleshooting database.

    d. Determine whether your solution will result in any other problems.

Lab 13.4 Troubleshooting Web Client Problems

Objectives

In this lab, you will troubleshoot a problem with a Web client. Because the connection between a client and a host on the Internet usually relies on a great number and type of connections, problems are common. They might also be difficult to identify and fix. Even if the nature of the problem is clear, you might not have any control over the network resources causing the problem. Coordination with other network administrators and other organizations is often essential to solving problems on the Internet.

In addition to basic physical and logical network connectivity, you must also make sure that DNS is working properly. Issues involving DNS are a common source of problems with Web servers and Web browsers. If the Web server is operating correctly but the client is unable to use DNS to find its address, the client will be unable to reach the Web server. The effect is the same as if the Web server were not functioning properly. However, the Web server will typically be reachable through its IP address (if its IP address is known at all). DNS problems can occur for a variety of reasons, including incorrect DNS entries, misconfigured DNS servers, or even failure to pay domain name registration fees.

After completing this lab, you will be able to:

- Use a methodical troubleshooting approach to identify and solve a problem involving a Web client

- Investigate potential problems caused by DNS errors

Materials Required

This lab will require the following:

- A computer running Windows Server 2008 named *SERVER1* with two NICs

- One NIC configured with an IP address of 192.168.54.1 and a subnet mask of 255.255.255.0, and the other NIC configured with an IP address of 172.16.1.1 and a subnet mask of 255.255.255.0

- Routing and Remote Access configured on *SERVER1* so that it acts as a router

- A hub named *HUB1* connected to the NIC on *SERVER1* that was configured with an IP address of 192.168.54.1 with a straight-through Cat 5 (or better) UTP cable

- A hub named *HUB2* connected to the NIC on *SERVER1* that was configured with an IP address of 172.16.1.1 with a straight-through Cat 5 (or better) UTP cable, as shown in Figure 13-4

- A computer running Windows XP Professional or Vista named *WORKSTATION1*, configured with an IP address of 192.168.54.2 and a subnet mask of 255.255.255.0, connected to *HUB1* with a straight-through Cat 5 (or better) UTP cable

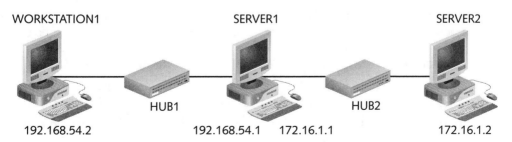

Figure 13-4   Network layout of Lab 13.4

Courtesy Course Technology/Cengage Learning

- A computer running Windows Server 2008, Standard Edition named *SERVER2*, con-figured with an IP address of 172.16.1.2 and a subnet mask of 255.255.255.0, con-nected to *HUB2* with a straight-through Cat 5 (or better) UTP cable

- IIS installed and running on *SERVER2*, with a file named default.htm containing the text "This is a test page" in C:\Inetpub\wwwroot

- The DNS server running on *SERVER1*, with an entry for *www.netpluslab.net* point-ing to 172.16.1.2

- *WORKSTATION1* configured to use *SERVER1* as its DNS server

- Administrative access to all three computers

- A faulty network cable that is the same color as the network cables used in the other labs

- An instructor or classmate assigned to cause a problem in the network

---

Estimated completion time: **60–90 minutes**

Activity

1. Log on to *WORKSTATION1* as an administrator. The Windows desktop appears.

2. Click **Start**, and then click **Internet Explorer**. Internet Explorer opens.

3. In the Address bar, type **www.netpluslab.net** and then press **Enter**. A Web page opens with the text "This is a test page."

4. Close Internet Explorer.

5. Leave the room and ask your instructor or classmate to cause a network problem by performing one of the actions listed in Table 13-2.

6. After you return to the room, attempt to repeat Steps 1 through 3 on *WORKSTATION1*. You are unable to open the Web page. Attempt to solve the problem using the following steps. If you solve the problem before completing all the steps, proceed to Step 17.

7. Attempt to determine the state of physical connectivity in the network. Check the status of the link lights on both hubs and the NICs in *WORKSTATION1*, the router, and the Web server.

8. Attempt to determine the state of network connectivity. On *WORKSTATION1*, click **Start**, point to **All Programs**, point to **Accessories**, and then click **Command Prompt**. (In Windows Vista, click **Start**, type **cmd** in the Start Search text box, and then press **Enter**.) A command prompt window opens. Type **ping 127.0.0.1** and then press **Enter**. Success indicates that the TCP/IP stack on *WORKSTATION1* is working.

9. At the command prompt on *WORKSTATION1*, type **ping 192.168.54.1** and then press **Enter**. Success indicates that you can connect to the near NIC on the router.

10. Type **ping 172.16.1.1** and then press **Enter**. Success indicates that you can connect to the far NIC on the router.

11. Type **ping 172.16.1.2** and then press **Enter**. Success indicates that you can connect to the Web server.

Table 13-2:   Possible actions to be performed by an instructor or classmate

Action	Instruction
Install faulty cable on server	Replace the network cable connecting the Web server to the hub with the faulty network cable.
Reconfigure the IP address on the Web server	a. Log on to *SERVER2* as the Administrator. The Windows Server 2008 desktop appears.
	b. Click **Start**, right-click **Network**, click **Properties**, and then click **Manage network connections**.
	c. Right-click **Local Area Connection** and click **Properties**. The Local Area Connection Properties window opens.
	d. Double-click **Internet Protocol (TCP/IP)**. The Internet Protocol (TCP/IP) Properties window opens.
	e. Click the **Use the following IP address** option button. In the IP address text box, type **172.16.1.5**. In the Subnet mask text box, type **255.255.255.0**.
	f. Click **OK** twice, and then close any open dialog boxes or windows.
Change the DNS server on *WORKSTATION1*	a. On *WORKSTATION1*, click **Start**, point to **All Programs**, point to Accessories, point to **Communications**, and then click **Network Connections**. (In Windows Vista, click **Start**, right-click **Network**, click **Properties**, and then click **Manage network connections**.) The Network Connections dialog box opens.
	b. Right-click **Local Area Connection** and click **Properties**. The Local Area Connection Properties window opens.
	c. Double-click **Internet Protocol (TCP/IP)**. (In Windows Vista, double-click **Internet Protocol Version 4 (TCP/IPv4)**). The Internet Protocol (TCP/IP) Properties window opens.
	d. Click the **Use the following DNS server addresses** option button. In the Preferred DNS server text box, type **192.168.154.1**.
	e. Click **OK** twice, and then close all open dialog boxes.
Change the DNS entry for *www. netpluslab.net*	a. Log on to *SERVER1* as the Administrator. The Windows Server 2008 desktop appears.
	b. Click **Start**, point to **Administrative Tools**, and then click **DNS**. The dnsmgmt window opens.
	c. In the tree in the left pane of the window, click the **plus sign (+)** next to *SERVER1* to expand the tree underneath it. Click **Forward Lookup Zones** in the tree in the left pane. Icons for the forward lookup zones appear in the right pane.

(Continued)

Table 13-2:   Possible actions to be performed by an instructor or classmate (Continued)

Action	Instruction
	d. In the right pane, double-click **netpluslab.net**. More icons appear, including an icon for www.
	e. Right-click the **www** icon and then click **Properties**. The www Properties window opens.
	f. Type **172.16.1.200** in the IP address text box, and then click **OK**.
	g. Close the DNS window.

12. If there is no network connectivity, at the command prompt on *WORKSTATION1*, type **ipconfig** and then press **Enter**. IP addressing information displays. Verify that the IP address is correct.

13. If you cannot find a problem with the IP addressing information on *WORKSTATION1*, repeat the previous step on *SERVER1* and *SERVER2*.

14. If you have verified network connectivity between *WORKSTATION1* and the Web server, on *WORKSTATION1* type **http://172.16.1.2** in the Address bar in Internet Explorer, and then press **Enter**. If you can open the Web page, this indicates a problem with DNS.

15. At the command prompt on *WORKSTATION1*, type **ipconfig /all** and then press **Enter**. Look through the IP addressing information to verify that *WORKSTATION1* is configured to use *SERVER1* (at 192.168.54.1) as its DNS server.

16. If *WORKSTATION1* is using the correct DNS server, type **nslookup www.netpluslab.net** and then press **Enter**. The IP address for www.netpluslab.net displays. Check to see if this matches the IP address of the Web server (172.16.1.2).

17. By this time, you should have been able to identify the problem. Fix it and repeat Steps 5 through 16, asking your instructor or classmate to perform a different action listed in Table 13-2.

Certification Objectives

Objectives for the Network+ Exam:

- Given a scenario, implement the following network troubleshooting methodology: information gathering—identify symptoms and problems, identify the affected areas of the network, determine if anything has changed, establish the most probable cause, determine if escalation is necessary, create an action plan and solution identifying potential effects, implement and test the solution, identify the results and effects of the solution, document the solution and the entire process

- Given a scenario, troubleshoot common connectivity issues and select an appropriate solution; *Physical issues*: cross talk, nearing crosstalk, near end crosstalk, attenuation, collisions, shorts, open impedance mismatch (echo), interference; *Logical issues*: port speed, port duplex mismatch, incorrect VLAN, incorrect IP address, wrong gateway, wrong DNS, wrong subnet mask; *Issues that should be identified but escalated*: switching loop, routing loop, route problems, proxy arp, broadcast storms; *Wireless issues*: interference (bleed, environmental factors), incorrect encryption, incorrect channel, incorrect frequency, ESSID mismatch, standard mismatch (802.11 a/b/g/n), distance, bounce, incorrect antenna placement

Review Questions

1. What does the Nslookup command reveal?

    a. a client's current connections

    b. a client's routing table entries

    c. the IP address of a given host name or vice versa

    d. the NetBIOS name based on a computer's IP address

2. If the link light on a hub port is not lit, what can you assume about the client connected to that hub's port?

    a. There are no connectivity problems with the client.

    b. The client cannot exchange data with the network.

    c. The client can exchange data only with other nodes on its segment.

    d. The client can exchange Network layer data, but not Transport layer data.

3. If a client does not have the correct DNS server address specified in its TCP/IP properties, which of the following will occur?

    a. The client cannot log on to or exchange data with the network.

    b. The client can exchange data with nodes on its local network, but not with nodes on other networks.

    c. The client can exchange data with nodes on local and external networks, but not by name.

    d. The client can exchange data with most, but not all, nodes on both its local and external networks by name.

4. What would happen if you assigned your Web server a new IP address that didn't match its DNS entry?

    a. It would be unavailable to clients.

    b. It would be available only to local clients, but not to clients accessing it over the Internet.

    c. It would be available to clients accessing it over the Internet, but not to local clients.

    d. It would still be available to all clients.

5. Which of the following tools will issue a simple pass/fail indication for a Cat 5 UTP cable?

   a. cable checker

   b. time domain reflectometer

   c. multimeter

   d. tone generator

6. True or False? Suppose you ping the IP address of a known Web server, and the response to your command indicates that the Web server is responding. It then follows that the Web server would successfully respond to HTTP requests from clients.

CHAPTER FOURTEEN

ENSURING INTEGRITY AND AVAILABILITY

Labs included in this chapter

- Lab 14.1 Understanding Malware
- Lab 14.2 Using Uninterruptible Power Supplies (UPSs)
- Lab 14.3 Configuring RAID
- Lab 14.4 Backing Up a Windows Server 2008 Computer
- Lab 14.5 Backing Up a Linux Computer

Net+ Exam Objectives

Objective	Lab
Conduct network monitoring to identify performance and connectivity issues	14.1
Explain different methods and rationales for network performance optimization	14.2, 14.3
Explain issues that affect device security	14.2, 14.3
Identify common security threats and mitigation techniques	14.1, 14.4, 14.5

Lab 14.1 Understanding Malware

Objectives

Malware can infect computers in a variety of ways. For instance, a malicious program can infect a client (or a server) by running an infected executable file, by previewing e-mail with an e-mail client that has not been upgraded with the latest patches, by browsing the Web with a Web browser that has not been upgraded with the latest patches, or even by running certain services on the Internet. Keeping a file server free of viruses can be even more challenging, as your users might try to store infected files on its shared drives. Sometimes users save infected files to a shared drive, have their computers cleared of viruses, and then reinfect their computers from the files on the shared drive.

Virus scanners are not helpful if you do not keep them up to date. Many virus scanners require that you periodically update the virus definition files they use to search for viruses. If you do not, the virus scanner will be unable to find newer viruses.

After completing this lab, you will be able to:

- Describe different types of malware
- Use malware-scanning software

Materials Required

This lab will require the following:

- A computer running Windows XP Professional or Vista named *WORKSTATION1* with an Internet connection
- AVG Free 8.5 Anti-Virus (available from *http://free.avg.com*), or the current version, installed on the computer

Estimated completion time: **30 minutes**

Activity

1. Log on to *WORKSTATION1* as an administrator. The Windows desktop appears. Connect to the Internet, if necessary.

2. Click **Start**, point to **All Programs**, point to **AVG Free 8.5**, and then click **AVG Free User Interface**.

3. Double-click the **Update Manager** icon and click **Update now**, as shown in Figure 14-1.

4. If new updates are found, click **Update**.

5. After AVG downloads and installs the updates, click **Close**.

6. Click the **Computer scanner** tab on the left to open the Scan for threats section.

7. Click the **Scan whole computer** icon. The scan begins showing the progress of the virus scan. Do not click any buttons or press any keys until the scan is finished; this might take several minutes. The amount of time required for the scan depends on the power of the computer's CPU and the number of files on the computer. After the scan is finished,

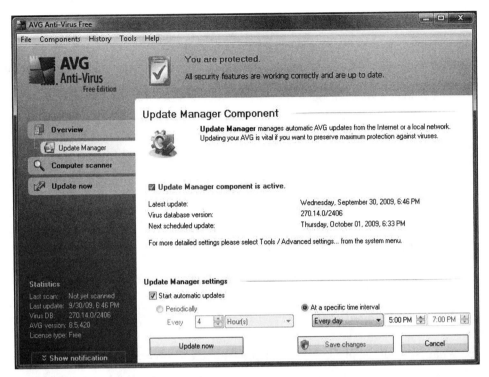

Figure 14-1   The AVG Free Update Manager

Courtesy Course Technology/Cengage Learning

the computer shows a summary of the scan, including the number of files scanned, the number of viruses found, and the number of files repaired, quarantined, deleted, or excluded.

8. Click **Close results** to return to the AVG Free main window.

9. Close AVG Anti-Virus Free.

10. To gain an understanding of virus-related terms, you will access the Webopedia Web site. Click **Start**, and then click **Internet Explorer**. Internet Explorer opens. In the Address bar, type **www.webopedia.com** and press **Enter**. The Webopedia home page opens.

11. In the "Enter a word for a definition" text box underneath SEARCH, type the term **macro virus** and then click **Go**. Record the definition in your own words.

12. Type **worm** into the "Enter a word for a definition" text box, and then click **Go**. Record the definition of worm (a type of virus) in your own words.

13. Type **Trojan horse** into the "Enter a word for a definition" text box, and then click **Go**. Record the definition of a Trojan horse (which technically is not a virus, but can cause similar damage) in your own words.

14. Log off.

Certification Objectives

Objectives for the Network+ Exam:

- Conduct network monitoring to identify performance and connectivity issues using the following: network monitoring utilities (e.g., packet sniffers, connectivity software, load testing, throughput testers); system logs, history logs, event logs
- Identify common security threats and mitigation techniques: *Security threats*: DoS, viruses, worms, attackers, man in the middle, smurf, rogue access points, social engineering (phishing); *Mitigation techniques*: policies and procedures, user training, patches and updates

Review Questions

1. If you receive an infected file as an executable program attached to an e-mail message, which of the following is this program likely to be?

    a. a macro virus

    b. a Trojan

    c. a worm

    d. a boot sector virus

2. What is the difference between a Trojan and a true virus?

    a. A Trojan does not automatically replicate itself, whereas a true virus does.

    b. A Trojan causes harm by simply being on the computer's hard disk, whereas a true virus file must be executed by the user.

    c. A Trojan often can't be detected by a virus-scanning program, whereas a true virus can almost always be detected by such a program.

    d. A Trojan changes its binary characteristics to avoid detection, whereas a true virus's binary characteristics remain static.

3. Which of the following types of virus checking requires frequent database updates to remain effective?

    a. signature scanning

    b. heuristic scanning

    c. rotation checking

    d. integrity checking

4. If a virus is polymorphic, what is it able to do?

    a. replicate itself over a network connection

    b. change its binary characteristics each time it's transferred to a new system

    c. modify the network properties of a client or server

    d. remain inactive until a particular date

5. What is unique about a time-dependent virus?

    a. It changes its binary characteristics at regularly scheduled intervals.

    b. It can only be eradicated by applying a virus fix at certain times of the day.

   c. It is alternately detectable, then undetectable, by virus-scanning software, depending on the date.

   d. It remains dormant until a particular date or time.

6. A macro virus is most apt to affect which of the following programs?

   a. Microsoft Client for Networks

   b. Microsoft Outlook

   c. Microsoft Excel

   d. Microsoft SQL Server

Lab 14.2 Using Uninterruptible Power Supplies (UPSs)

Objectives

A sudden power failure or outage can cause numerous computer problems. If power were interrupted while a computer's files were open, for instance, those files might be corrupted. An uninterruptible power supply (UPS) is a power supply that uses a battery to ensure that any device attached to it will be able to function for some length of time despite a power failure. If the power outage lasts only a few seconds, the UPS prevents the attached devices from losing power. If the power outage lasts more than a few seconds, the UPS affords you (or a software program) the opportunity to shut down the attached devices gracefully. Alternately, use of a UPS might allow a backup generator time to get up to full operating power.

   Depending on the power requirements of your network devices and servers and the amount of power produced by a UPS, you might be able to use one UPS with multiple devices. However, you should check the power requirements of each device against the specifications of the UPS before attempting to do this. You should usually overestimate the power consumption to provide a healthy margin of error. A device's power consumption is commonly measured by its Volt-Amp (VA) rating. It can also be measured in amps. The VA rating can be found by multiplying the current consumed by the device (measured in amps) by the incoming voltage. For devices in the United States, this is 120 volts, but for international devices, this is usually 220 volts. In general, estimating the actual power consumption of a network device is difficult, as an individual device might use more or less power than its manufacturer indicates that it should.

   Some servers come with multiple power supplies. If one power supply fails, the other power supply continues to power the computer. For truly critical servers or network devices, you might find that attaching multiple power supplies to a single UPS is insufficient. If the UPS fails, the device would also fail during a power outage. However, if you plugged each power supply into a separate UPS, the failure of a single UPS would not cause the computer to lose power in the event of an overall power failure. Some data centers might also plug each UPS into a different circuit, and each circuit into a different generator. However, these fault-tolerance measures increase costs considerably.

   In addition to the smaller UPSs you will investigate in this lab, you can also purchase large models designed to support many devices in large data centers.

   After completing this lab, you will be able to:

   - Perform a cost comparison of UPSs
   - Discuss the characteristics of UPSs

Materials Required

This lab will require the following:

- A pencil or pen
- A computer with access to the Internet and online retailers who sell UPSs, such as *www.apcc.com*, *www.tripplite.com*, or *www.liebert.com*

Estimated completion time: **60-90 minutes**

Activity

1. You are the network administrator for Hollisville Manufacturing. Table 14-1 shows the types of devices in your data center, the number of each device, and the VA rating per each device. Calculate and record the total VA rating of the devices in the data center.

2. Using the Internet to perform research, choose a model of UPS that exceeds the total power rating for all of the devices in the data center. Record the vendor name.

3. Record the model number.

4. Record the price.

5. Record the amount of time that the UPS will keep a device running after a power failure.

6. Record whether the UPS comes with software that will automatically shut down a computer after a power failure.

7. Repeat Steps 2 through 6 with two other models of UPS.

Certification Objectives

Objectives for the Network+ Exam:

- Explain different methods and rationales for network performance optimization: *Methods*: QoS, traffic shaping, load balancing, high availability, caching engines, fault tolerance; *Reasons*: latency sensitivity, high bandwidth applications, VoIP, video applications, uptime

- Explain issues that affect device security: physical security; restricting local and remote access; secure methods vs. unsecure methods; SSH, HTTPS, SNMPv3, SFTP, SCP; TELNET, HTTP, FTP, RSH, RCP, SNMPv1/2

Table 14-1 Power consumption of network devices in the Hollisville Manufacturing data center

Device	Number of devices	Volt Amp (VA) rating per device
Router	2	120
Server	8	285
Workstation	20	150
Hub	5	60

Review Questions

1. What is line conditioning?

    a. the regular testing of the integrity of electrical systems

    b. the periodic application of a large amount of voltage to electrical systems to clean the lines

    c. the continuous filtering of an electrical circuit to protect against noise

    d. the intermittent fluctuation of voltage on a circuit, which over time will cause power flaws for connected devices

2. Which of the following devices, when used in conjunction with one or more UPSs, will allow other devices to continue running indefinitely after a power outage?

    a. surge protector

    b. circuit breaker

    c. generator

    d. circuit mirror

3. Which of the following power conditions equates to a power failure?

    a. sag

    b. line noise

    c. surge

    d. blackout

4. Which of the following power conditions would not necessarily cause a power failure, but might adversely affect computer equipment? (Choose all that apply.)

    a. sag

    b. line noise

    c. brownout

    d. blackout

5. What specification is necessary for you to determine the amount of electrical power that your computer devices require?

    a. capacitance

    b. impedance

    c. resistance

    d. wattage

6. What is the difference between a standby UPS and an online UPS?

    a. A standby UPS engages when it detects a power failure, whereas an online UPS continuously provides power to its connected devices.

    b. A standby UPS requires that the network administrator connect it to key devices when a power failure is detected, whereas an online UPS can remain connected to devices indefinitely, even when not in use.

   c. A standby UPS continuously provides power to its connected devices, whereas an online UPS engages when it detects a power failure.

   d. A standby UPS can remain connected to devices indefinitely, even when not in use, whereas an online UPS requires that the network administrator connect it to the devices when a power failure is detected.

7. Suppose you are working on several documents in Microsoft Word when your Windows XP Professional workstation loses power. Suppose also that you are not relying on a UPS or other alternate power source. Which of the following is a significant risk?

   a. The installation of the Word program on your hard disk might become corrupt and require replacement.

   b. Your computer's operating system might fail to recognize the Word program in the future.

   c. The Word documents you were working on when the power failed might become corrupt.

   d. Your computer's power source might become damaged.

Lab 14.3 Configuring RAID

Objectives

If a hard drive on a computer fails, either the computer itself will fail or the computer will lose data. Redundant array of independent disks, or RAID, allows you to improve disk reliability by combining multiple disks. Depending on how RAID is configured for a computer, it can also help improve disk performance. In this lab, you will configure RAID in software. Keep in mind, however, that RAID is also commonly available in hardware. Hardware RAID has several advantages over software RAID, including greater reliability, better performance, and often the ability to swap out hard drives while the computer is still running. Most modern network operating systems (NOSs), including Windows, Linux, and UNIX, support software RAID. Windows server operating systems such as Windows Server 2008 support software RAID, but workstation operating systems such as Windows XP Professional do not.

Each possible RAID configuration involves a different arrangement of disks and is called a level. RAID level 0 is called disk striping and requires at least two physical disks (almost always of the same size). Because the computer writes parts of each file to both physical disks at the same time, RAID level 0 results in higher performance. As in all levels of RAID, the disadvantage is that less disk space is available to the computer because it sees only one logical disk that is the size of just one of the physical disks. RAID level 0 does not provide any fault tolerance, and data on both disks will be lost if either of the physical disks fail.

RAID level 1, which you will configure in this lab, is known as disk mirroring. It requires at least two physical disks and provides 100% redundancy. Each time the computer writes data to its hard disks, the same data is written to each disk at the same time. If one disk fails, the computer can continue running normally because the other disk has precisely the same data. As in RAID level 0, the computer sees only one logical disk that is the size of one of the physical disks. In a variation of disk mirroring known as disk duplexing, the disks also have redundant disk controllers so that the failure of a single controller will not result in the loss of data.

RAID level 5 (commonly known as RAID 5) writes data to three or more physical disks. It also writes parity data to each disk. If one of the physical disks fails, the data and parity data written to the other disks can be used to recover any lost data. In RAID level 5, an amount of disk space equal to the space on one physical disk is unavailable. Although disks in a RAID level 5 configuration take longer to recover from the failure of a disk than disks in a RAID level 1 configuration, RAID level 5 allows the computer to have more disk space than RAID level 1.

To configure a RAID array in software in Windows Server 2008, you must use two or more dynamic disks. The exact number of disks required depends on the level of RAID you want to use. A dynamic disk can be used in volumes that can be resized as needed without rebooting the server, or they can be included in RAID arrays. The disadvantage of using dynamic disks is that other operating systems, including versions of Windows prior to Windows 2000, cannot locally read these disks (although they can read data stored on them if it is shared over a network). In contrast, a basic disk can have primary and extended partitions and logical volumes, which can be read by other operating systems.

After completing this lab, you will be able to:

- Configure RAID level 1 on a Windows Server 2008 computer

Materials Required

This lab will require the following:

- A computer running Windows Server 2008 named *SERVER1* with two hard disks of equal size installed; one of the hard disks should contain the Windows Server 2008 installation
- The second hard disk should have no partitions or logical volumes configured
- Access as the Administrator to the computer

Estimated completion time: **45 minutes**

Activity

1. Log on to *SERVER1* as the Administrator. The Windows Server 2008 desktop appears.

2. Click **Start**, point to **Administrative Tools**, and then click **Computer Management**. The Computer Management console appears.

3. In the left pane, click **Disk Management**. Information about the disks installed in the computer appears in the right pane, as shown in Figure 14-2. If the Initialize Disk Wizard opens, ensure that the **Disk 1** check box is checked. Click **OK**.

4. In the middle pane, you see a list of the physical disks on the system. Right-click an area in the gray box around Disk 0, and then click **Convert to Dynamic Disk**. The Convert to Dynamic Disk dialog box opens.

5. Click the **Disk 1** check box so that both the Disk 0 and Disk 1 check boxes are checked. Click **OK**. The Disks to Convert dialog box opens, listing the disks to be converted to dynamic disks.

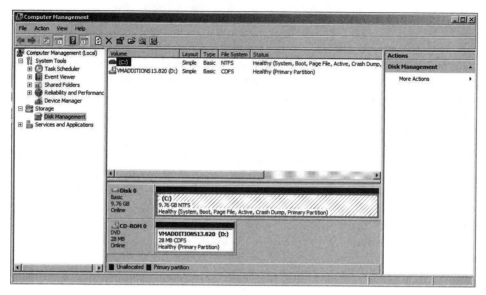

Figure 14-2 Computer Management console

Courtesy Course Technology/Cengage Learning

6. Click **Convert**. The Disk Management dialog box opens, indicating that after conversion you will be unable to start other operating systems installed on those disks. Click **Yes**.

7. If the Convert Disk to Dynamic dialog box opens, indicating that any file systems on these disks will need to be unmounted, complete the following steps. Otherwise, skip ahead to Step 13.

8. Click **Yes**. The Confirm dialog box opens, indicating that the computer will be rebooted to finish the conversion process.

9. Click **OK**. The computer reboots.

10. After the computer has rebooted, press **Ctrl+Alt+Del** to display the Log On to Windows dialog box. Log on as the Administrator. The Windows Server 2008 desktop appears. The System Settings Change dialog box opens, indicating that you must restart the computer before the changes you have made can take effect.

11. Click **Yes**. The computer reboots again.

12. After the computer has rebooted for a second time, repeat Steps 1 through 3. Both Disk 0 and Disk 1 now appear as dynamic disks.

13. Right-click the rectangle with the green bar at the top next to Disk 0, and click **Add Mirror** on the shortcut menu. The Add Mirror dialog box opens.

14. Click **Disk 1** to select it. Click **Add Mirror**. The bar at the top of the rectangles next to both Disk 0 and Disk 1 turns red, and text in each rectangle indicates that each disk is resyncing. After a few minutes, each disk is marked C: with a status of healthy. You have successfully created a RAID level 1 set of disk mirrors.

15. Close the Computer Management dialog box and log off *SERVER1*.

Certification Objectives

Objectives for the Network+ Exam:

- Explain different methods and rationales for network performance optimization: *Methods*: QoS, traffic shaping, load balancing, high availability, caching engines, fault tolerance; *Reasons*: latency sensitivity, high bandwidth applications, VoIP, video applications, uptime

- Explain issues that affect device security: physical security; restricting local and remote access; secure methods vs. unsecure methods; SSH, HTTPS, SNMPv3, SFTP, SCP; TELNET, HTTP, FTP, RSH, RCP, SNMPv1/2

Review Questions

1. Which of the following levels of RAID offers disk mirroring?

   a. 0

   b. 1

   c. 3

   d. 5

2. Why is RAID level 0 not considered fully fault tolerant?

   a. If a hard disk fails, its data will be inaccessible.

   b. It cannot stripe files whose size exceeds 64 MB.

   c. It is incompatible with modern NOSs.

   d. It cannot verify whether its fault-tolerance activities are successful.

3. RAID level 0 achieves performance benefits by simultaneously writing to multiple _____.

   a. NICs

   b. hard disks

   c. processors

   d. instances of RAID software

4. Which of the following RAID levels provides fault tolerance while also making a large amount of disk space available?

   a. 0

   b. 1

   c. 3

   d. 5

5. What is the minimum number of physical hard disks required for disk mirroring?

   a. 1

   b. 2

   c. 4

   d. 5

14

6. What is one disadvantage of using RAID level 1 compared with using RAID level 5?

   a. RAID level 1 is not fault tolerant, whereas RAID level 5 offers at least some fault tolerance.

   b. RAID level 5 requires a third-party software program, whereas RAID level 1 is provided with every NOS.

   c. RAID level 1 requires more physical hard disks than RAID level 5.

   d. RAID level 1 makes a higher percentage of disk space unavailable when compared with RAID level 5.

Lab 14.4 Backing Up a Windows Server 2008 Computer

Objectives

In this lab, you will use the Backup utility on a Windows Server 2008 computer to back up files to a shared network folder or a second hard drive. Then you will restore the files from the backup media. Many companies supply software for backing up data. Examples include Symantec Backup Exec and Tivoli Storage Manager. The capabilities (and the cost) of these programs vary widely. Some software allows you to back up a single machine, while other software allows you to back up an entire data center. Almost all backup software allows you to schedule a backup for a time when activity on the machine is low.

The usefulness of backups is limited if they are not performed regularly. If you need to restore a user's file and you have not backed that file up in six months, the file will not contain any changes the user has made in the last six months. This might be as unhelpful to the user as no backup at all.

Backups should be stored in a safe, offsite location because they are useless if the backup media have been destroyed. For instance, if backup media are kept near the servers that store the original data, a fire in the data center could destroy both the server and the backup tapes. For this reason, many organizations regularly rotate copies of their backups to offsite locations or back up to remote drives over the Internet so that at least one good copy will be available even after a disaster. Your backup location should also be secure, as your backup tapes will contain any sensitive information on your servers.

After completing this lab, you will be able to:

- Back up data
- Restore data

Materials Required

This lab will require the following:

- A computer running Windows Server 2008 named *SERVER1* with Windows Server Backup installed
- Access as the Administrator to the computer
- Access to a remote shared folder or a second local drive large enough to back up the local volume

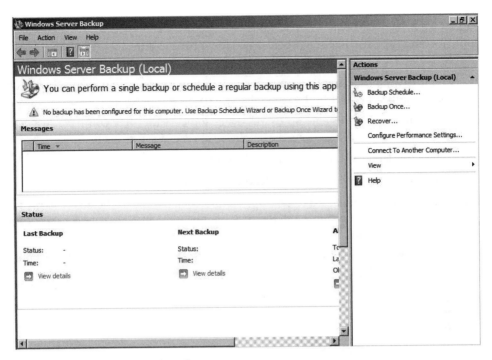

Figure 14-3   Windows Server Backup

Courtesy Course Technology/Cengage Learning

Estimated completion time: **30 minutes**

Activity

1. Log on to *SERVER1* as the Administrator. The Windows Server 2008 desktop appears.

2. Click **Start**, point to **Administrative Tools**, and then click **Windows Server Backup**. The Windows Server Backup interface opens, as shown in Figure 14-3.

3. Click **Backup Once** in the Actions pane. The Backup Once Wizard opens.

4. Make sure that the **Different options** option button is selected, and click **Next**. The wizard asks what you want to back up.

5. Click the **Custom** option button, and then click **Next**. The wizard asks you what volumes you want to back up. Select only your system volume and click **Next**.

6. The wizard asks you to specify the destination media. Choose the backup media appropriate to your system and click **Next**.

7. Choose the destination volume. Click **Next**.

8. If a message appears noting that the selected volume is also included in the list of items to back up, click **Yes** to exclude the volume.

9. Click **Next** to accept the default VSS copy backup option.

10. Click **Backup**. The Backup progress window opens and the status box indicates the various backup states being completed.

11. After a few minutes, the Backup progress window indicates that the backup is complete. Click **Close**. The Backup progress dialog box closes.

12. Now you will test the backup by restoring some of the files you have just backed up. Click **Recover** in the Actions pane. The Recovery Wizard opens.

13. Choose the server you are on and click **Next**.

14. Select the date and time that the backup was made and click **Next**.

15. Click the **Files and folders** option and click **Next**. In the Select items to recover window, expand the **server1** node, click the **Local disk** node, select **autoexec.bat**, and then click **Next**.

16. Click **Next** again to accept the recovery options and click **Recover**.

17. When the recovery has completed, click **Close**.

18. Log off *SERVER1*.

Certification Objectives

Objectives for the Network+ Exam:

- Identify common security threats and mitigation techniques: *Security threats*: DoS, viruses, worms, attackers, man in the middle, smurf, rogue access points, social engineering (phishing), mitigation techniques, policies and procedures, user training, patches and updates

Review Questions

1. Assume that a company has 50 users (at a single location), a limited budget, and significant security concerns. What method would it most likely use to back up its server data?

   a. online backup

   b. DASD

   c. RAID level 5

   d. DVD

2. Which of the following types of backup requires the most attention to the security of data while the backup is taking place?

   a. online backup

   b. DASD

   c. RAID level 5

   d. DVD

3. Why do network administrators prefer not to back up every file on their servers every day? (Choose all that apply.)

   a. It would take too much time.

   b. It would be less accurate than periodic backups.

   c. It would be more costly.

   d. It's hard to configure backup software to perform daily backups.

4. Which of the following methods will back up only data that has been changed since the last backup?

   a. full

   b. incremental

   c. differential

   d. interval

5. Which backup method will back up data regardless of whether the data has been changed?

   a. full

   b. incremental

   c. differential

   d. interval

Lab 14.5 Backing Up a Linux Computer

Objectives

As with Windows, you can back up a Linux server with either commercial software or built-in commands. The tar command, short for "tape archiver," is one of the most common methods for making a backup. In addition to making backups of files on tape, the tar command (like the zip program) is also commonly used to package software for distribution. A file created with the tar program is often called a tar file. A tar file can be updated incrementally with any files that have changed since the tar file was created.

The tar command is commonly used with one of two compression programs, gzip and bzip2. Each program uses a different algorithm to compress files. The bzip2 program creates smaller compressed files, but the gzip program is faster. A compressed tar file made with the gzip program usually ends with the suffix .tar.gz or .tgz, whereas a compressed tar file made with the bzip2 program usually ends with the suffix .bz2.

Another useful command for backing up files on a Linux server is the rsync command. The name rsync is short for "remote synchronization." This command can be used to copy files from one machine to another and to copy files incrementally. An incremental backup copies only the files that have changed since the last backup. To copy files remotely, the rsync command typically uses the capabilities of another command. In this lab, the rsync command will use the ssh command to copy files to the remote server.

After completing this lab, you will be able to:

- Back up files on a Linux server with the tar command
- Back up files on a Linux server with the rsync command
- Compress files on a Linux server with the gzip and bzip2 commands

Materials Required

This lab will require the following:

- A computer running a current version of Fedora Linux named *LINUX1. NETPLUSLAB.NET*, configured with no firewall, and the GNOME Desktop Environment
- *LINUX1.NETPLUSLAB.NET* configured with an IP address of 192.168.54.5 and a subnet mask of 255.255.255.0
- A computer running a current version of Fedora Linux named *LINUX2. NETPLUSLAB.NET*, configured with no firewall, and the GNOME Desktop Environment
- *LINUX2.NETPLUSLAB.NET* configured with an IP address of 192.168.54.6 and a subnet mask of 255.255.255.0
- Access as the netplus user and as root to both *LINUX1.NETPLUSLAB.NET* and *LINUX2.NETPLUSLAB.NET*
- Both computers connected to a hub with straight-through Cat 5 (or better) UTP cables
- No firewall software enabled on either computer

Estimated completion time: **35 minutes**

Activity

1. Log on to *LINUX1.NETPLUSLAB.NET* as the netplus user.
2. Open a terminal window, type **su -**, and press **Enter**. The Password prompt appears.
3. Enter the password for the root account and press **Enter**. The prompt now ends in a pound sign (#), indicating that you are logged on as the root user.
4. Type **echo "Your name" >/usr/local/netplus.txt**, replacing "*Your name*" with your name, and press **Enter**. The computer creates a text file named netplus.txt containing your name.
5. Type **ls /usr/local** and press **Enter**. The computer displays a list of the files in the /usr/local directory, including the file netplus.txt.
6. In the terminal window, type **tar -zcvf backup.tar.gz /usr/local** and press **Enter**. As shown in Figure 14-4, the computer creates a tar file named backup.tar.gz, backs up all the files in the /usr/local directory, and compresses the files with the gzip program. It displays a list of files as it backs them up. Note that all the files and directories located within the /usr/local directory are included in the archive.

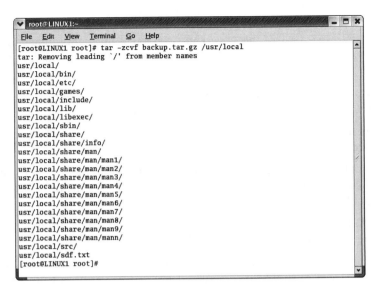

Figure 14-4   Creation of a tar file

Courtesy Course Technology/Cengage Learning

7. Type **mv backup.tar.gz /tmp** and press **Enter**. The computer moves the file backup. tar.gz to the /tmpdirectory.

8. Type **cd /tmp** and press **Enter**. The computer changes your directory to /tmp.

9. Type **tar –zxvf backup.tar.gz** and press **Enter**. The computer unarchives and uncompresses all the files contained in backup.tar.gz.

10. Type **ls /tmp/usr/local** and press **Enter**. The computer displays a list of the files that you have just extracted from the tar archive. Note that the tar command has preserved the directory structure of all the files it has archived.

11. Type **cd usr** and press **Enter**. The computer changes your current directory to the /tmp/usr directory.

12. Type **cd local** and press **Enter**. The computer changes your current directory to the /tmp/usr/local directory that was created when backup.tar.gz was untarred. (Do not type cd /local, as that will change your current directory to the /local directory instead.)

13. Type **cat netplus.txt** and press **Enter**. The computer displays the contents of the netplus.txt file.

14. Type **tar –jcvf backup.tar.bz2 /usr/local** and press **Enter**. The computer creates an archive as it did in Step 8, with a name of backup.tar.bz2 and using the bzip2 program.

15. Now you will back up files to a remote machine. Type **rsync -zav -e ssh /usr /local 192.168.54.6:/tmp** and press **Enter**. The -z option tells the rsync command to compress the files like the gzip command, the -a option tells the rsync command to archive all the files, and the -v option tells it to be verbose, or display detailed messages explaining what the command is doing. The -e option tells the rsync command to use

the ssh command. The last two options tell it to copy the /usr/local directory to the /tmp directory on 192.168.54.6. If the "Are you sure you want to continue connecting (yes/no):" prompt appears, type **yes** and press **Enter**. The password prompt appears.

16. Enter the password for the root account and press **Enter**. The rsync command indicates that it is building a list of files to transfer to the remote computer, lists the files it transfers, and then summarizes the size and speed of the transfer.

17. Type **echo "New file" >/usr/local/newfile.txt** and press **Enter**. The computer creates a text file containing the text "New file."

18. Repeat Steps 15 and 16. The rsync command indicates that it is building a list of files to be copied and displays the names of the files and directories that have changed. (A directory in Linux changes when files are added to or removed from it.)

19. Log on to *LINUX2.NETPLUSLAB.NET* as the netplus user. Open a terminal window, type **su -**, and press **Enter**. Enter the password for the root account and press **Enter**.

20. In the terminal window on *LINUX2.NETPLUSLAB.NET*, type **cd /tmp** and press **Enter**. This is the directory to which the rsync command copied files from *LINUX1.NETPLUSLAB.NET*.

21. Type **cd local** and press **Enter**. The computer changes the current directory to /tmp/local.

22. Type **ls** and press **Enter**. The computer displays a list of all the files and directories copied from *LINUX1.NETPLUSLAB.NET*.

23. Type **cat netplus.txt** and press **Enter**. The computer displays the contents of the netplus.txt file.

24. Type **cat newfile.txt** and press **Enter**. The computer displays the contents of the newfile.txt file.

25. Log off both computers.

Certification Objectives

Objectives for the Network+ Exam:

- Identify common security threats and mitigation techniques: *Security threats*: DoS, viruses, worms, attackers, man in the middle, smurf, rogue access points, social engineering (phishing), mitigation techniques, policies and procedures, user training, patches and updates

Review Questions

1. Which of the following commands could *not* be used in the process of creating backups on a Linux computer?

   a. tar

   b. rsync

   c. bzip2

   d. cat

2. Which of the following commands would create an archive file named march13.tar.gz containing the directory /usr and all of the files and directories within it and compressed by the gzip command?

   a. tar -jzvf march13.tar.gz /usr

   b. tar -zxvf march13.tar.gz /usr

   c. tar -jcvf march13.tar.gz /usr

   d. tar -zcf march13.tar.gz /usr

3. Which programs are likely to have made a file named foo.tar.bz2?

   a. rsync and bz2

   b. ssh and bz2

   c. tar and gzip

   d. tar and bzip2

4. Which of the following programs would be used to back up data to a tape drive on a Linux computer?

   a. tar

   b. gzip

   c. rsync

   d. cat

5. You are a network administrator working for Red Rectangle Manufacturing. Red Rectangle has 12 servers, which it would like to back up to a single server attached to a tape library capable of backing up many computers. How would you use the tools in this lab to accomplish this task?

   a. Use the tar command every night to back up each server individually, then transfer the tar files to the backup server with floppies.

   b. Use the tar command every night to back up each server individually, then transfer the files using the ssh command.

   c. Use the rsync command each night to back up each server to the backup server, then use the tar command to create an archive file for each server.

   d. Use the rsync command each night to back up each server to the backup server, then use the tar command to write each backup to a separate tape.

14

CHAPTER FIFTEEN

IMPLEMENTING AND MANAGING NETWORKS

Labs included in this chapter

- Lab 15.1 Creating a Project Plan

- Lab 15.2 Planning an Upgrade

- Lab 15.3 Observing a Network Upgrade

- Lab 15.4 Installing and Removing Updates on Windows Server 2008

- Lab 15.5 Researching Network Solutions

Net+ Exam Objectives

Objective	Lab
Identify types of configuration management documentation	15.1, 15.2
Given a scenario, evaluate the network based on configuration management documentation	15.2, 15.3
Given a scenario, implement the following network troubleshooting methodology	15.1, 15.5
Identify common security threats and mitigation techniques	15.4

Lab 15.1 Creating a Project Plan

Objectives

When planning a project—particularly a large, technical project—you must keep track of details pertaining not only to the hardware and software involved, but also to the people responsible for tasks, the time each task might take, and which tasks rely on other tasks. To track all these details, it's helpful to use project planning software.

Microsoft Office Project Professional 2007 is one of several project planning software packages available. An advantage of using such software is its ability to create charts and timelines easily. For example, you could create a Gantt chart that displays the timelines of all project tasks and their relationships.

After completing this lab, you will be able to:

- Create a project plan using Microsoft Office Project Professional 2007

Materials Required

This lab will require the following:

- A Windows XP Professional or Vista computer with Microsoft Office Project Professional 2007 installed
- Access to the Windows computer as an ordinary user

Estimated completion time: **20 minutes**

Activity

1. In this lab, you will use Microsoft Office Project Professional 2007 to create a Gantt chart, which provides a graphical diagram of a project. Review the task list in Table 15-1.

Table 15-1 Project task list

Number	Task description	Predecessors	Duration
1	Order and ship server hardware	None	7 days
2	Order and ship server software	None	7 days
3	Install server hardware	1	1 day
4	Install server software	2, 3	1 day
5	Add server to LAN	4	1 day

2. Log on to the Windows XP or Vista computer. The Windows desktop appears.

3. To open Microsoft Project, click **Start**, point to **All Programs**, point to **Microsoft Office**, and then click **Microsoft Office Project 2007**. (You might find Microsoft Project located elsewhere on your Start menu.)

4. If a new project does not open, click **File** on the menu bar, and then click **New**. The New Project Tasks pane is displayed on the left side of the window. Click **Blank Project**. A new project opens. Close the Tasks pane, if necessary.

5. On the left side of the window, look for the Task Name column. You can enter task information in this column. On the right side of the window, a chart will appear after tasks have been entered, marking the tasks on the calendar with boxes and showing precedence information. Figure 15-1 shows the window after task information has already been entered. You will enter the same information in the following steps.

6. In the Task Name column, enter the first task description given in Table 15-1 and press **Tab**. Microsoft Project automatically fills in the Duration, Start, and Finish columns.

7. If necessary, click the cell in the Duration column next to the first entry you've made. Up and down arrows appear in the cell. Click the up arrow until the duration matches the number of days given for that task in Table 15-1.

8. In the Predecessors column, enter the appropriate number(s) from the Predecessors column in Table 15-1. (Leave the column blank if Table 15-1 indicates that the task has no predecessors.)

9. Right-click the first task and click **Task Information** on the shortcut menu. The Task Information dialog box opens.

10. Click the **Resources** tab. In the top line of the Resources text box, enter your name or the name of your lab partner and then click the **green check mark**.

11. Click **OK**. The name you entered in Step 10 appears in the chart in the right pane of the Microsoft Project window.

12. Repeat Steps 6 through 11 with the remaining tasks. When repeating Step 8, be sure to enter the appropriate information in the Predecessors column.

13. On the menu bar, click **File**, then click **Save As**. The Save As dialog box opens.

14. Enter a unique filename in the File name text box. Click **Save**. The computer saves your project.

15. Close Microsoft Project and log off the computer.

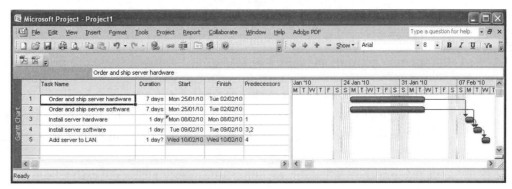

Figure 15-1 Microsoft Office Project Professional 2007

Certification Objectives

Objectives for the Network+ Exam:

- Identify types of configuration management documentation: wiring schematics; physical and logical network diagrams; baselines; policies, procedures, and configurations; regulations

- Given a scenario, implement the following network troubleshooting methodology: information gathering—identify symptoms and problems, identify the affected areas of the network, determine if anything has changed, establish the most probable cause, determine if escalation is necessary, create an action plan and solution identifying potential effects, implement and test the solution, identify the results and effects of the solution, document the solution and the entire process

Review Questions

1. The task that must be completed before another task is begun is called a(n) _____.

   a. successor

   b. predecessor

   c. antecedent

   d. dependent

2. In a significant network upgrade project, which of the following tasks takes place first?

   a. Identify which tasks are dependent on other tasks.

   b. Complete a needs assessment survey.

   c. Test the proposed solution on a pilot network.

   d. Assign tasks to the most qualified or appropriate people on the project team.

3. Which of the following best describes contingency planning?

   a. obtaining support from high-level project sponsors before committing resources to the project

   b. installing identical software and hardware, on a smaller scale, as the project's proposed solution will require, to test the feasibility of the solution

   c. identifying a team and assigning roles to that team in case of disaster

   d. identifying steps that will minimize the impact of unforeseen obstacles

4. You are a network administrator managing a network backbone upgrade. Your supervisor has scheduled a meeting to discuss the project's status with you. What is the advantage of taking a Gantt chart to the meeting?

   a. A Gantt chart will help the supervisor better understand the project's costs.

   b. A Gantt chart will determine the maximum possible amount of each employee's time to be spent on each task.

   c. A Gantt chart will allow the supervisor to see timelines of each task in addition to the project as a whole.

   d. A Gantt chart will demonstrate why some tasks have taken longer to complete than first anticipated.

5. True or False? One way of predicting how long a task might take is by examining the time taken to complete previous similar tasks.

Lab 15.2 Planning an Upgrade

Objectives

Even when you make relatively minor changes, a project plan can be helpful. The potential benefits include minimizing downtime, creating an efficient implementation, and planning for when something goes wrong. For instance, a project plan for changing the NIC on a server might include contingency plans in case the new NIC is defective, the NIC is accidentally damaged during installation, or the server does not boot after installation. Alternately, a configuration change made on a remote router might cut you off from the router. By having included contingency plans in your project plan, you are better prepared to solve the problem quickly and efficiently.

In environments in which downtime must be minimized at all costs, contingency planning is even more important. Although the odds of a problem occurring might be low, you must be prepared just in case. During a server upgrade, for example, you might have a spare server ready in case the server fails. (Note that you can also use network design to minimize potential downtime. For instance, you might use redundant servers.)

In this lab, you will create a project plan for replacing the NIC in a Windows Server 2008 computer. Your project plan should include a task breakdown, which divides the project into smaller parts, and a list of dependencies—that is, a list of tasks that depend on the completion of previous tasks. Your contingency planning should cover situations such as a defective NIC, drivers that are not available for the NIC, a NIC or server that is damaged during installation, and a server that cannot boot after installation of the NIC. Also include a testing plan, in which you outline your plans for determining whether the project or change was successful and whether the results of the project include any unforeseen side effects. Finally, your plan should contain a timeline, the resources required, and the project milestones.

After completing this lab, you will be able to:

- Make a project for a network upgrade
- Perform a network upgrade

Materials Required

This lab will require the following:

- Pencil and paper, or planning software such as Microsoft Office Project Professional 2007
- A computer running Windows Server 2008, Standard Edition named *SERVER1,* configured as a domain controller for the netpluslab.net domain with an IP address of 192.168.54.1 and a subnet mask of 255.255.255.0
- A shared folder on *SERVER1* named NETPLUS
- Access as the Administrator to *SERVER1*
- An extra NIC (with a driver disk, if necessary)
- A computer running Windows XP Professional or Vista named *WORKSTATION1,* configured as a member of the netpluslab.net domain, with an IP address of 192.168.54.3 and a subnet mask of 255.255.255.0

- An ordinary user account in the Domain Users group in the netpluslab.net domain
- Both computers connected to a hub with straight-through Cat 5 (or better) UTP cables
- A toolkit with a Phillips screwdriver, a ground mat, and a ground strap

Estimated completion time: **60 minutes**

Activity

1. First, you will verify that the network works properly. Log on to *WORKSTATION1* with an ordinary user account. The Windows desktop appears.

2. Click **Start**, and then click **My Computer**. (Click **Computer** in Windows Vista.) The My Computer (or Computer) window opens.

3. Click **Tools** on the menu bar, and then click **Map Network Drive**. (In Windows Vista, click **Map network drive** on the toolbar.) The Map Network Drive dialog box opens.

4. If necessary, select **Z:** (or the first available drive letter) from the Drive drop-down menu. In the Folder text box, type **\\192.168.54.1\netplus** and click **Finish**. The computer maps the NETPLUS shared folder.

5. If necessary, return to My Computer (or Computer). The netplus on '192.168.54.1' (Z:) icon now appears underneath Network Drives.

6. Right-click the **netplus on '192.168.54.1' (Z:)** icon and click **Disconnect** on the shortcut menu. The drive mapping disappears as the computer disconnects the network drive.

7. On a separate piece of paper, or in project planning software such as Microsoft Office Project Professional 2007, write the project plan that will cover the activities in Steps 8 through 17. Use Steps 2 through 5 as your testing plan.

8. Power down *SERVER1* and remove the power cable. Place the computer on the ground mat.

9. Place the ground strap on your wrist and attach the strap to the ground mat underneath the computer.

10. Remove any screws, as necessary, to open the cover of the computer case.

11. Remove the computer case cover.

12. Unscrew the NIC from its slot in the computer, and carefully remove it.

13. Place the new NIC in the slot.

14. Attach the NIC to the system unit with the Phillips screwdriver to secure the NIC in place.

15. Replace the computer case and reinsert any screws you removed in Step 10. Remove the ground strap and the ground mat.

16. Plug in the computer and turn it on.

17. To verify that the network is working properly, perform the steps in your testing plan.

18. Review your project plan and note anything that did not work according to the plan.

Certification Objectives

Objectives for the Network+ Exam:

- Identify types of configuration management documentation: wiring schematics; physical and logical network diagrams; baselines; policies, procedures, and configurations; regulations

- Given a scenario, evaluate the network based on configuration management documentation: compare wiring schematics, physical and logical network diagrams, baselines, policies, and procedures and configurations to network devices and infrastructure; update wiring schematics, physical and logical network diagrams, configurations, and job logs as needed

Review Questions

1. What is the purpose of identifying milestones in a project plan?
   a. They indicate when project staff changes must occur.
   b. They mark significant events of the project's progress.
   c. They offer a quick assessment of how successfully the project is staying within budget.
   d. They help predict the result of a project.

2. Which of the following are examples of resources related to a project plan that proposes to upgrade the network cards inside each workstation on a network from 100 Mbps to 1000 Mbps? (Choose all that apply.)
   a. NIC device drivers
   b. a team member's time
   c. IP addresses
   d. NICs
   e. switches

3. Which of the following are examples of stakeholders of a project whose purpose is to upgrade an entire network from 100 Mbps to 1000 Mbps? (Choose all that apply.)
   a. network users
   b. software vendors of applications running on the client machines
   c. high-level managers who approved the project
   d. IT staff who helped implement the change
   e. network cabling vendors

4. Which of the following tools might you use to assess the success of a project whose purpose is to upgrade an entire network from 100 Mbps to 1000 Mbps?

   a. Network Monitor

   b. sniffer or packet analyzer

   c. Microsoft SQL Server

   d. System Monitor

5. Which of the following obstacles could halt or seriously impair the progress of a project whose purpose is to upgrade the NICs in all workstations on a network from 100 Mbps to 1000 Mbps?

   a. the use of two different NIC models

   b. the use of different installation personnel on different shifts

   c. management's requirement that the cost of each NIC remain under $75

   d. a large group of defective NICs

Lab 15.3 Observing a Network Upgrade

Objectives

Observing a network upgrade will help you appreciate the complexities that can arise in a real-world situation. Depending on the project, you might be able to observe only a small part of an upgrade at any one time. For larger projects, the networking professional is more likely to have a formal project plan; for smaller projects, the plan might be very informal.

After completing this lab, you will be able to:

- Explain how a network upgrade is performed

Materials Required

This lab will require the following:

- Pencil and paper
- A person (such as a network professional) willing to allow you to observe a network upgrade
- Alternatively, an instructor can play the role of a network administrator and demonstrate a network upgrade in the classroom environment

Estimated completion time: **2 hours**

Activity

1. Visit the site where the network upgrade will be performed.
2. Ask the network engineer who is allowing you to observe the upgrade to discuss any project plans that might be used during the upgrade.

3. Ask the network engineer to discuss any contingency planning that might have been done as part of the upgrade.

4. Record any changes occurring at the site. For example, the upgrade might involve replacing Cat 5 cable with Cat 6 cable. Another change might involve altering the IP addressing scheme.

5. Record the time required for the network upgrade.

6. Thank the network engineer who allowed you to observe the upgrade.

Certification Objectives

Objectives for the Network+ Exam:

- Given a scenario, evaluate the network based on configuration management documentation: compare wiring schematics, physical and logical network diagrams, baselines, policies, and procedures and configurations to network devices and infrastructure; update wiring schematics, physical and logical network diagrams, configurations, and job logs as needed

Review Questions

1. Which of the following best describes project management?

    a. recording and analyzing the time and resources required for each task in a project

    b. assessing network statistics before and after a project is completed

    c. monitoring the needs of users prior to the beginning of a project, then later assessing how the project's completion met their needs

    d. planning for and handling the steps required to accomplish a goal in a systematic way

2. Which of the following projects is most likely to be driven by a company's security needs?

    a. doubling the RAM in a key file server

    b. installing a firewall on a connection to the Internet

    c. upgrading the version of client software on each workstation

    d. changing from the use of static IP addressing to DHCP on an entire network

3. What is one good technique for assessing the feasibility of a suggested project deadline before the project begins?

    a. Begin calculating task timelines from the deadline, working back to the start of a project.

    b. Issue a survey to key staff asking their opinion of the suggested deadline.

    c. Use the Web to research similar projects completed by other companies.

    d. Calculate the ratio of the number of project milestones to the proposed project duration, in months, to check that it does not exceed 2:1.

4. In a very large company (for example, one with over 10,000 employees), which of the following staff is most likely to decide whether a project such as an entire network upgrade will be funded?

a. network administrator

b. personnel director

c. chief information officer

d. accountant

5. Which of the following situations might necessitate changing all the IP addresses on a company's networked workstations?

a. The company has divided its network into several smaller subnets.

b. The company has hired 50 new employees.

c. The company has decided to use Network Address Translation (NAT) for all connections to public networks.

d. The company has decided to establish a Web server with e-commerce capability.

Lab 15.4 Installing and Removing Updates on Windows Server 2008

Objectives

Keeping software up to date on both servers and network devices is an important part of maintaining and upgrading a network. Usually software updates consist of patches or other fixes to problems that users and administrators have encountered when using the software. In other cases, a software update might solve a potential security problem, or it might even add a new feature.

Microsoft typically releases its software updates in one of two forms. The first form is a hot fix, which is an update to a specific piece of software, often used to correct a specific problem. For instance, a hot fix might solve a problem with Internet Information Services (IIS), which is the Web server sold by Microsoft. The second form is a service pack, which is a group of numerous software updates. You might install a service pack as part of a server's regular maintenance.

Both forms of updates are accessible through Microsoft's Windows Update service. Additionally, you can automate the installation of hot fixes so that no user intervention is required. Automatic updates can often prevent security problems from occurring, as they can fix a security vulnerability as soon as it is discovered. However, a software update might cause problems. For instance, you might run a certain application on your Windows Server 2008 computers. If this application relies on a piece of software that has been changed in a service pack or hot fix, the application might no longer work after the update has been applied. As a result, you might have to backlevel, or revert to the previous version of the software, after the upgrade. Thus, if at all possible, you should verify that a software upgrade will work in a test environment prior to applying it to production machines. Additionally, you should carefully consider the implications before scheduling automatic updates on important servers. Automatic updates are more safely scheduled for workstations, but it is also possible that an update installed automatically could cause problems on all workstations in your organization. You should carefully weigh the benefits of scheduling automatic updates before you implement them.

After completing this lab, you will be able to:

- Install updates to a computer running Windows Server 2008
- Remove updates from a computer running Windows Server 2008

Materials Required

This lab will require the following:

- A computer running Windows Server 2008, Standard Edition with access to the Internet
- At least one update or hot fix that needs to be installed on the computer
- Administrator access to the computer
- Internet Explorer security set to High (the default)

Estimated completion time: **30 minutes**

Activity

1. Log on to the server as the Administrator. The Windows Server 2008 desktop appears.

2. Click **Start**, click **Control Panel**, and then double-click **Windows Update** to open the Windows Update window shown in Figure 15-2.

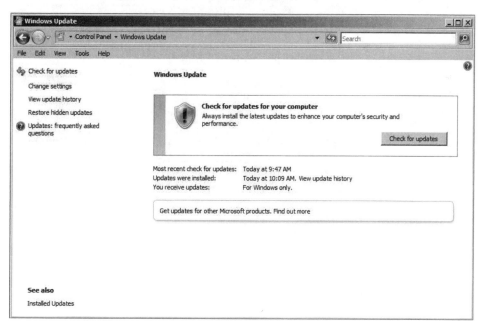

Figure 15-2 Microsoft Windows Update

Courtesy Course Technology/Cengage Learning

3. Click **Check for updates** and click **Install Now**. The Windows Update dialog box indicates that it is checking for updates.

4. When Windows has finished checking for updates, click **Install Now**.

5. Select **I accept the license terms** and click **Finish**.

6. Depending on the updates required, the installation process might vary somewhat from this step. Often not all of the required updates can be installed at the same time. Some of the updates might require other updates to be installed first and the computer rebooted before they can be installed. As a result, you might have to update your computer in stages.

7. If Windows indicates that you need to restart the computer to finish installing the updates, click **OK**. After the computer reboots, press **Ctrl+Alt+Del** to display the Log On to Windows dialog box. Log on as the Administrator. The Windows Server 2008 desktop appears.

8. Now you will remove an update added earlier. Click **Start**, point to **Control Panel**, and then double-click **Programs and Features**.

9. Click **View installed updates**. A list of installed updates appears, as shown in Figure 15-3.

10. A number of hot fixes are listed, followed by the number of a Microsoft Knowledge Base article describing the problem solved by the hot fix. Click a hot fix chosen by your instructor.

11. Click **Uninstall** for the selected hot fix and then click **Yes**. Windows begins to remove the hot fix. Depending on the hot fix to be removed, additional steps might be required.

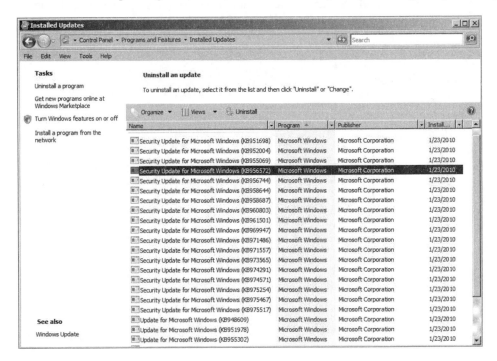

Figure 15-3   Installed Updates window

Courtesy Course Technology/Cengage Learning

If a dialog box opens, indicating that some programs might not function properly after the removal of the hot fix, click **Yes**. The wizard finishes.

12. Click **Finish**. The wizard closes.

13. Repeat Steps 2 through 7 to reapply any necessary hot fixes.

Certification Objectives

Objectives for the Network+ Exam:

- Identify common security threats and mitigation techniques: *Security threats*: DoS, viruses, worms, attackers, man in the middle, smurf, rogue access points, social engineering (phishing); *Mitigation techniques*: policies and procedures, user training, patches and updates

Review Questions

1. In which of the following situations would it be wise to backlevel?

   a. You have just performed a complete backup of your server's data directories, and you cannot confirm that the backup was successful.

   b. You have just applied a fix to your network operating system (NOS) and have discovered that the fix resulted in a lack of network access for half of your users.

   c. You have just installed a database program on one of your servers and have discovered that you neglected to install an optional component that your users will need.

   d. You have just installed Windows Server 2008 on a new computer and you cannot get the operating system to recognize the NIC.

2. Which two of the following can typically be accomplished by applying a patch to an NOS?

   a. replacing all the NOS's program files

   b. modifying an existing feature

   c. removing an old feature

   d. fixing a known bug

3. Before installing a major NOS patch, you should _____ .

   a. Remove all protocols installed on the server.

   b. Prevent users from logging on.

   c. Disable Internet services.

   d. Disable network connectivity.

4. In Microsoft terminology, what is a hot fix?

   a. a patch that replaces all or a portion of the NOS

   b. a patch that requires that the server be connected to Microsoft's Web site as it is installed

   c. a patch that updates a specific type of software, often the operating system

   d. a patch that can be installed while users are logged on without causing adverse effects

5. What is the primary difference between a software upgrade and a patch?

    a. The software manufacturer issues a patch, whereas an upgrade may be issued by any organization that has the software's source code.

    b. A patch fixes a specific part of a software program, whereas an upgrade typically replaces much or all of a software program.

    c. A patch typically does not require that the network administrator test its changes before applying it to a server; an upgrade does.

    d. A patch typically is not supported by the software manufacturer; an upgrade is.

Lab 15.5 Researching Network Solutions

Objectives

In this lab, you will research network solutions by examining business case studies on vendor Web sites. By examining these case studies, you can get an idea of how each vendor uses its product line to help customers solve problems or fulfill business needs. It is important to keep in mind, however, that few vendors are objective about their products. When considering a solution, you should look for information from multiple sources. Additionally, you might find it helpful to talk to someone who has attempted to implement a solution such as the one you are considering.

When looking at case studies, you will often find it helpful to look for organizations that are similar to your own. For instance, a large bank with thousands of employees and a high-security network environment is likely to have different needs than a small, nonprofit organization. Seeing how an organization similar to your own has solved certain problems might help you solve similar problems in your organization.

It is also important to try to anticipate future network trends when researching network solutions. A solution that might help you solve future problems will tend to be more cost effective in the long run than a solution that only addresses an immediate problem. For instance, suppose you are researching software packages that diagnose potential problems in business productivity software on user workstations. If you have noticed a trend toward greater user support of personal digital assistant (PDA) applications, then software packages that also diagnose potential problems in PDA software might prove more useful than ones that do not.

After completing this lab, you will be able to:

- Review case studies of networking companies
- Identify the needs of the customer in a case study
- Identify the solutions provided by the networking companies

Materials Required

This lab will require the following:

- Pencil and paper
- A computer running Windows XP Professional or Vista with Internet access
- An ordinary user account on the computer

Estimated completion time: **20 minutes**

Activity

1. Log on to Windows as an ordinary user. The Windows desktop appears.
2. Perform whatever steps are necessary for the computer to access the Internet.
3. Start Internet Explorer.
4. Go to **www.microsoft.com**.
5. In the Search text box, type **case study**, and then press **Enter**. A list of links for this search term displays.
6. Select a case study from the search results by clicking the case study's title. The case study's page appears. Scroll through the page and read the details of the study. Record the name of the customer and the type of business you reviewed.
7. Record background information on the company in the case study. This information might include the type of business, its size, and the networking hardware or software used.
8. Record the business need or challenge for the company that was the customer in the case study.
9. Record the Microsoft solution. Be sure to identify the software or hardware solution used.
10. Record the results of the solution.
11. Close your Web browser.

Certification Objectives

Objectives for the Network+ Exam:

- Given a scenario, implement the following network troubleshooting methodology: information gathering—identify symptoms and problems, identify the affected areas of the network, determine if anything has changed, establish the most probable cause, determine if escalation is necessary, create an action plan and solution identifying potential effects, implement and test the solution, identify the results and effects of the solution, document the solution and the entire process

Review Questions

1. You are trying to decide whether to purchase a software package from a vendor. Who among the following is most likely to provide objective information about the software package?

   a. the vendor's sales staff

   b. a business partner of the vendor

   c. a current customer of the vendor

   d. a vendor who makes a competing product

2. You are researching a new Internet access router for your company's network. You have also noticed a trend toward greater use of your company's network resources from home. Given this, which of the following features would you expect to be most valuable in a new Internet access router?

   a. support for additional routing protocols

   b. support for virtual private networks

   c. support for additional security features

   d. support for multiple protocols

3. When implementing a network solution, why is it important to anticipate future trends as much as possible?

   a. so that the solutions you implement meet the future needs of your users

   b. so that the solutions you implement meet the current needs of your users

   c. so that the solutions you implement are more scalable

   d. so that you can justify the purchase of the solution to management

4. You work for the Best Roast Coffee Company, which has 100 employees in nine retail stores. You are looking at case studies for a product you are researching. Which of the following case studies is most likely to be helpful?

   a. a case study for an automobile manufacturer with hundreds of thousands of employees

   b. a candy maker with 200 employees that sells candy in 13 malls across the country

   c. an insurance company with thousands of employees in three locations, plus hundreds of agents all over the country

   d. a small school district with 300 employees and 10,000 students

5. When investigating a network solution, which two of the following should you do?

   a. Get information about possible solutions from only one source.

   b. Get information about possible solutions from multiple sources.

   c. Look at the product lines from only one vendor.

   d. Talk to someone who has implemented a similar solution.

INDEX